PROFESSIONAL
TEST-DRIVEN DEVELOPMENT WITH C#

PROFESSIONAL

Test-Driven Development with C#

PROFESSIONAL

Test-Driven Development with C#

DEVELOPING REAL WORLD APPLICATIONS WITH TDD

James Bender
Jeff McWherter

WILEY

Wiley Publishing, Inc.

Professional Test-Driven Development with C#: Developing Real World Applications with TDD

Published by
Wiley Publishing, Inc.
10475 Crosspoint Boulevard
Indianapolis, IN 46256
www.wiley.com

Copyright © 2011 by Wiley Publishing, Inc., Indianapolis, Indiana

Published simultaneously in Canada

ISBN: 978-0-470-64320-4
ISBN: 978-1-118-10210-7 (ebk)
ISBN: 978-1-118-10211-4 (ebk)
ISBN: 978-1-118-10212-1 (ebk)

Manufactured in the United States of America

10 9 8 7 6 5 4 3

For general information on our other products and services please contact our Customer Care Department within the United States at (877) 762-2974, outside the United States at (317) 572-3993 or fax (317) 572-4002.

Wiley also publishes its books in a variety of electronic formats. Some content that appears in print may not be available in electronic books.

Library of Congress Control Number: 2011924919

For Gayle. Thank you for being so awesome!

—JAMES

To everyone who has believed in me.

—JEFF

To my wonderful wife Courtney and my two amazing kids, Katie and Jacob.

—MICHAEL

ABOUT THE AUTHORS

JAMES BENDER is Vice Present of Technology for Improving Enterprises and has been involved in software development and architecture for 17 years. He has worked as a developer and architect on everything from small, single-user applications to Enterprise-scale, multi-user systems. His specialties are .NET development and architecture, SOA, WCF, WF, cloud computing, and agile development methodologies. He is an experienced mentor and author.

James has spent his career pushing the envelope of software development and pursuing new and better ways of building applications. He began his career developing credit card processing applications in C++ on SCO Unix based systems. In the late 90's James began exploring web development with both Java based JSP pages and Microsoft's ASP technologies. He was an early adopter of .NET starting with the first public beta. He continued exploring the .NET technology stack, focusing on the distributed computing paradigm made possible by .NET web services, which naturally evolved into a somewhat obsessive interest in Microsoft's Windows Communication Foundation (WCF).

James has been practicing agile-based methodologies since 2003, including Scrum and eXtreme Programming (XP). At part of this interest in agile methodologies, James began exploring test-driven development at the same time. He was instrumental in introducing the concepts and techniques used in agile software development and test-driven development to many developers at his clients and in the software development community in general.

James is a Microsoft MVP for Visual C#. James is an active member of the development community. He is the current president of the Central Ohio .NET Developers Group (www.condg.org) and continues to lead the Columbus Architects Group (www.colarc.org) and is the senior editor of first-party content for nplus1.org, an educational website aimed toward architects and aspiring architects. His blog can be found at www.jamescbender.com.

JEFF MCWHERTER is a partner and director of development at Gravity Works Design and Development, based in a historic office in Lansing Michigan's Old Town District. A graduate of Michigan State University with over 12 years of professional software development experience, Jeff holds numerous certifications from Microsoft including Microsoft Certified Solutions Developer (MCSD), Microsoft Certified Database Administrator (MCDBA), Microsoft Certified Application Developer (MCAD), and Microsoft Technology Specialist (MCTS).

In 2010 Jeff was awarded with the Microsoft Most Valuable Professional (MVP) for the third year in a row. Also in 2010, Jeff received the Ten Over The Next Ten award presented by the Lansing Regional Chamber of Commerce, which recognizes 10 young professionals to "watch" over the next 10 years. Jeff is also a published author, with *Testing ASP.NET Web Applications* published by Wrox Press.

Along with being an author and software developer, Jeff is very active in developing programming communities across the country by speaking at conferences and organizing events such as the Lansing Give Camp, which pairs developers with non-profit organizations for volunteer projects.

MICHAEL EATON has been developing awesome solutions using Microsoft tools and technologies since 1994, but in 2001 he broke free from the confines of the cube farm to go out on his own. While he lives in the middle-of-nowhere Michigan, he serves clients throughout the Midwest. Well known for his dislike of web development and box lunches, his focus over the past few years has been on XAML-based technologies like WPF and Silverlight. He speaks at regional events and user groups, runs the Kalamazoo X Conference and helps with the Ann Arbor Give Camp. He is also a C# MVP. When not working on projects or spending time with his family, he treats his World of Warcraft addiction with ample doses of time on his XBox 360.

ABOUT THE TECHNICAL EDITOR

MITCHEL SELLERS specializes in software development using Microsoft technologies. He is the CEO of IowaComputerGurus Inc., a Microsoft C# MVP, a Microsoft Certified Professional, has served as an author on two books, and served as technical editor on many other books. You will often find Mitchel interacting with the greater software development community either at events/conferences or in online discussion forums. To obtain additional information on Mitchel's professional experience, certifications, and publications refer to his resume at `MitchelSellers.com`.

CREDITS

ACKNOWLEDGMENTS

I WANT TO START BY THANKING MY GIRLFRIEND (with any luck, fiancé by the time you are reading this) Gayle. She has been very supportive and EXTREMELY understanding during the process of writing this book. More than she should have had to be. Thank you.

I want to thank my parents for making this book possible by making me possible. My mother is so proud she'll read every page of this book. Bless her heart. I hope she's still proud when she realizes I lied and this is NOTHING like a Stephen King novel.

In the understanding and supporting department I would also like to thank Daniel Grey, Mark Kovacevich, Jeff Perry and everyone else at Improving Enterprises. I'd also like to thank Pete Klassen. We miss you man!

I'd like to thank Jeff McWherter and Michael Eaton for their contributions to this book. Jeff; thanks for taking some of the load off. Mike; thank you for pushing me to include the "non-web" people. I'd also like to thank my editor Sydney for making this book look like I know how to write.

Brian Prince; thank you for pushing me to get involved in the development community. I was going to write something funny here, but I couldn't think of anything. I'll getcha in the next one.

When I was presented with the opportunity to write this book, I almost said no. I want to thank Ted Neward for talking me into it. So, this is kinda your fault too.

I want to thank my partners in NPlus1.org Mike Wood and Chris Woodruff for picking up my slack of the past several months while I worked on this.

Long list of general thanks: Brahma Ghosh, Brian Sherwin, Bill Sempf, Jeff Blankenburg, Carey Payette, Caleb Jenkins, Jennifer Marsman, Sarah & Kevin Dutkiewicz, Steve Harman, Josh Holmes. Thanks to Matt Groves for pimping this book almost as much as I did. I'm sure I forgot someone, so I apologize.

—JAMES

FIRST AND FOREMOST I WOULD LIKE TO THANK my very patient wife Carla. Thank you for all the support, patience, and understanding you have provided to me for all of my endeavors. Thank you to the staff at Gravity Works — Amelia Marschall, Lauren Colton, Scott Gowell and Dave Smith — for answering my random questions that appeared to come out of nowhere. And lastly I would like to thank James for his hard work, dedication, and friendship.

—JEFF

CONTENTS

INTRODUCTION

AS A CONSULTANT, I WORK WITH MANY DEVELOPERS. At each client I get to meet a new team and see how they develop software. I've seen great teams, and I've seen teams that are so broken they have never had a successful project. Over the years I've noticed that different teams along this success continuum have different traits. And I've started to formulate an idea of what makes a development team able to develop and deploy applications that are high-quality and deliver value to the business.

The observation that most people expect me to make is that the successful teams had smarter, more competent people, and certainly they did. But the teams that failed had plenty of smart people as well. Clearly intelligence is not a key factor in success.

What I observed about the successful teams was that they had a passion for technology and pride in the work they produced. They were always learning about new tools and techniques, with the aim of developing software faster and with fewer bugs. On the other hand, the less successful teams were content to stick with their old ways of doing things and never took an interest in the changes that were going on around them.

Not all those successful, passionate development teams were practicing test-driven development (TDD) when I first found them. However, most of them quickly and eagerly latched on to it when introduced to the concept. These teams have found that adding the practice of test-driven development to their process of building software produced immediate, measurable results by increasing quality and reducing the number of defects in the delivered application.

Passion is difficult to create but easy to kill. In teams that lack passion, the introduction of test-driven development has, in many cases, reignited passion in developers. This is particularly true of developers who have grown tired of doing the same kind of development day in and day out.

Passion aside, there is another very compelling reason to investigate test-driven development. Arguably the two biggest changes in recent years with the potential to reach the largest number of developers are the rise of agile methodologies and test-driven development. Often the two go hand in hand. I don't believe that an agile methodology can succeed in the long term without the use of test-driven development, and I have great difficulty seeing how test-driven development could work in a waterfall environment.

Agile is here to stay. It's no longer a "crazy cowboy coding" way of working practiced by small development shops. Large companies that have made huge investments in structuring their IT departments around waterfalls are starting to build more and more projects with an agile methodology. Even the most bureaucratic organization in existence, government, is starting to investigate agile with great success. These developments spell out a clear reality: Developers who can work in agile environments, including the practice of test-driven development, soon will be more valuable than those who can't.

Test-driven development has not existed in a vacuum. In the past several years, many groups and movements have been aimed at raising the quality of the software being developed and bringing business into the process. New principles and ways of doing things have been advanced to help developers build maintainable applications that serve the needs of the business. Terms such as software craftsmanship and SOLID have made their way into the lexicon of passionate developers all over the world. Some developers have even gone so far as to call themselves software artisans or craftsmen.

Many books, websites, and workshops have appeared to feed the need to learn test-driven development and all its supporting pieces. Many of these are very good. But others are nothing more than commercials for a common and transportable way of doing things that is dressed up as an expensive and proprietary solution. Many smart, passionate developers talk about and evangelize test-driven development. However, no "one-stop shopping" resource has been able to take a developer — specifically, a .NET developer — from neophyte to, well, still a neophyte, but a neophyte with some information.

The fact that you are reading this book indicates that you have some interest in test-driven development. Maybe you're a developer who's heard a lot about test-driven development but never really had an opportunity to explore it. Perhaps you're an experienced test-driven developer who is curious to see how this book is different from all the other books on the subject. In either case, the fact that you are reading this book indicates that test-driven development has become mainstream and is worthy of your time to learn, practice, and promote.

WHO THIS BOOK IS FOR

Test-driven development is an effective way to build quality into your application from the start. The supporting principles and practices of test-driven development will enable you and your development team to quickly write maintainable software that is more aligned with the needs of the business. If you are a developer interested in improving your skills, this book is for you.

If you're new to test-driven development, start with Chapter 1. Doing so will give you a good background in why test-driven development has become such a compelling practice. It will also introduce you to the concepts of object-oriented programming, the SOLID Principles, and refactoring. These skills are a crucial foundation for the practice of test-driven development.

If you've dabbled in test-driven development, you might want to start with Chapter 3, which provides a refresher on object-oriented development, the SOLID Principles, and refactoring. Even seasoned developers sometimes need a reminder of how these concepts relate to application development. The rest of the book, starting with Chapter 4, provides form and structure for test-driven development for these developers.

Developers who are experienced with test-driven development will probably want to start with Part III. Doing so assumes that you have a high degree of skill with test-driven development, object-oriented programming (OOP), and SOLID. This part focuses on specific scenarios that .NET developers face. It covers how to practice test-driven development in web-based applications (including web forms, ASP.NET MVC, and JavaScript), applications built on Windows Presentation

Foundation (WPF) with the Model-View-ViewModel (MVVM) pattern, and service applications built using Microsoft's Windows Communication Foundation (WCF). The most difficult part of an application to test is the edge. These chapters will show you how to make the edges around your application as thin as possible and therefore more testable.

WHAT THIS BOOK COVERS

This book starts by covering the conditions that brought the software industry to the point where test-driven development could flourish. It's important to understand this history and the conditions that brought software development to its current state. Avoiding the mistakes of the past is important. But identifying these antipatterns in your current development practice is even more important.

To support your practice of test-driven development, this book also includes extensive coverage of object-oriented programming, agile methodologies, and the SOLID software design and coding principles.

Of course, this book covers the concepts inherent in and necessary to test-driven development. The first tests you will be exposed to are simple and easy to understand. You'll see how the NUnit unit-testing framework can be used to write unit tests in Visual Studio.

Later, the dependency injection pattern is introduced. You will see how this pattern is implemented and how dependency injection frameworks such as Ninject can help manage the dependencies in your application. The practice of mocking and mocking frameworks also are covered, including an introduction to the mocking framework Moq.

The basics of behavior-driven development are covered, but a deep discussion of this topic is not included. This book explains the idea behind behavior-driven development and showcases the business-driven development style of naming tests. This book also introduces the NBehave testing framework. NBehave has many features, but this book simply uses it to provide syntactic sugar for the tests.

HOW THIS BOOK IS STRUCTURED

A great deal of effort has been expended to structure the information in this book so that each chapter builds upon the lessons in the previous one. The first chapters are designed to provide a foundation built on the importance of test-driven development and the underlying skills needed to effectively practice it. Each chapter and section build on a concept such as dependency injection and mocking until you've been exposed to all the necessary tools and techniques to practice test-driven development.

Incorporating the test-driven development skills taught in the previous chapters, Part III demonstrates how to practice test-driven development with several of Microsoft's frameworks aimed at developing interfaces for applications, including ASP.NET MVC, WPF, and WCF.

The book ends with an appendix that lists some alternative tools that can help you develop applications using test-driven development. It also lists potential user stories to use as practice if you are not in a position to use test-driven development in your everyday work.

WHAT YOU NEED TO USE THIS BOOK

To follow along with the examples in this book and use the demonstration application available for download at www.wrox.com, you need the following tools:

➤ Visual Studio 2010 (any version)

➤ NUnit version 2.5.2.9222 or later, available at nunit.org

➤ Moq version 4 beta 4 (build 4.0.10827.0) or later, available at code.google.com/p/moq

➤ Ninject version 2 (build 2.1.0.91) or later, available at ninject.org

➤ NBehave version 0.4.5.183 or later, available at nbehave.org

➤ Fluent NHibernate version 1.1 or later, available at fluentnhibernate.org

➤ A Database Management System (DBMS) is required for the sample applications. The examples in this book use Microsoft SQL Server Developer, but any relational database system will suffice.

CONVENTIONS

To help you get the most from the text and keep track of what's happening, we use a number of conventions throughout the book: As for styles in the text:

➤ We *italicize* new terms and important words when we introduce them.

➤ We show keyboard strokes like this: Ctrl+A.

➤ We show filenames, URLs, and code within the text like so: persistence.properties.

We present code in two different ways:

```
We use a monofont type with no highlighting for most code examples.
We use bold to emphasize code that's particularly important in the present context.
```

The pencil icon indicates notes, tips, hints, tricks, or asides to the current discussion.

Boxes with a warning icon like this one hold important, not-to-be forgotten information that is directly relevant to the surrounding text.

SOURCE CODE

As you work through the examples in this book, you may choose either to type in all the code manually, or to use the source code files that accompany the book. All the source code used in this book is available for download at `www.wrox.com`. When at the site, simply locate the book's title (use the Search box or one of the title lists) and click the Download Code link on the book's detail page to obtain all the source code for the book. Code that is included on the website is highlighted by the following icon:

Available for download on Wrox.com

Listings include the filename in the title. If it is just a code snippet, you'll find the filename in a code note such as this:

Code snippet filename

 Because many books have similar titles, you may find it easiest to search by ISBN; this book's ISBN is 978-0-470-64320-4.

Once you download the code, just decompress it with your favorite compression tool. Alternately, you can go to the main Wrox code download page at `www.wrox.com/dynamic/books/download .aspx` to see the code available for this book and all other Wrox books.

ERRATA

We make every effort to ensure that there are no errors in the text or in the code. However, no one is perfect, and mistakes do occur. If you find an error in one of our books, like a spelling mistake or faulty piece of code, we would be very grateful for your feedback. By sending in errata you may save another reader hours of frustration and at the same time you will be helping us provide even higher quality information.

To find the errata page for this book, go to www.wrox.com and locate the title using the Search box or one of the title lists. Then, on the book details page, click the Book Errata link. On this page you can view all errata that has been submitted for this book and posted by Wrox editors. A complete book list including links to each book's errata is also available at www.wrox.com/misc-pages/ booklist.shtml.

If you don't spot "your" error on the Book Errata page, go to www.wrox.com/contact/ techsupport.shtml and complete the form there to send us the error you have found. We'll check the information and, if appropriate, post a message to the book's errata page and fix the problem in subsequent editions of the book.

P2P.WROX.COM

For author and peer discussion, join the P2P forums at p2p.wrox.com. The forums are a Web-based system for you to post messages relating to Wrox books and related technologies and interact with other readers and technology users. The forums offer a subscription feature to e-mail you topics of interest of your choosing when new posts are made to the forums. Wrox authors, editors, other industry experts, and your fellow readers are present on these forums.

At p2p.wrox.com you will find a number of different forums that will help you not only as you read this book, but also as you develop your own applications. To join the forums, just follow these steps:

1.   Go to p2p.wrox.com and click the Register link.

2.   Read the terms of use and click Agree.

3.   Complete the required information to join as well as any optional information you wish to provide and click Submit.

4.   You will receive an e-mail with information describing how to verify your account and complete the joining process.

 You can read messages in the forums without joining P2P but in order to post your own messages, you must join.

Once you join, you can post new messages and respond to messages other users post. You can read messages at any time on the Web. If you would like to have new messages from a particular forum e-mailed to you, click the Subscribe to this Forum icon by the forum name in the forum listing.

For more information about how to use the Wrox P2P, be sure to read the P2P FAQs for answers to questions about how the forum software works as well as many common questions specific to P2P and Wrox books. To read the FAQs, click the FAQ link on any P2P page.

PROFESSIONAL

Test-Driven Development with C#

PART I
Getting Started

The Road to Test-Driven Development

WHAT'S IN THIS CHAPTER?

➤ How has software development evolved to bring us to TDD

➤ What an Agile methodology is and how does it differs from traditional waterfall-based technologies

➤ What TDD is and what the benefits of using it are

Test-Driven Development (TDD) has become one of the most important concepts and practices in modern software development. To understand why this is, consider the history of the practice of creating software. TDD was created through an almost evolutionary process. It came about as a response to the difficulties and challenges of writing software, but there was no real plan for its creation. It's a classic case of the traits of a thing that make that thing more successful and stronger being propagated and the traits that lead to failure being discarded. The practices of TDD were not created by any single company or individual; they rose from countless discussions (or, more likely, arguments) about what was done in the past, why it failed, and what could be done better. If TDD is a structure, such as a house, its foundation is created from failure. Failed projects, whose developers knew there had to be a better way, are what TDD has been built upon.

In this chapter you learn about the history of software development and how the methodology of managing software projects has moved from favoring waterfall to iterative to agile methodologies. You'll learn how the practice of Test-Driven Development is a key component of agile methodologies to ensure that quality code that addresses the business needs is being produced. I will explain the tenets of Test-Driven Development, outline its benefits, and show you an example of how Test-Driven Development is done.

THE CLASSICAL APPROACH TO SOFTWARE DEVELOPMENT

To understand the importance of TDD, it's necessary to see the road that led to it. Over the past 50 years the practice of software development has constantly evolved in an effort to find a balance between the needs of the business, the capabilities of the current technology, and the methodology in which developers are most productive. Missteps have occurred along the way, but even they were important as a means of determining which techniques and methodologies were evolutionary dead ends. This chapter reviews the road to TDD.

A Brief History of Software Engineering

Software development for business began during the age of the mainframe. Each hardware vendor seemed to have its own unique platform and paradigm for developing software. Sometimes these systems were similar enough to each other that developers could move from job to job and platform to platform with very little friction. Other times it was like starting from scratch. Although the basic concepts of computing were the same, each vendor had its own, sometimes very unique take on those concepts. Languages were archaic, often requiring many lines of code to do the simplest things that we take for granted today. And many times what worked in one implementation of a language or platform didn't work quite the same way in another.

The mainframe was a large, expensive piece of equipment. Many companies didn't own one, so the concept of the service bureau was born: Companies with a mainframe would lease time on their computer to customers. Unfortunately, this sometimes meant waiting for access to the computer. Imagine if you wrote a program today but couldn't compile it until next Monday. It would be very hard to be a productive developer with that kind of constraint. Suppose you attempted to compile on Monday but encountered an error. You could fix it, but you wouldn't know if your fix was correct for three more days. The limited access to computing resources often meant that testing, out of necessity, took a backseat to getting the product out the door.

These were also the days before the concept of *waterfall* development. Developers, left to their own devices, often worked in an iterative manner, scoping out specific pieces of a system and completing those, and then adding new features and functionality later. This method worked well, because it allowed developers to approach application development in a logical manner that kept things in terms they could understand and manage. Unfortunately, business users and what was logical and comprehensible to them often were not taken into consideration.

The second generation of mini-computers emerged in 1977, but they didn't really take off in business until 1979 with the release of VisiCalc. VisiCalc was the first spreadsheet application available for the personal computer. It demonstrated that PCs weren't just toys for the home, but machines that could provide real value to business. PCs offered many advantages over mainframes, the first one being that they were much less expensive. A business that couldn't afford even one dedicated mainframe could afford dozens of PCs. And although PCs weren't as fast as mainframes, their availability made them ideal for day-to-day tasks that didn't require the power of the mainframe. Developers could write applications for the PC and know right away if their code worked. They also didn't have to wait days to have their jobs scheduled and run.

Things got even better with third- and fourth-generation programming languages. They abstracted some of the more mundane tasks of their predecessors and allowed developers to be more productive by focusing on the business problem at hand. These languages also opened software development to a wider audience who didn't want to deal with the friction of languages such as Assembler and C. Business and the business computer industry ultimately settled on a few base languages and their derivatives. This helped developers become more attractive and marketable to business as their skills became more portable.

Ultimately business's need to plan brought about the waterfall project methodology. The concept behind waterfall was that every software project, whose average time span was about two years, should have every phase from inception to delivery planned from the start. This necessitated a long period at the beginning for requirements gathering. After all the requirements were gathered, they were "thrown over the wall" to the architects. The architects took the requirements and designed the system that would be built down to the smallest detail. When they completed this task, they threw the design over the wall to the developers, who built the system. After the developers completed their work, they threw the system to the Quality Assurance (QA) department, which tested the application. As soon as the application was validated, it was deployed to the users.

Software testing in a waterfall methodology was often a long, difficult, inefficient, and expensive process. QA testers would test applications by manually running through test scripts, which were documents that instructed the tester to carry out an action in the system and described the result the tester should observe. Sometimes these scripts ran into hundreds of pages. When a change was made to the system, it could take a tester two or more weeks to completely regression-test the system. Another issue was that often these test scripts were written by the developer who created the system. In these cases the scripts usually described how the system *would* act, not how it *should* act.

The first step toward TDD happened with the proliferation of automated QA testing tools. These recorded a series of actions a user takes on a user interface (UI) and allowed them to be played back later. This verified that the UI worked correctly. After the initial tests were recorded, the QA tools also allowed much faster regression testing than manual tests and could be run repeatedly. A large failing of many of these early tools was that the tests they created were brittle. When an aspect of the UI changed, the test usually couldn't handle the change, and the test would break. For tools that used the record/playback model, that meant the test had to be discarded and a new one created. Later versions of these tools allowed for scripting that would make some of these changes easier to absorb, but the tests still remained fragile.

From Waterfall to Iterative and Incremental

Software development doesn't happen in a void. It doesn't matter if it's an 18-month project to create an application to collate the Enterprise's Testing Procedure Specification (TPS) reports or a website that you built for your child's peewee hockey team; you are using a methodology. You have requirements, you plan features, and you build the application. After it's tested, you deploy it to a grateful user base.

A problem with the waterfall methodology is that all the requirements are gathered early on. In business, requirements often change for a variety of reasons. Changes in the law, a shift in the company's strategic direction, or even something as simple as a mistake in the requirements-gathering phase could have serious repercussions for the downstream process. The planned-out nature of waterfall does not respond well to change. A change request to the system generally must go through the same requirements/design/development/QA process that the rest of the system did. This creates a ripple effect that causes the rest of the plan to become inaccurate.

To create the upfront plan, the work must be estimated early — sometimes years before the actual work is to be done, and usually by someone who won't actually do the work. This creates a house of cards in which one wrong estimate can again wreak havoc across the rest of the project plan.

The architects aren't blameless either. This era led to "ivory tower architects" who created designs for applications that in practice were impractical or, in some cases, impossible. Developers didn't help the case either, because many of them simply carried out the architect's design vision, whether or not it made sense. Many times what was delivered to the business (two years after it had been requested) did not remotely resemble what was wanted or needed.

In an effort to solve some of the issues with waterfall, some development shops turned to the concept of *iterative* or *incremental* development. The idea was to take a large waterfall project and divide it into several smaller waterfall projects. Each subproject would have a defined scope and delivery target and upon completion would feed into the next iteration of the larger project. This was an improvement, because it resulted in smaller projects that were easier to define and got software in front of users much faster. However, in the end this was really just several linked waterfall projects, albeit shorter ones. The individual subproject still did not have a good mechanism for dealing with the constant change of business and technology. Another step was needed.

A QUICK INTRODUCTION TO AGILE METHODOLOGIES

Unlike waterfall, which seeks to control and constrain the realities of software development, *agile* methodologies embrace them. Change in business is inevitable, and software development methodologies must be able to adapt. A key failure of the large up-front plan is that estimates by their very definition are always wrong. If they were correct, they wouldn't be estimates; they would be "the number." An iterative process shows promise, but the iterations themselves, and the methodology as a whole, must be flexible and open to change.

A Brief History of Agile Methodologies

In February 2001 several proponents of new methodologies such as Scrum, Extreme Programming (XP), Pragmatic Programming, Feature Driven Development, and others met and drafted the Agile Manifesto. It reads as follows:

> *"We are uncovering better ways of developing software by doing it and helping others do it. Through this work we have come to value:*
>
> ➤ *Individuals and interactions over processes and tools*
>
> ➤ *Working software over comprehensive documentation*

> ➤ *Customer collaboration over contract negotiation*

> ➤ *Responding to change over following a plan*

> *That is, while there is value in the items on the right, we value the items on the left more."*

The Agile Manifesto itself is not a development methodology. It doesn't prescribe how software should be developed. It simply states a set of key values that can be used to create and describe lighter and faster application development methodologies that are more focused on people, working software, and results than meticulous multiyear project plans and mountains of documentation.

Many branded agile development methodologies are in use today:

- ➤ Scrum
- ➤ Extreme Programming (XP)
- ➤ Feature Driven Development
- ➤ Clear Case
- ➤ Adaptive Software Development

The Principles and Practices of Test-Driven Development

These methodologies are all different in how they are implemented, but they share some characteristics:

- ➤ They all make communication across the team a high priority. Developers, business users, and testers are all encouraged to communicate frequently.

- ➤ They focus on transparency in the project. The development team does not live in a black box that obscures their actions from the rest of the team. They use very public artifacts (a Kanban board, a big visible chart, and so on) to keep the team informed.

- ➤ The members of the team are all accountable to each other. The team does not succeed or fail because of one person; they either succeed or fail as a team.

- ➤ Individual developers do not own sections of the code base. The whole team owns the entire code base, and everyone is responsible for its quality.

- ➤ Work is done in short, iterative development cycles, ideally with a release at the end of each cycle.

- ➤ The ability to handle change is a cornerstone of the methodology.

- ➤ Broad strokes of a system are defined up front, but detailed design is deferred until the feature is actually scheduled to be developed.

Agile methodologies are not a silver bullet. They are also not about chaos or "cowboy coding." In fact, agile methodologies require a larger degree of discipline to administer correctly. Furthermore, no one true agile methodology exists. Ultimately, each team needs to do what works best for them. This may mean starting with a branded agile methodology and changing it, or combining aspects of several. You should constantly evaluate your methodology and do more of what works and less of what doesn't.

THE CONCEPTS BEHIND TDD

The history of TDD starts in 1999 with a group of developers who championed a set of concepts known as Extreme Programing (XP). XP is an agile based methodology that is based on recognizing what practices in software development are beneficial and dedicating the bulk of the developers time and effort to those practices under the philosophy "if some is good, more is better." A key component of XP is test-first programming. TDD grew out of XP as some developers found they were not ready to embrace some of the more, at the time, radical concepts, yet found the promise of improved quality that was delivered by the practice of TDD compelling.

As mentioned, agile methodologies do not incorporate a big upfront design. Business requirements are distilled into features for the system. The detailed design for each feature is done when the feature is scheduled. Features, and their resulting libraries and code, are kept short and simple.

TDD as a Design Methodology

When used as an application design methodology, TDD works best when the business user is engaged in the process to help the developer define the logic that is being created, sometimes going so far as to define a set of input and its expected output. This is necessary to ensure that the developers understand the business requirements behind the feature they are developing. TDD ensures that the final product is in line with the needs of the business. It also helps ensure that the scope of the feature is adhered to and helps the developer understand what *done* really means with respect to the current feature in development.

TDD as a Development Practice

As a development practice, TDD is deceptively simple. Unlike development you've done in the past, where you may sit down and start by creating a window, a web page, or even a class, in TDD you start by writing a test. This is known as *test first development*, and initially it might seem a bit awkward. However, by writing your test first, what you really are doing is creating the requirement you are designing for in code. As you work with the business user to define what these tests should be, you create an executable version of the requirement that is composed of your test. Until these tests pass, your code does not satisfy the business requirement.

When you write your first test, the first indication that it fails is the fact that the application does not compile. This is because your test is attempting to instantiate a class that has not been defined, or it wants to use a method on an object that does not exist. The first step is simply to create the class you are testing and define whatever method on that class you are attempting to test. At this point your test will still fail, because the class and method you just created don't do anything. The next step is to write just enough code to make your test pass. This should be the simplest code you can create that causes the test to pass. The goal is not to write code based on what might be coming in the requirement. Until that requirement changes, or a test is added to expose that lack of functionality, it doesn't get written. This prevents you from writing overly complicated code where a simple algorithm would suffice. Remember, one of the goals of TDD is to create code that is easy to understand and maintain.

As soon as your first test is passing, add more tests. You should try to have enough tests to ensure that all the requirements of the feature being tested are being met. As part of this process, you want to ensure that you are testing your methods for multiple input combinations. This includes values that fall outside the approved range. These are called *negative tests*. If your requirement says that your interest calculation method should handle only percentage rates up to 20%, see what happens if you try to call it with 21%. Usually this should cause an exception of some sort to be thrown. If your method takes string arguments, what happens if you pass in an empty string? What happens if you pass in nulls? Although it's important to keep your tests inside the realm of reality, triangulating tests to ensure the durability of your code is important too. When the entire requirement has been expressed in tests, and all the tests pass, you're done.

THE BENEFITS OF TDD

When describing TDD to developers, development managers, and project managers who have never experienced it, I am usually met with skepticism. On paper, creating code does seem like a long and convoluted process. The benefits cannot be ignored, however:

➤ TDD ensures quality code from the start. Developers are encouraged to write only the code needed to make the test pass and thus fulfill the requirement. If a method has less code, it's only logical that the code has fewer opportunities for error.

➤ Whether by design or by coincidence, most TDD practitioners write code that follows the SOLID principals. These are a set of practices that help developers ensure they are writing quality software. While the tests generated by the practice of TDD are extremely valuable, the quality that results as a side-effect is an incredibly important benefit of TDD. The SOLID principals will be covered in Chapter 3.

➤ TDD ensures a high degree of fidelity between the code and the business requirements. If your requirements are written as tests, and your tests all pass, you can say with a high degree of confidence that your code meets the needs of the business.

➤ TDD encourages the creation of simpler, more focused libraries and APIs. TDD turns development a bit on its head, because the developer writing the interface to the library or API is also its first consumer. This gives you a new perspective on how the interface should be written, and you know instantly if the interface makes sense.

➤ TDD encourages communication with the business. To create these tests, you are encouraged to interact with the business users. This way, you can make sure that the input and output combinations make sense, and you can help the users understand what they are building.

➤ TDD helps keep unused code out of the system. Most developers have written applications in which they designed interfaces and wrote methods based on what might happen. This leads to systems with large parts of code or functionality that are never used. This code is expensive. You expend effort writing it, and even though that code does nothing, it still has to be maintained. It also makes things cluttered, distracting you from the important working code. TDD helps keep this parasite code out of your system.

➤ TDD provides built-in regression testing. As changes are made to the system and your code, you always have the suite of tests you created to ensure that tomorrow's changes do not damage today's functionality.

➤ TDD puts a stop to recurring bugs. You've probably been in situations where you are developing a system and the same bug seems to come back from QA repeatedly. You think you've finally tracked it down and put a stop to it, only to see it return two weeks later. With TDD, as soon as a defect is reported, a new test is written to expose it. When this test passes, and continues to pass, you know the defect is gone for good.

➤ When developing applications with testability in mind, the result is an architecture that is open, extensible and flexible. Dependency Injection (covered in Chapter 5) is a key component of both TDD and a loosely coupled architecture. This results in a system that by virtue of its architecture is robust, easy to change, and resistant to defects.

A QUICK EXAMPLE OF THE TDD APPROACH

The following exercise takes you through an example of what it's like to develop a feature for a system using TDD. For this example, imagine you have been asked to create a feature that counts occurrences of a character in a string. Assume that you are working in an existing solution, with an existing project structure, but the class you'll implement this method on does not exist. Also assume for this example that your unit-testing frameworks have been referenced in your project. Don't worry; I cover how to do this in Chapter 6. Currently, the solution looks like Figure 1-1.

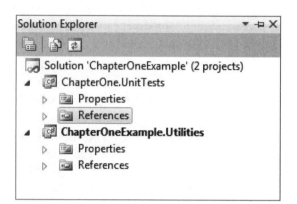

FIGURE 1-1

The ChapterOne.UnitTests project will contain our unit tests. The ChapterOneExample.Utilities project will be where our completed class will be placed. The first step is to create a class in our unit test project that will contain our unit tests, as shown in Figure 1-2.

You have a variety of ways to arrange your unit test classes within your unit test project. Some developers prefer to place each test class in a separate code file. Some developers like to create a code file for all the test classes for a specific feature. A more common approach, which is the one taken here, is to create a code file class for all the unit test classes for a specific section of the application—in this case, the utilities project. If you had a business logic library with several business/domain-based services, you could

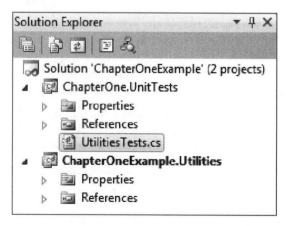

FIGURE 1-2

create a separate code file for each domain service's test classes. For this example that would be overkill, so you'll use one test class for the whole project.

When you created the `UtilitiesTest.cs` class, Visual Studio created some boilerplate code:

```
namespace ChapterOne.UnitTests
{
    public class UtilitiesTests
    {

    }
}
```

 For the purposes of this example, the name UtilitiesTests is fine, but in a real business development situation it might not be descriptive enough for the other developers on your team. It definitely won't mean much to a nontechnical business user. Subsequent examples in this book will employ a method for naming and constructing tests that is more in line with a Business Driven Development style. It provides human-friendly names and makes the actual test easier to understand and follow for nontechnical people.

Now you write your first test. This can be the simplest expression of what your requirements are. This test passes in the string `mysterious` and asks the library to count the occurrences of the letter `y`:

```
using NUnit.Framework;

namespace ChapterOne.UnitTests
{
    public class UtilitiesTests
    {
        [Test]
        public void ShouldFindOneYInMysterious()
        {
            var stringToCheck = "mysterious";
            var stringToFind = "y";
            var expectedResult = 1;
            var classUnderTest = new StringUtilities();

            var actualResult =
                classUnderTest.CountOccurences(stringToCheck, stringToFind);

            Assert.AreEqual(expectedResult, actualResult);
        }
    }
}
```

The test method `ShouldFindOneYInMysterious` is decorated with the attribute `Test` to tell the unit test framework that this is a test. The test conditions are set up by defining the string to search and the character to find in it. They also define the expected result. Next the method is invoked under test and captures the actual result. Finally, an `Assert` statement determines whether the expected and actual values are the same.

The first indication that the test does not pass is the fact that the application does not compile. This tells you that no one has implemented a `StringUtilities` class in the application. That's what you must do first. To do so you simply add a new class called `StringUtilities` to your utilities project. The class that Visual Studio creates looks like this:

```
namespace ChapterOneExample.Utilities
{
    public class StringUtilities
    {

    }
}
```

The test still fails, because you haven't created a `CountOccurences` method on this class. The next step in making this test pass is adding that method:

```
using System;

namespace ChapterOneExample.Utilities
{
    public class StringUtilities
    {
        public int CountOccurences(string stringToCheck,
                                   string stringToFind)
        {
            throw new NotImplementedException();
        }
    }
}
```

This method initially throws an exception because so far the only reason this test has failed is due to a failure to compile. This might seem silly, but in TDD you don't take anything for granted; it's important to see your tests fail before you write your methods. This ensures that you are writing only enough code to make the test pass. When you run the test, it fails, as shown in Figure 1-3.

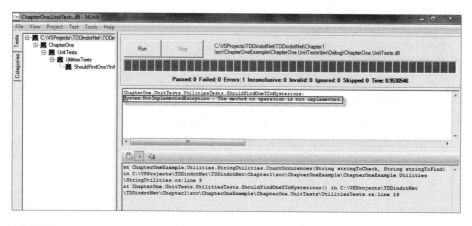

FIGURE 1-3

The reason for the test failure (as shown by the highlighted text) is that you have not implemented the method. The next step is to write code to make this test pass:

```
using System;

namespace ChapterOneExample.Utilities
{
    public class StringUtilities
    {
        public int CountOccurences(string stringToCheck,
                                   string stringToFind)
        {
            var stringAsCharArray = stringToCheck.ToCharArray();
            var stringToCheckForAsChar =
                                    stringToFind.ToCharArray()[0];
            var occuranceCount = 0;

            for (var characterIndex = 0;
                 characterIndex < stringAsCharArray.GetUpperBound(0);
                 characterIndex++)
            {
                if (stringAsCharArray[characterIndex] ==
                                            stringToCheckForAsChar)
                {
                    occuranceCount++;
                }
            }

            return occuranceCount;
        }
    }
}
```

This may or may not be the best way to implement this method, but if you run the test you can see in Figure 1-4 that it's enough to satisfy this requirement.

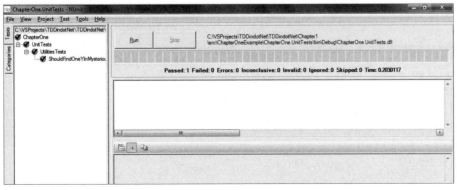

FIGURE 1-4

So, right now you know it works when there is one instance of the character you're looking for in the target word. In the interest of triangulating tests, you need to write another one to verify that it finds multiple instances:

```
[Test]
public void ShouldFindTwoSInMysterious()
{
    var stringToCheck = "mysterious";
    var stringToFind = "s";
    var expectedResult = 2;
    var classUnderTest = new StringUtilities();

    var actualResult = classUnderTest.CountOccurences(stringToCheck, stringToFind);

    Assert.AreEqual(expectedResult, actualResult);
}
```

When you run both tests, you can see that the code has a problem, as shown in Figure 1-5.

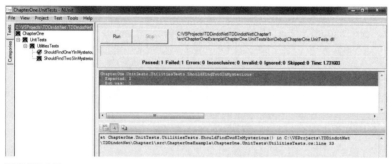

FIGURE 1-5

The test has uncovered a bug in the code. Specifically, the for loop is looping through the target string one fewer time than is needed (string length - 1). After the defect has been found, you can fix the code:

```
for (var characterIndex = 0;
    characterIndex <= stringAsCharArray.GetUpperBound(0);
    characterIndex++)
```

Now when you run the test, the code behaves the way it should, as shown in Figure 1-6.

FIGURE 1-6

Now imagine that as you continue to develop your character counter method, you are given a new requirement. Your business user wants the search to be case-insensitive. That is, the algorithm shouldn't care if letters are uppercase or lowercase. Your first step is to write a test that expresses this new requirement:

```
public void SearchShouldBeCaseSenstive()
        {
            var stringToCheck = "mySterious";
            var stringToFind = "s";
            var expectedResult = 2;
            var classUnderTest = new StringUtilities();

            var actualResult =
                classUnderTest.CountOccurences(stringToCheck,
                                               stringToFind);

            Assert.AreEqual(expectedResult, actualResult);
        }
```

Figure 1-7 shows that when you run this test, the current implementation does not meet this new requirement.

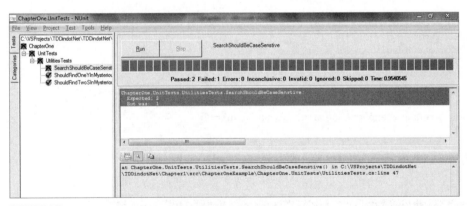

FIGURE 1-7

The next step is to update your method to make this test pass while making sure that the other two tests do not start to fail. This change is easy enough; you simply convert both the string you are searching and the character you are searching for to uppercase before you run the search algorithm:

```
var stringAsCharArray = stringToCheck.ToUpper().ToCharArray();
var stringToCheckForAsChar = stringToFind.ToUpper().ToCharArray()[0];
```

Figure 1-8 shows the results of running this test again. This change was all that was needed to make the new test pass, without causing the existing tests to fail, so this requirement is complete.

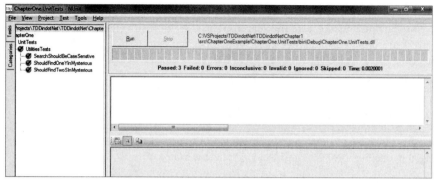

FIGURE 1-8

You deploy version one of your string utility class, and before long you have your first defect. When a user passes in a null as the string to be searched, a null reference exception is thrown. You can question the responsibility of the calling code to check its values before making the call, or argue that a null reference exception is appropriate; the string *is* null, after all. But the truth is that good developers realize that all input is evil and must be validated independently. And in the end, the business user would rather have the value –1 returned. You write a test to demonstrate this defect:

```
public void ShouldBeAbleToHandleNulls()
{
    string stringToCheck = null;
    var stringToFind = "s";
    var expectedResult = -1;
    var classUnderTest = new StringUtilities();

    var actualResult = classUnderTest.CountOccurences(stringToCheck, stringToFind);

    Assert.AreEqual(expectedResult, actualResult);
}
```

As expected, you can see in Figure 1-9 that this test fails when it is run.

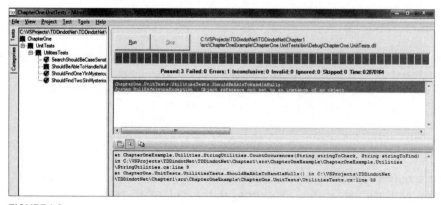

FIGURE 1-9

Another code change is needed, this time to validate the incoming arguments and return the appropriate response if the data fails validation:

```
public int CountOccurences(string stringToCheck, string stringToFind)
{
    if (stringToCheck == null) return -1;
    var stringAsCharArray = stringToCheck.ToUpper().ToCharArray();
```

When you run the test again, the code change corrects the defect, as shown in Figure 1-10.

FIGURE 1-10

In addition to ensuring that you have fixed the defect, this test ensures that the defect doesn't reappear in the future.

SUMMARY

In this chapter you have seen how the history of software development has come full circle to a preference for iterative development. You also saw how the Agile Manifesto has created a framework for today's new breed of iterative methodologies. Software developers have also had to learn the value of change and find ways to adapt their work to the pace of change in the rest of the business. You saw a basic example of how Test-Driven Development (TDD) can be used to write robust software that is simple to implement and easy to maintain. You also learned how these tests can insulate you from introducing new defects while providing a framework for you to add new features without disrupting current ones. Finally, you learned what tools you need to start working with TDD.

An Introduction to Unit Testing

➤   What a unit test is

➤   How unit testing differs from other types of tests

➤   How unit testing frameworks can help you write unit tests quickly and easily

➤   Why mocking external resources in your test is important when practicing TDD

➤   A brief overview of the NUnit unit testing framework and the Moq mocking framework, two very popular TDD tools in the .NET world

Unit testing (UT) is the cornerstone of test-driven development (TDD). When your unit tests are properly aligned with and correctly reflect your business requirements, they almost become a living design document — one that can validate the code you've written with the push of a button. Unit tests are not difficult to write, although they do require a minor change to how you usually approach writing software. They also represent a few new concepts to master, such as code isolation and the idea of having stand-in or mock objects to enable your tests to focus on only the code that is being tested. These new concepts are integral to TDD. The ability to write isolated, repeatable, and focused tests allows you to ensure that your code is meeting the business's needs and can continue to evolve without those changes disrupting the code's fidelity to the business's needs. To help you with these concepts, tools and frameworks such as NUnit and Moq can make your development process easier, faster, and more rewarding.

WHAT IS A UNIT TEST?

Over the years, many different and mutually exclusive definitions of the term *unit test* have arisen. Many people say "unit test" when they really mean component test, integration test, or even user acceptance test (UAT). This can lead to a lot of confusion in software development in general. In TDD that confusion takes on a whole new dimension when you consider just how central to the practice of TDD unit tests are. It's important for the sake of communicating with our fellow developers that we maintain a consistent definition of the term "unit test."

Unit Test Definition

In the simplest terms, a *unit test* is a test designed to test one unit of work. In this case "one unit of work" means one requirement for one method. The example from Chapter 1 tested an algorithm to count the number of occurrences of a given character in a given string. You didn't know where the string or character came from; that detail was unimportant to the given unit of work, which was counting the occurrences of the character in the string. Everything else was out of scope for the unit of work.

The benefit of this type of test is the fact that it is confined to only one specific unit of work. You can focus your efforts on your unit of work. You don't need to know the details of the other players in the system (unless you have a direct dependency on them). This makes writing the tests, and the resulting code, easier. Additionally, if a defect does appear in your code that causes your test to fail, you can be fairly sure that the defect is isolated to your specific unit of work. You don't have to "go down the rabbit hole" searching for which layer of code your defect occurred in. If your character-counting tests fail, you know that's where the problem is.

Stylistically, unit tests can be written in a variety of ways, but all unit tests share some common characteristics. They are:

➤ Isolated from other code

➤ Isolated from other developers

➤ Targeted

➤ Repeatable

➤ Predictable

Now that you know the characteristics of a true unit test, the next section discusses some patterns and characteristics you should avoid.

What Is Not a Unit Test?

For starters, you want to avoid tests that cross the boundaries between the code you are testing and the other parts of the system. This pertains to everything from other classes and services in the same application to databases, web services, and any other external dependency. When your tests start to bleed into these other classes, services, and systems, your tests start to lose their focus, and when they fail, it becomes more difficult to target the defective code. The idea behind a unit test is that you test only what's in that method. When it fails, you don't want to have to hunt through several layers of code, database tables, or the documentation for third-party products to find a possible answer.

Another issue arises when you cross these boundaries, especially if that boundary is a shared resource such as a database. When you share resources with other developers on your team, you potentially can pollute their test results, and your test results can be affected by them. If a test writes a value to a database, reads it, and then deletes it, the test has clearly broken the boundary. If you are the only developer on that system, this may not appear to be a problem. But if other developers are working on the same code, and they all attempt to run the same test that creates and/or deletes the same record on the same table in the same database, the tests may very well interfere with each other. This creates an unstable testing environment.

This is not to say that tests that extend beyond the boundaries of your classes and methods under test are not of value. A unit of code that cannot be integrated into a larger system is of limited value. Integration tests are extremely important for gauging a system's overall health and ensuring that as each component is being developed they can all be combined to form a system. Integration tests should be created during development as well. A common practice is to complete a feature-based unit of work (unit tests are complete and passing) and then create integration tests to ensure that the code you just created can be consumed by (or consume) the rest of the application. A good motto is "Integrate early; integrate often."

In the interest of keeping your tests focused, you also want to be sure that they test only one thing. According to the Single Responsibility Principle (covered in Chapter 3), each class or method should have one reason to change. A logical and practical extension of this principle is that each class and method should have one purpose and do only one thing. As a result, each unit test should test only one set of requirements. In the example in Chapter 1, the method did one thing: It counted the occurrences of a particular character in a string. It didn't tell you where the character was found in the string, if the instances were of the same case, or any information other than how many occurrences of the character there were. According to the Single Responsibility Principle, those functions should be served by other methods in the StringUtility class. In turn, the StringUtility class should not provide functionality for working with numbers, dates, or complex data types. They are not strings, and by definition the StringUtility class works only with strings.

If you find yourself in a situation where your tests are testing more than one thing, you probably have violated the Single Responsibility Principle. What this means in terms of unit testing is that you have unfocused tests that are difficult to understand. Also, your tests are likely to become brittle and fragile over time as more inappropriate functionality is added to the method or class. Diagnosing problems also becomes a challenge, because your functionality can take multiple paths. Determining which of these paths contains the defect can be difficult. Many times the interaction of these branches can be the cause of the defects. Defects of this type are also difficult to fix, because a change to one branch can cause unpredictable behavior in the other.

Another situation you may find yourself in where you are violating this concept is by mixing your unit tests and integration test. Remember, a good unit test does not break the boundaries around what is being tested. If you find you are testing more than one thing in your unit tests, look at the test itself. You may be pushing too hard against those boundaries.

Unit tests should be predictable. When you call a method on a class for a given set of input parameters, the result should always be consistent. Sometimes this principle may seem hard to adhere to. For example, if you are writing a commodity trading application, it's likely that the price of gold will be one value at 9 a.m. and a different value at 2:30 p.m. There are also potential situations where you may need to build the ability to create randomization functionality into your system.

In these cases a good design principle is to abstract the functionality that provides unpredictable data into another class or method that can be mocked in your unit test. (Mocking is covered in more detail later in this chapter in the section "Decoupling with Mock Objects.") In the case of your commodity system, the service that provides the time-sensitive price should be mocked. Depending on your needs, you may want that test implementation to always return the same value. Or you may want it to provide a predetermined value given a specific time. In the case of randomization, it would be a good design practice to wrap the randomization in a service class that can also be mocked by your tests to always return the same value or sequence of values. These predictable sets of data allow you to write tests that are specific and exercise your code effectively without your having to worry about getting different results in each test run.

Other Types of Tests

The focus of this book is unit tests, but those are not the only tests that are important to software development. Unit tests verify one set of a system's aspects — that the internal classes, methods, and services meet the business requirements and provide the necessary functionality. A complete application has many more dimensions than the business-based internals.

User interface tests verify that the application's user interface operates correctly, that it can be used by the application's audience, and that it provides a way to access all the necessary functionality. Within each of these criteria are a myriad of things to consider. Is the application a web-based application that the user will access with a web browser? Is it a Windows forms-based application similar to Microsoft Word or Excel? What about Silverlight? What are the usability requirements? Do you need to make your application accessible to visually impaired people? Who is your audience, and how computer savvy are they? Are they employees of your company, or are they external customers? What about security?

User interface testing clearly is not a trivial matter. Nor is it unimportant when developing a high-quality application. Many tools can help you automate various types of user interface testing. Some are targeted to web-based applications, and others are focused on Windows forms. Ultimately the best way to perform these types of tests is to employ an experienced and knowledgeable Quality Assurance department. A skilled QA engineer who understands the business is worth his or her weight in gold. Often these individuals are the final arbiters of whether a system is ready to be deployed to production or must be sent back for rework.

Integration tests are an important step in software development and should not be skipped or left until the end of development. Many a developer has spent the night before a system was supposed to be deployed fighting defects raised when he attempted to unite the pieces of a system into one application. This can be alleviated by integrating features with the rest of the systems as they are completed. In fact, a common practice in agile methodologies is to get software, even if it's not entirely complete, in front of users quickly. Clearly, this is not possible without integrating your application. Therefore, you can infer that thorough integration testing is a key component of a successful agile methodology.

Unit tests and even integration tests verify that your individual features and your application as a whole work with one user. But what will happen to your application when 100 users try to access it at once? This concern is addressed by stress testing your application. Stress testing is simply creating test conditions that simulate multiple users interacting with your application concurrently. Stress testing is designed to measure response time under load as well as how well an application scales when it is spread across multiple resources. Most user interface (UI) tools provide some form of stress testing.

Stress testing traditionally has been delayed until an application is deployed to some sort of QA environment. Granted, until the application is deployed to the actual production hardware, it is difficult to determine a baseline performance metric. I feel, though, that stress testing should be done in some form throughout application development. The numbers generated by stress testing so early and on nonproduction hardware cannot be used to state the actual application's expected performance in production. However, stress-testing an application early in its development process and continuing to gather metrics has an advantage. As the application is built, the development team knows immediately if new functionality creates a sudden and negative effect on the application's performance or scalability.

For example, suppose that, in an application that is undergoing development, the average operation takes 2 seconds with 100 concurrent users. The team checks in two new features, and suddenly the average time for the same number of users jumps to 5 seconds. Clearly something in one of those two features has impacted the application's performance. Because you performed stress testing along the way, you know that it had to be something in one of the two recently completed features. If stress testing had been delayed until the end, this information would have been lost in a fog, and users would simply complain that the system is slow. By performing stress testing along the way, you can focus on where the problem is and resolve it much more quickly and efficiently.

An important step in stress testing is determining a usable performance metric. How many transactions per hour should the system be able to process? How many concurrent users should the system support? What are acceptable response times for the system? All developers have worked on applications where the users have complained that "It's just slow." No doubt many systems can be optimized, but without some form of metric to measure performance and some idea of what the target performance is, meaningful optimization is difficult to perform for such a subjective complaint. You need to ask, "In what way is it slow?"

Most applications go through some form of user acceptance testing (UAT), usually at the end of the application development process. This testing occurs when the business users finally get to use the software in real-world scenarios and evaluate its performance. If the application fulfills their needs, the users sign off on the application, and the next stop usually is production.

In waterfall methodologies UAT was usually the last step in the project plan before the application was deployed to production. And in most cases it was also the first time any user saw any part of the new application. Because the project team normally was working in their own silo away from the business users, the first round of UAT often ended with long lists of things that the users didn't like. Some of these got fixed. Others were deemed low priority, and the users were told they would just have to live with these issues. Usually a long period of time had transpired between the project's inception and UAT, and the application may not even have reflected the current needs of the business.

Imagine for a moment that you are building a house. For most of us, a house is the most expensive thing we will ever buy. The opportunity to have a house built to your desires and specifications is something to be excited about. Imagine, though, that when you leave the architect's office for the last time, you will not be allowed to see the house's progress or make changes to the blueprints or design until the house is completed. Imagine that the first time you get to see the house is the day you move in. How well do you think the house would reflect what you actually wanted? It may reflect what's on the blueprints, but there's a big difference between a drawing and a physical structure. Amazingly, this is how many companies still develop software.

In organizations that use agile development methodologies, the users are shown the application as a work in progress many times before UAT. This allows them to spot features or aspects of the application that are not working how they want and ensures that as the application is built it remains aligned with the needs of the business. Developers and development managers benefit from this short feedback loop as well, because defects that are found quickly after they have been introduced to the system are quicker, easier, and less expensive to repair.

A BRIEF LOOK AT NUNIT

Many tools can help you perform unit testing. Since TDD's rise in popularity in 2005, the market for frameworks and tools has exploded. One of the most popular types of unit testing tools are unit test frameworks. These frameworks let you define your unit test code, control the execution of the tests, and provide an application to run the tests and report on the success of each test in your test suite. NUnit is one of the most popular and mature of the .NET unit test frameworks.

What Is a Unit Test Framework?

Before unit test frameworks, developers had a difficult time creating executable tests. The initial practice was to create a window in your application that was dubbed the "test harness." This was simply a window with a button for each test. The results of the tests were either a message box or some sort of readout on the form itself. With a button for each test, these windows soon became crowded and unmanageable. Some enterprising developers moved to using console applications that would execute each test and output the results to the console. This was a step forward in that developers could spend more time on their test and less on their test harness. It also had the benefit that you could easily have it run automatically from a build server.

These methods worked to a degree, but they didn't provide a common means for creating, executing, and interrogating tests. Unit test frameworks such as NUnit sought to provide those features. Unit test frameworks provide a unified programming model to define your tests as simple classes with methods that call the application code that you want to test. Developers do not need to write their own test harness; the unit test frameworks provide test runners that allow you to execute all your tests with the click of a button. With a unit test framework, you can easily insert, set up, and tear down functionality around your tests. When a test fails, the test runner provides you with information about the failure, including any exception information that is available and a stack trace.

As mentioned, NUnit is arguably the most popular unit testing framework for .NET. There is a good reason for this. NUnit, which is based on JUnit a Java-based unit testing tool. NUnit is stable, easy to use, and executes quickly. NUnit has an active user community around it. This community provides the base framework with new features and enhancements while creating many popular add-ons that make NUnit an appropriate choice for almost any unit testing need. NUnit is easy to learn and use and has become a standard tool in almost every TDD practitioner's toolbox.

The Basics of NUnit

Most unit tests you write will have a very simple pattern:

➤ Perform some activity to set up your test.

➤ Execute your test.

➤ Verify its result.

➤ If necessary, reset your environment.

Your tests themselves are methods that execute and call the methods you are testing. These methods must reside in a class, which is called a test fixture. The following example shows a class using the TestFixture attribute to indicate that it is a test class, and the Test attribute to indicate the method that is our test:

```
namespace NUnitExample
{
    [TestFixture]
    public class ExampleTests
    {
        [Test]
        public void TestMethod()
        {
            Debug.WriteLine("This is a test");
        }
    }
}
```

Occasionally some setup needs to happen before you run your test, such as populating a dataset, instantiating a class, or setting up an environment variable. In such a case, you can use the Setup attribute to define a method that will execute before your test runs:

```
namespace NUnitExample
{
    [TestFixture]
    public class ExampleTests
    {
        private string _testMessage;

        [SetUp]
        public void SetupForTest()
        {
            _testMessage = "This is a test.";
        }

        [Test]
        public void TestMethod()
        {
            Debug.WriteLine(_testMessage);
        }
    }
}
```

In this example, the variable _testMessage is initialized in the `SetupForTest` method. When `TestMethod` executes, the value that was assigned to the variable _testMessage (`"This is a test."`) is written to the Debug console. Of course, if you can have setup code for your tests, it only makes sense that you have code to reset resources used by your tests when they are finished. NUnit provides the `TearDown` attribute to give you this ability:

```
namespace NUnitExample
{
    [TestFixture]
    public class ExampleTests
    {
        private string _testMessage;

        [SetUp]
        public void SetupForTest()
        {
            _testMessage = "This is a test.";
        }

        [Test]
        public void TestMethod()
        {
            Debug.WriteLine(_testMessage);
        }

        [TearDown]
        public void TearDownAfterTest()
        {
            _testMessage = string.Empty;
        }
    }
}
```

This example replicates a situation in which you may want or need to reset a resource after a test has finished running. You probably won't need to reset an instance variable, but you might need to reset an environment variable or roll back a database transaction.

Right now the test executes, but it doesn't really test anything. You can change that by using an *assert* — a way of telling the test runner application the final result of the test. Many different types of asserts available in NUnit test conditions such as equality of two values, whether two reference type variables point to same object, and whether various conditions are met. Some examples later in the book demonstrate how to use a framework called NBehave to write the asserts in your tests; that syntax is covered in Chapter 7. For now, because these tests don't use NUnit asserts extensively, I'll just cover the most basic ones. In the first example, the test simply verifies whether the length of _testMessage is greater than 0:

```
[Test]
public void MessageLengthGreaterThanZero()
{
    if (_testMessage.Length > 0)
    {
```

```
        Assert.Pass();
    }
    else
    {
        Assert.Fail();
    }
}
```

There is an NUnit assert that would verify that the length of _testMessage is more than 0, but this example just focuses on the basic asserts that you could use for general purposes. This test checks the length of _testMessage. If it's more than 0, the test calls Assert.Pass, which tells the test runner that the test passes, as shown in Figure 2-1.

To see Assert.Fail work, you add a test to see if the length of the value in _testMessage is greater than 100:

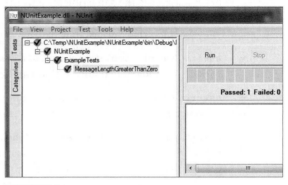

FIGURE 2-1

```
[Test]
public void MessageLengthGreaterThan100()
{
    if (_testMessage.Length > 100)
    {
        Assert.Pass();
    }
    else
    {
        Assert.Fail();
    }
}
```

When the test is run, it fails because Assert .Fail is called, as shown in Figure 2-2.

Many other types of asserts are available in NUnit. For the project that I'll be building in later chapters, I'll use NBehave to write the asserts, which will provide a more business-friendly syntax. But with knowledge of Assert.Pass and Assert.Fail, you could opt out to native NUnit if needed without

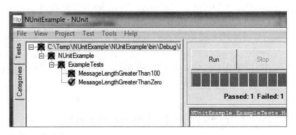

FIGURE 2-2

having to know the other types of asserts. Some other asserts available from the NUnit library are:

➤ **Assert.AreEqual(expected, actual)** — This method is overloaded to take any type of value for expected or actual, so long as both arguments are of the same type. Passing in different types of numerical arguments for each parameter will still work as the method can up-cast or down-cast as needed. For example, passing in an integer and a double will not cause an error. For value types, this assert will verify that the expected and actual parameters have the same value. When passing in a reference type (an object) the method will use the result of the objects `Equals` method to determine if this assert succeeds. There is a corollary assert called `AreNotEqual` which verifies that the two values are not equal.

➤ **`Assert.AreSame(expected, actual)`** — This assert takes reference types as its arguments. It is used to determine whether the object passed in for expected and the argument passed in for actual are the same object. This means that both objects occupy the same space in memory and are not simply copies of one another. There is a corollary assert called `Assert .AreNotSame` that verifies that the two objects are not the same object.

➤ **`Assert.IsTrue(bool)/Assert.IsFalse(bool)`** — This assert takes either a Boolean variable or a logical condition that can be evaluated to a Boolean result.

➤ **`Assert.IsNull(object)/Assert.IsNotNull(object)`** — This assert will examine a reference type and determine whether it is null.

➤ **`Assert.Greater(x,y)/Assert.GreaterOrEqual(x,y)`** — Evaluates either two value types or two reference types that implement the `IComparable` interface to determine if x is greater that y (x > y) or if x is greater than or equal to y (x >= y). Like AreEqual, `Greater/ GreaterOrEqual` can take two different types of numbers, provided it was up-cast/ down-cast appropriately to make the comparison. NUnit also provides `Assert.Less` and `Assert.LessOrEqual` which behave in the same way, but verify that x is less than y (x < y) or that x is less than or equal to y (x <= y).

The asserts listed here are the most commonly used asserts in NUnit, but there are many more available in the NUnit library. If you are interested in the full list of asserts available in NUnit, www.nunit.org has extensive documentation organized by version.

DECOUPLING WITH MOCK OBJECTS

A well-written piece of software tries to limit dependencies. There comes a point, however, where each of your components must be coupled with another to form a greater whole. These couplings create a web of dependencies within your application that usually end in an external resource, be it a database, web service, file system, or other resource. Mock objects are designed to stand in for these other components in your application and the external resources they sometimes represent. This allows you to test your code without having to worry about the consequences of interacting with other resources.

Why Mocking Is Important

When you write unit tests for a method, your intention is to test only the code in that method. This is by design; you are attempting to isolate the code under test. The reason for this is that you want to assess the validity of only that piece of code for a given condition. A condition can be defined as not only the input data for that method, but also the context and environment that the code will execute in.

By isolating that code, you can ensure that any failing tests point squarely to a problem with that specific method, not a method in a far-flung corner of the system. For this example, it's okay to assume that the other components your method works with are correct and have been tested themselves and that you can rely on the quality of these components and tests. (I'll talk more about dealing with third-party components in Chapter 5.) You care about only the method in front of you at that point in time.

Unit tests should also be able to be run quickly. Even in a small application, if TDD is applied correctly, is it not unusual to have hundreds of unit tests. Your goal is to have developers run these tests frequently during their development to ensure that changes they are making to their methods and classes are not negatively impacting other parts of the system. If only a small amount of work is done between a successful test and a failed test, you need to examine only that small amount of work to determine what went wrong. If these tests take several hours or even just minutes to run, they will not be run frequently enough.

A test that is never run is worthless. Most tests that take a long time to run do so because they are interacting with an external resource, such as a database. Database calls can be slow, especially if you are executing hundreds at once against a development database. An object that mocks that database can return predefined values for predefined parameters instantly without having to connect to a database and execute a SQL query. This provides much faster execution than querying the database directly.

Unit tests should be predictable and consistent. When writing a method and its corresponding tests, you should be able to be certain that if your method receives X and Y as arguments, Z will always be returned. External resources, and the data they contain, change over time. If your method and the test that invokes it rely on an external resource, you can't guarantee that you will always get the same results for the same input parameters. By mocking this resource, you can be sure that you're always getting consistent and reliable data to test your method against.

Finally, most development projects are undertaken by teams of more than one person. In these cases, your unit tests should be able to run without impacting the test results of your teammates. Perhaps your test suite contains tests that change the state of a database table and other tests that rely on the data in that table. If so, there is a good chance that if two or more developers run the tests concurrently, they will all have failing tests. They are stepping on each other's data, and none are getting the data they are expecting. Mocking these external resources ensures that you won't cause tests run by other developers to fail based on incorrect or unexpected data.

Dummy, Fake, Stub, and Mock

Mock is somewhat of a generic term that covers a family of stand-in objects for use in unit testing. Dummy objects are simple mocks that stand in for an external resource. They usually return a predefined response for a method when that method is invoked, but they usually can't vary that response based on the input parameters. Many developers who don't want to incur the overhead of a mocking framework and don't need the functionality provided by one use hand-rolled dummy objects in their tests.

 For the purposes of these examples I will not be using a mocking framework. I will be hand-rolling these mocks, which will enable you to see the internals of each type of mock and have a better understanding of what is going on in each type of mock. The mocking framework used for the examples in this book, Moq, will be introduced later in this chapter in the section, "A Brief Look at Moq."

The examples in this section, include tests for a class called DependentClass. DependentClass has a dependency on a class that implements the interface IDependency. DependentClass has a method called get GetValue that takes a string as a parameter. The implementation of GetValue in the DependentClass class calls the GetValue method on the implementation of IDependency that is provided to the DependentClass as a constructor argument when an instance of DependentClass is created. The definition of DependentClass and IDependency are shown here:

```csharp
internal interface IDependency
{
    int GetValue();
}

internal class DependentClass
{
    private readonly IDependency _dependency;

    public DependentClass(IDependency dependency)
    {
        _dependency = dependency;
    }

    public int GetValue(string s)
    {
        return _dependency.GetValue(s);
    }
}
```

In the following code, you can see that I have a test that will test the implementation of DependentClass when it has been passed an instance of DummyDependency, a dummy object that implements the IDependency interface:

```csharp
[TestFixture]
public class DummyTestClass
{
    [Test]
    public void TestWithADummy()
    {
        var dependency = new DummyDependency();
        var dependentClass = new DependentClass(dependency);
        const string param = "abc";
        const int expectedResultOne = 1;

        var resultOne = dependentClass.GetValue(param);
        Assert.AreEqual(expectedResultOne, resultOne);
    }
}

public class DummyDependency : IDependency
{
    public int GetValue(string s)
    {
        return 1;
    }
}
```

The test method creates an instance of the DummyDependency class and passes it in as the implementation of IDependency that DependentClass needs at instantiation. The test calls GetValue on the instance of DependentClass and passes the string "abc" as its parameter.

The DummyDependency class has an implementation of GetValue that simply returns the value one. This satisfies the test; the value one is the expected result and the dummy object DummyDependency satisfies that requirement.

But you can easily see the limitations of the dummy object. In spite of whatever value is passed in by the test, the dummy object can react only one way; by returning a value of one. There are occasions where this limitation is not an issue. But for most tests that are verifying business domain logic, a more robust means of mocking is necessary.

Fakes and stubs are a step up from dummy objects in that they can vary their response based on input parameters. For example, a stub of a database may return the name Rick Nash for user ID 61 and the name Steve Mason for user ID 1. Aside from that, no logic is invoked. A stub generally cannot track how many times a method was called or in what order a sequence of methods were called. An example of a stub is provided here:

```
[TestFixture]
public class StubTestClass
{
    [Test]
    public void TestWithAStub()
    {
        var dependency = new StubDependency();
        var dependentClass = new DependentClass(dependency);
        const string param1 = "abc";
        const string param2 = "xyz";
        const int expectedResultOne = 1;
        const int expectedResultTwo = 2;

        var resultOne = dependentClass.GetValue(param1);
        var resultTwo = dependentClass.GetValue(param2);
        Assert.AreEqual(expectedResultOne, resultOne);
        Assert.AreEqual(expectedResultTwo, resultTwo);
    }
}

public class StubDependency : IDependency
{
    public int GetValue(string s)
    {
        if (s == "abc")
            return 1;
        if (s == "xyz")
            return 2;
        return 0;
    }
}
```

The preceding example creates a new class called StubDependency that implements the IDependency interface. Unlike the DummyDependency, the implementation of GetValue on

StubDependency has some logic to returned different values based on different input parameters. This stub is able to respond to different stimuli in different specific ways. This provides a much more robust way of mocking than dummy objects.

A mock is a step up from fakes and stubs. Mocks provide the same functionality as stubs but are more complex. They can have rules defined for them that dictate in what order methods on their API must be called. Most mocks can track how many times a method was called and can react based on that information. Mocks generally know the context of each call and can react differently in different situations. Because of this, mocks require some knowledge of the class they are mocking.

For the example of a mock, I've added a few members to the IDependency interface and DependentClass class:

```
internal interface IDependency
{
    int GetValue(string s);
    void CallMeFirst();
    int CallMeTwice(string s);
    void CallMeLast();
}

internal class DependentClass
{
    private readonly IDependency _dependency;

    public DependentClass(IDependency dependency)
    {
        _dependency = dependency;
    }

    public int GetValue(string s)
    {
        return _dependency.GetValue(s);
    }

    public void CallMeFirst()
    {
        _dependency.CallMeFirst();
    }

    public void CallMeLast()
    {
        _dependency.CallMeLast();
    }

    public int CallMeTwice(string s)
    {
        return _dependency.CallMeTwice(s);
    }
}
```

IDependency interface and the DependentClass class include three methods: CallMeFirst, CallMeTwice, and CallMeLast. In many APIs you work with as a developer, specific methods have to be called in a specific order and methods need to be called a specific number of times. As is indicated by the new method names of the IDependency interface and the DependentClass class, the method CallMeFirst must be called first, the CallMeTwice method must be called two times and the CallMeLast method must be the last method called for a particular transaction.

To enforce these rules, you need to write a somewhat more sophisticated and complex mocking class that the previous two examples:

```
public class MockDependency : IDependency
{
    private int _callMeTwiceCalled;
    private bool _callMeLastCalled;
    private bool _callMeFirstCalled;

    public int GetValue(string s)
    {
        if (s == "abc")
            return 1;
        if (s == "xyz")
            return 2;
        return 0;
    }

    public void CallMeFirst()
    {
        if ((_callMeTwiceCalled > 0)|| _callMeLastCalled)
            throw new AssertionException("CallMeFirst not first method called");
        _callMeFirstCalled = true;
    }

    public int CallMeTwice(string s)
    {
        if (!_callMeFirstCalled)
            throw new AssertionException("CallMeTwice called before CallMeFirst");
        if (_callMeLastCalled)
            throw new AssertionException("CallMeTwice called after CallMeLast");
        if (_callMeTwiceCalled >= 2)
            throw new AssertionException("CallMeTwice called more than twice");
        _callMeTwiceCalled++;
        return GetValue(s);
    }

    public void CallMeLast()
    {
        if (!_callMeFirstCalled)
            throw new AssertionException("CallMeLast called before CallMeFirst");
        if (_callMeTwiceCalled !=2 )
            throw new AssertionException(
                string.Format("CallMeTwice not called {0} times",
_callMeTwiceCalled));
        _callMeLastCalled = true;
    }
}
```

To be sure that the methods of the implementation of IDependency used by the DummyClass are used correctly it's necessary to build a mock that not only returns values, but encapsulates all the rules of the API. Each method must check to make sure that it's been called in the correct order. In the case of CallMeTwice the method must also verify that it has been called the appropriate number of times.

Before I show you the test based on the MockDependency mocking class, I want to make a couple of points. Clearly based on the code in this example, hand-rolling mocks is inefficient, time consuming and introduces a profound amount of brittleness to your code base. It is for that reason that most developers choose to employ a mocking framework and avoid hand-rolling mocks.

Secondly, you can see in this example that the MockDependency class is required to have quite a bit of knowledge of how the DependentClass uses it. The amount of and type of knowledge necessary in most cases clearly violates many principals of object-oriented programming and good coding practices. In some cases, using a mock that has this level of knowledge is necessary, but if you find yourself doing this kind of mocking often you should take another look at your application design and your code.

The test that tests the DependentClass implementation that uses an implementation of IDependency based on MockDependency is listed here:

```
[TestFixture]
public class MockTestClass
{
    [Test]
    public void TestWithAMock()
    {
        var dependency = new MockDependency();
        var dependentClass = new DependentClass(dependency);

        const string param1 = "abc";
        const string param2 = "xyz";
        const int expectedResultOne = 1;
        const int expectedResultTwo = 2;

        dependentClass.CallMeFirst();
        var resultOne = dependentClass.CallMeTwice(param1);
        var resultTwo = dependentClass.CallMeTwice(param2);
        dependentClass.CallMeLast();

        Assert.AreEqual(expectedResultOne, resultOne);
        Assert.AreEqual(expectedResultTwo, resultTwo);
    }
}
```

With so many options when it comes to types of mocks, a common question is which one to use. The answer is that it depends. In general, you'll want to favor fakes and stubs. Mocks are useful when you need to replicate a more complex interaction with a component, but they usually require more configuration and overhead than is needed for most unit tests. Favoring stubs also ensures that you are designing your system to be loosely coupled; requiring a calling method to know an extensive set of rules to use an API is not very loose. Finally, you should use a spy when a method on a mocked resource does not have a conventional output.

Best and Worst Practices

When using mocks in TDD, you should be aware of some concepts and guidelines:

➤ **Dependency Injection** — Mocking is a key concept that makes TDD a viable way of writing software. To use mocking effectively, your application should use Dependency Injection. In short, this means that instead of statically creating objects that your class is dependent on as part of the class's internal instantiation process, you should provide the class with instances of those objects that conform to the interface needed by the dependency. These instances should be passed in as constructor arguments to the object as it is being created. This makes it easy to substitute mocked objects for actual objects that would be used by the fully integrated application. Dependency Injection is explained in more detail in Chapter 5.

➤ **Design for the interface, not the implementation** — When consuming another class or resource as a dependency, your concern should not be how it performs its tasks, just what the interface is. Likewise, you should use interfaces when designing and building your service's classes to abstract the functionality from the API. This design not only makes your code less brittle and more open for extension, but it also makes mocking easier and more efficient.

➤ **Try to limit dependencies** — Most code needs to be dependent on something. It could be a database to store and retrieve data, or a web service to authenticate a user, or another domain service in your application. Given that, you should work to limit the things that your code is dependent on. Not only do a large number of dependencies signify a brittle system, but such a system also is more difficult to mock and test effectively.

➤ **Do not mock private methods** — When you are writing a test and your code is dependent on another class, you should mock only the public methods. And even then, you should mock only those you will use directly; don't overmock. Mocking private methods requires knowledge of the internal function of the service you are mocking — knowledge that, according to the encapsulation rule, you should not have. As a consumer of a service, you should only concern yourself with the methods on the public interface; the protected and private methods should be invisible to you.

➤ **Don't cheat** — As you continue with your practice of TDD, you'll be tempted at times to take shortcuts with your mocking. Maybe it's because a particular dependency requires a mock that is a little more complicated than you're used to. Maybe the stubbed method must return a complex data or object graph that you just don't feel like creating. Don't let yourself get caught in that trap. Tests form the quality baseline for your applications. Your tests rely on mocks and stubs to ensure that they can correctly interact with the various dependencies your system will contain. If you take shortcuts with your mocks, your tests and, by extension, your software will suffer.

A BRIEF LOOK AT MOQ

.NET has many mocking frameworks. For years Rhino Mocks was *the* mocking framework for .NET, and many applications used it extensively in test suites. In addition to Rhino Mocks, other mocking frameworks such as NUnit Mocks, TypeMock, and Easy Mock have gained popularity. They are all good frameworks and offer various features that may make them more or less appealing to various developers and development teams. Some developers still prefer to hand-roll their own mocks, but this is becoming less frequent as mocking frameworks have become more widespread, full-featured, and easy to use. A mocking framework is definitely preferable to rolling your own mocks, and it can make your TDD experience more efficient and fulfilling. Moq is quickly becoming one of the most popular mocking frameworks for .NET. It has a solid list of features, is easy to use, and has a large community support base, which ensures constant improvement and development of Moq's features.

What Does a Mocking Framework Do?

A mocking framework gives you the facilities to quickly create and consume stubs and mocks. Using a mocking frameworks API, you can create your mocks and inject your own testing functionality at runtime. Mocking frameworks also give you a Domain-Specific Language (DSL) for defining execution rules for your mocked resources.

A Bit About Moq

Moq is an open-source .NET mocking framework that is published under the BSD license. Moq was built to take advantage of new language features in .NET 3.5 and C# 3.0 — specifically, lambdas. Moq eschews the record/playback functionality that many mocking frameworks use in favor of a more declarative syntax. Moq was developed to be lightweight and simple to use. Moq has a very active user and supporter community, with updates and bug fixes being checked in to the code bases almost daily.

Moq Basics

Moq is easy to use. The following example shows you how to create mocks and stubs for tests based on this class and interface:

```
public interface ILongRunningLibrary
{
    string RunForALongTime(int interval);
}

public class LongRunningLibrary : ILongRunningLibrary
{
    public string RunForALongTime(int interval)
    {
        var timeToWait = interval*1000;
```

```
        Thread.Sleep(timeToWait);
        return string.Format("Waited {0} seconds", interval);
    }
}
```

The purpose of this method is to simulate a long-running process, such as a database query. In this example I start by showing you how a long-running process can make the process of testing very slow as the test must wait for the long running test to execute. Later in this example, I replace the long running process that simulates accessing a database with a mock that stands in for the database call without actually accessing the database. This example shows how to run it without using a stub:

```
[TestFixture]
public class MoqExamples
{
    private ILongRunningLibrary _longRunningLibrary;

    [SetUp]
    public void SetupForTest()
    {
        _longRunningLibrary = new LongRunningLibrary();
    }

    [Test]
    public void TestLongRunningLibrary()
    {
        const int interval = 30;
        var result = _longRunningLibrary.RunForALongTime(interval);
        Debug.WriteLine("Return from method was '{0}'", result);
    }
}
```

As you can see, this test simply instantiates the LongRunningLibrary and calls the RunForALongTime method. The test then writes the results of this method to the debug console. If you run this test in the test runner, the test waits while the method executes and then writes the output to the debug console, as shown in Figure 2-3.

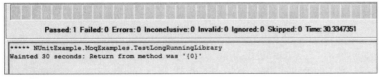

FIGURE 2-3

The test passed, but 30 seconds is a long time to wait. Imagine if you were running 10 of these. Or even 100! You're also a bit at the mercy of the implementation of the RunForALongTime method and the rest of the LongRunningLibrary class. If that class were to change or have a defect, you may not get a meaningful pass or failure of your test.

The first thing you must do is declare a new type for the variable _longRunningLibrary. Instead of creating a concrete instance, you will ask Moq to create a mocked instance based on the ILongRunningLibrary interface:

```
private Mock<ILongRunningLibrary> _longRunningLibrary;

[SetUp]
public void SetupForTest()
{
    _longRunningLibrary = new Mock<ILongRunningLibrary>();
}
```

Because _longRunningLibrary is now a mock, you have to deal with it a bit differently in the test method. To access the methods on the mocked instance, you need to use the Object property of the mocked object:

```
[Test]
public void TestLongRunningLibrary()
{
    const int interval = 30;
    var result = _longRunningLibrary.Object.RunForALongTime(interval);
    Debug.WriteLine("Return from method was '{0}'", result);
}
```

If you run it now, you don't get quite the result you expected, as shown in Figure 2-4.

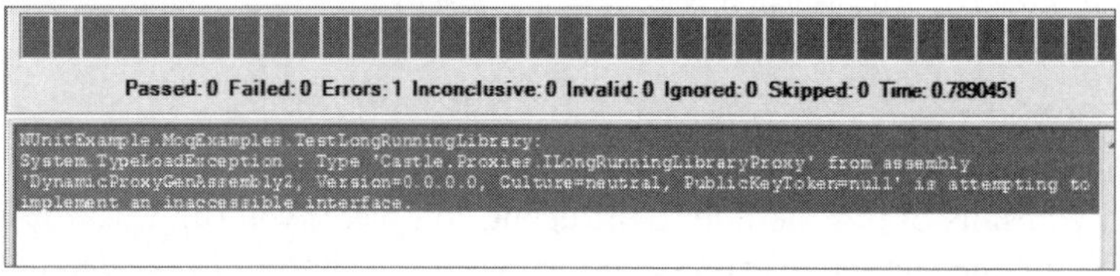

Passed: 0 Failed: 0 Errors: 1 Inconclusive: 0 Invalid: 0 Ignored: 0 Skipped: 0 Time: 0.7890451

```
NUnitExample.MoqExamples.TestLongRunningLibrary:
System.TypeLoadException : Type 'Castle.Proxies.ILongRunningLibraryProxy' from assembly
'DynamicProxyGenAssembly2, Version=0.0.0.0, Culture=neutral, PublicKeyToken=null' is attempting to
implement an inaccessible interface.
```

FIGURE 2-4

The test failed because a mocked instance of LongRunningLibrary was provided, but not an implementation for the mocked method. This is easily corrected:

```
_longRunningLibrary
                .Setup(lrl => lrl.RunForALongTime(30))
                .Returns("This method has been mocked!");
```

In this example, you are telling Moq that when the RunForALongTime method is called on the mocked instance of LongRunningLibrary with an argument of 30, you just want it to return the string "This method has been mocked!". If you run this in the test runner now, the test passes, as shown in Figure 2-5.

```
Passed: 1 Failed: 0 Errors: 0 Inconclusive: 0 Invalid: 0 Ignored: 0 Skipped: 0 Time: 0.5430311

***** NUnitExample.MoqExamples.TestLongRunningLibrary
Return from method was 'This method has been mocked!'
```

FIGURE 2-5

Right now your stub is only set up to take a value of 30 as its input parameter. If you were to run the test again, but this time pass in 100, you would see that although your test passes, you don't get the response from the stubbed method you expected, as shown in Figure 2-6.

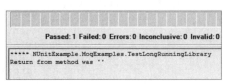

```
Passed: 1 Failed: 0 Errors: 0 Inconclusive: 0 Invalid: 0

***** NUnitExample.MoqExamples.TestLongRunningLibrary
Return from method was ''
```

FIGURE 2-6

Generally, you should use static values when mocking your methods. You want to make sure you have expected outputs for expected inputs when testing. But there will be times when this is impractical. In these cases Moq gives you a couple of options.

The first is to use Moq's It.IsAny method to specify that although your stub expects a value of a specific type, any value of that type is acceptable. For example, if you make this change to the stub method setup code:

```
_longRunningLibrary
        .Setup(lrl => lrl.RunForALongTime(It.IsAny<int>()))
        .Returns("This method has been mocked!");
```

and then run the same test where you pass 100 as the interval instead of 30, you get the response in your test runner shown in Figure 2-7.

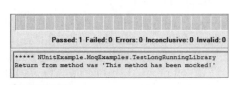

```
Passed: 1 Failed: 0 Errors: 0 Inconclusive: 0 Invalid: 0

***** NUnitExample.MoqExamples.TestLongRunningLibrary
Return from method was 'This method has been mocked!'
```

FIGURE 2-7

The ability to accept any value of a specified type is powerful and should not be overused. Traditionally, an issue with this type of stub has been that because most stubs return a static value, there was no way to verify on the other side that a valid value was passed into the stub. Moq provides a facility to access the input parameters of a stubbed method and use them however you like in the return value. In this case, you append the value to the end of your return value:

```
_longRunningLibrary
        .Setup(lrl => lrl.RunForALongTime(It.IsAny<int>()))
        .Returns((int s) =>
            string.Format(
                "This method has been mocked! The input value was {0}", s));
```

Now when you run your test in the test runner, you can see that your input parameter has been included in the return string value, as shown in Figure 2-8.

```
Passed: 1 Failed: 0 Errors: 0 Inconclusive: 0 Invalid: 0 Ignored: 0 Skipped: 0 Time

***** NUnitExample.MoqExamples.TestLongRunningLibrary
Return from method was 'This method has been mocked! The input value was 100'
```

FIGURE 2-8

In some situations you will want to verify that a method throws an exception for a specified set of conditions. For this example let's assume that 0 is an invalid interval and should throw an `ArgumentException`. You can add a setup for your stub to specify that 0 as an argument should cause `ArgumentException` to be thrown from your stub:

```
_longRunningLibrary = new Mock<ILongRunningLibrary>();
_longRunningLibrary
                .Setup(lrl => lrl.RunForALongTime(It.IsAny<int>()))
                .Returns((int s) =>
                    string.Format(
                        "This method has been mocked!
                        The input value was {0}", s));
_longRunningLibrary
                .Setup(lrl => lrl.RunForALongTime(0))
                .Throws(new ArgumentException("0 is not a valid interval"));
```

The order in which you call your setup methods is important. Moq stacks these rules, so if you were to put the setup that has a rule for 0 as a parameter first, it would be overwritten by the rule that covers any integer being passed in. Therefore, the exception would never happen. In general, you want to put the least-specific setups first in the stack, followed by the most-specific. You can think of this stack as a sort of sieve; you want to catch every combination you can at the correct level. If the first levels are too restrictive, the condition will be caught too soon and at the incorrect level. Creating these stacks can be a bit of an art, but with practice it will become simple.

When I change the interval to 0 and rerun the test, I get the result shown in Figure 2-9.

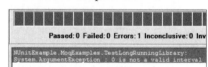

FIGURE 2-9

Moq is a powerful mocking framework that provides mocking and stubbing for a wide variety of scenarios. This chapter has covered only a small number of Moq's features. As you progress through this book, I'll demonstrate other features of Moq as needed. But the ability to create stubs that respond to value arguments and return static or dynamic value, along with the ability to throw exceptions, should cover the vast majority of situations you find yourself creating stubs for.

SUMMARY

Unit tests should be designed to isolate and verify small parts of code. If your test strays into calls across multiple methods, you should think about your test and class design. Integration tests are important, but they serve a different purpose than unit tests. Don't confuse the purpose of unit tests with these other types of tests. Keep your unit tests small and simple and reflective of the business needs. Only write unit tests against your class's public interface, and use interfaces liberally.

NUnit and Moq are crucial tools for effectively practicing TDD. NUnit is an easy-to-use and widely popular unit testing framework for .NET. It provides facilities to write unit tests that can be executed by a test running, quickly giving you results of your test run. Moq lets you create mocks and stubs of external resources and intra-application dependencies so that you know you're focusing on only the specific code under test. Moq lets you create objects that stand in for these resources and provide some limited functionality for the code under test to verify its functionality.

3

A Quick Review of Refactoring

WHAT'S IN THIS CHAPTER?

➤ Why Refactoring application code is important

➤ How Clean Code principals such as OOP and SOLID help you build robust applications

➤ How to identify and fix some of the most common design and coding mistakes in application development

No code is perfect. For developers, accepting this fact is very freeing. There will always be something you could have done better, although maybe you don't realize it at the time. Looking at code you've written in previous years, you may sometimes find small, subtle things you would like to change to make the code faster, more aligned with the business, or simply easier to maintain. Other times you may say, "If only I knew then what I know now, I would have done this completely different."

Refactoring is the act of changing the internal implementation of a class or method with the aim of making the code more readable and maintainable. Refactoring also reduces the code's overall complexity without changing the external behavior of the class or method. These alterations can be as simple as changing the name of a method or variable to moving methods from one class to another or even splitting large classes into several smaller ones. Refactoring allows you to continuously change and improve your code.

This chapter explains why refactoring your code is important. It reviews object-oriented programming and the SOLID Principles. It also shows you some common coding and design problems, colloquially referred to as "code smells," and demonstrates common patterns for eliminating them from your code.

WHY REFACTOR?

When practicing TDD, the goal when initially writing a method or creating a class is to simply make the test pass and nothing more. At this point you're not necessarily looking for style points or to make your code reusable or elegant. You're simply trying to make the tests "all green," meaning that the tests all pass. Once you've accomplished this, the next step is to improve your code. In practice this is a very practical approach. Many developers spend too much time trying to make their code elegant and beautiful the first time through. They end up missing some important pieces of business functionality that they then have to somehow work into their code. By starting from a point of complete business functionality before making your code beautiful, you ensure that the top priority — working business code — is met before anything else. Unit tests help you make sure that no matter what you change in the name of refactoring, your code still meets the business need. This is the genesis of the term *fearless refactoring*.

A Project's Lifecycle

TDD involves a lot of new concepts for many developers, such as mocking and dependency injection (covered in Chapter 5). These are relatively simple to understand and to get comfortable with compared to one of the major (if not the prime) tenets of TDD: Write a test before you write your code. The idea behind TDD (remember, the first D stands for driven) is that your tests become living, breathing executable versions of your business (and sometimes your nonfunctional or technical) requirements. By employing this test-first philosophy, you can ensure that you never write code that does not add some value to the application. An example of using test-first development is the focus of Chapter 6.

Once you have a test, your goal is to write just enough code to make that test pass. No more, no less. Your strategy should be how to get from point A (a failing test) to point B (all tests passing) with the shortest and straightest line possible. Don't worry about other aspects of the system yet.

Also, don't worry about an aspect of the feature that is not in the tests but that you are almost certain the business will want. For example; a feature specifies that a method take an integer as an input parameter. You *just know* that that input parameter has be a value of 100 or less. Your test should *only* test for numbers; there is nothing in the feature about limiting to numbers with values of 100 or less. Until that feature gets scheduled, and a unit test is created for it, it's not a requirement. What happens if that feature never actually gets scheduled? At best you've written code that provides no value but that must be maintained along with the rest of the code base. At worst you've needlessly overcomplicated what should have been a simple piece of functionality. The software development term YAGNI stands for You Aren't Going to Need It. If that feature gets scheduled, at that point you can write those tests and the necessary code to make them pass. For now, worry only about the test for the current feature you are working on.

After you've concluded that your test passes and you haven't broken anything else in the application (all tests pass), it's time to look at potential areas to improve. Maybe your variable or method names no longer reflect the true intent of the value or functionality provided. Perhaps you've duplicated some functionality in your new code. Maybe you have a function that is a bit long, and breaking it up would improve its readability. In any case, now is the time to refactor.

Start by making a small improvement to your code, such as renaming a variable. Once you've done that, run your tests to verify that the external functionality of your class or method has not changed. Don't run the tests for only the code you just wrote; run them all. This is necessary to ensure that you have not caused an adverse side effect somewhere else in the code base. When you're satisfied that your change has not had any adverse effect, improve the next issue with your code, and run the tests again. Repeat as needed. This practice is known as "red, green, refactor." This means that you start with a test that fails because you haven't implemented the logic to make it pass yet. Then you implement the test so that it passes. Finally, you refactor to improve the code while not breaking the test.

Maintainability

It's been established that when practicing TDD, your initial goal when writing code is simply to make the tests pass. As time goes on and the application and the business it supports evolve, the application must change to either support new functionality or change how the current business logic performs its function. The ability to quickly and easily make these changes is important. Refactoring code for readability is an important step in managing an application. Not just for other developers, but for ourselves. Every developer has had the unfortunate experience of looking at code he or she wrote in the past and not remembering what, how, or why the code does what it does.

Refactoring for maintainability should work to simplify the code wherever possible. This includes making sure that methods are short, control structures are simple, and variable and method names are descriptive and clear. Think of refactoring for maintainability as leaving your future self a hint so that you can remember what motivated you to write the code in the first place.

Code Metrics

Measuring the quality of a code base is a subjective task. There are almost as many ideas of what constitutes quality as there are developers. However, a few specifics can give you some hints about what's under the hood in your application.

Code test coverage (code coverage) measures how much of your code base is exercised by your unit test suite. This metric is controversial, because the number tells only part of the story. A code base with less than 100% coverage does not necessarily mean that the code lacks quality. A code base with 100% coverage ensures only that its quality is as good as the tests that exercise it.

The first question to ask when looking at code coverage is what parts of the code base are being measured. In most cases I find that it is more important to write tests based on the functional parts of the source code. This encompasses almost everything except entity objects, data transfer objects, and any object or structure whose sole purpose is to contain data. The reason for this is that my tests test only functionality; a structure that holds data should have no moving parts. Therefore, I could argue that these should not be included in my code coverage metric because they could skew the result low.

On the other hand, the goal of TDD is to write only the code that you need to make the tests pass. If you have several fields on a data structure that a test is not using, why do you need them? Code coverage will quickly uncover what is not being used, allowing you to examine the need for those fields. Of course, there are situations in which your data structures interact with external systems that use the fields in question. In the end you have to use some intelligence and be prepared to do some research when examining code coverage numbers for data entities.

Luckily, the story with functional code in your application is a little more cut and dried. For starters, you should always include any functional code in your code coverage metric. This code should exist only because a test requires it to; therefore, it should have a high code coverage number. Any code in this category that is not covered should be examined. This examination will always reveal one of two outcomes: You are missing a test, or the code is unneeded and should be deleted.

Missing tests are clearly a problem and should be addressed immediately. This also uncovers a significant issue with relying too much on code coverage as an indicator of code quality: Your code coverage number is only as good and reliable as your tests are. If your tests are of low quality, a 100% code coverage number is worthless.

If you have a complete set of tests for your requirements, but you still have code that is not covered by a unit test, that code is probably not needed and can be deleted. Notice I said deleted, not commented out. Unused code is like a parasite in your code base; it provides no value, yet it must be maintained as if it were a contributing part of the application. The only thing this code contributes is noise, so it should be removed to make development easier. If you are using a version control system (and you absolutely should be), you can always replace the code later if you need it (be sure to write a test for it at this time). So it's never really gone forever, but it doesn't belong in your working code.

A metric that has seen a bit of a comeback in recent years (but not in how it was used in the past) is the lines-of-code count. Previously this number was expected to be high and was a bit of a bragging point for some developers and managers, because it indicated that the developers were doing a lot of work. Unfortunately, this perception is a bit backwards. Developers should be looking for ways to do more with fewer lines of code.

It's a fact that the more lines of code you have in a method or class, the greater the chance that defects will emerge. Keeping your methods shorter and more focused reduces the complexity and the likelihood that the code has a flaw. The more lines of code you write, the more chances you give yourself to write the wrong code.

It's also more likely that if you are writing more lines of code, you are duplicating functionality that already exists somewhere in the application. The concept of don't repeat yourself (DRY) in software development states that each unit of functionality should appear in a code base only once. I'll explain this concept more in the discussion of the Single Responsibility Principle later in this chapter.

Cyclomatic complexity is a metric that has been around for a long time. But due to an influx of metric tools, it has only recently become widely used as a code metric in the business world. Cyclomatic complexity measures the number of unique paths that exist in a method, class, or application. A higher number indicates more possible unique paths and therefore a higher degree of complexity in the code.

Code is complex. There is no way around it. At some point your code evaluates a condition and branches off in another direction. The less complex a system is, the easier it is to understand and maintain. Code that has a high cyclomatic complexity number should be refactored to make it simpler. A couple of ways you can do this are to locate methods with several unique paths and to extract some of that branch logic to other methods. Another approach would be to utilize polymorphism (covered later in this chapter) to help remove any control structures that exist only to determine an object's exact concrete type.

CLEAN CODE PRINCIPLES

A growing software craftsmanship movement has, among other things, begun to champion the idea of developers continuing to study their craft, with a goal of being able to write clean code. In summary, the point of this movement and philosophy is that developers should always strive to learn and try to write the best possible code they can based on a set of prescribed practices and principles.

OOP Principles

Object-oriented programming (OOP) is a method of abstracting real-world objects into classes that code can use. The idea is that if you can model your business problems in code, it will be easier to create applications that correctly address those business problems in a way that is more reflective of the real world. Most modern development languages support OOP. OOP makes it easier to conceptualize and develop your applications to meet the business's needs while keeping your individual units of code small and reusable. Having a solid basis in OOP will make many of the concepts you'll use in TDD easier to understand and work with.

In general terms, OOP has three major tenets. Over the years many people have insisted that there are others. These people are not necessarily wrong. But when you scratch the surface of these claims, you quickly find that these additional tenets are intended to either tout the advantages of one language over another or disparage a language or platform as not being truly OOP. Or perhaps they constitute a wish list a developer may have for features he wants to see in his language of choice. These other tenets are not necessarily invalid; binding and messaging are important concepts and in some languages are just as important as the tenets discussed here. But OOP's three universal tenets are encapsulation, inheritance, and polymorphism.

Encapsulation

The *encapsulation rule* states that the classes you create should be black boxes. In other words, the internals of a class should be inaccessible to a client. The client's only means of interacting with or changing the state of a class should be that class's public interface. At no time should the client have or need any knowledge of how a class performs its actions. The client knows only what methods and/or properties to use to get the information or interaction it needs.

You really don't care how the client of a class does its work, so long as you get the results you need. The class also needs to be assured that it is free to perform its work without the risk of unauthorized changes to its internal state. When you design your classes, it is important to scope your methods, properties, and variables correctly. Only members that are part of the public interface should be declared public. Only members that must be used by a descendant of the class should be declared protected. Everything else is private. A good rule of thumb for developers new to this concept is to make everything private until it needs to be public. Also, you should never allow a member variable to be anything other than private; if a descendant class needs to use the variable, make it accessible through a protected property. If the variable needs to be part of the public interface, wrap it in a public property. You should never simply allow unmonitored or uncontrolled access to an internal variable.

Inheritance

As you build the classes in your application, you will soon find that some classes have natural hierarchical relationships to each other. These classes may be similar, but they are not quite equal in functionality. In these cases you can place the common functionality in a base class and have your more-specific classes derive from that class. This is called *inheritance* and is a very important concept in OOP.

Assume that you are writing a payroll application that has entities for hourly employees, salaried employees, and seasonal employees. (See Figure 3-1.)

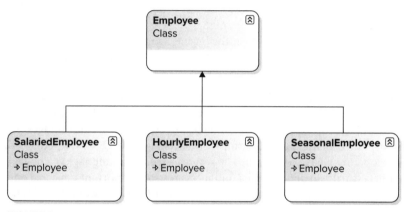

FIGURE 3-1

Your business rules indicate that compensation (salary, benefits, insurance) is computed differently for each type of employee. However, all three have many things in common. Each employee has some biographical information (name, address, work history, tax information), and certain processes are the same for each, such as getting the employee's information from the database.

By utilizing inheritance, you can create an Employee base class that encapsulates all the common functionality for all three employee types. You then create classes for Hourly, Salary, and Seasonal employees. These three more-specific classes derive from, or inherit from, your Employee base class. Your derived classes have access to the functionality of the Employee base class simply by virtue of their ancestor/descendant relationship.

Classes that inherit from a base class have a few options as to how they handle the functionality provided in the base class. They can take that functionality as is, simply allowing clients to call those methods on their instantiated objects as if the derived class contained the same functionality locally. The derived class may choose to override the base class's implementation and extend it by calling the base class's implementation from its own implementation, or simply ignore the functionality provided by the base class.

Base classes also have some say in how their functionality is consumed by the derived class. The base class can declare some or all of its methods as abstract methods. This means that the derived class must provide its own implementation based on the interface defined in the base class.

Inheritance clearly gives developers a lot of power to reuse and leverage existing code. It's important, however, to make sure that inheritance is not overused. Deep inheritance trees can introduce new types of complexities. They can end up making the code brittle and difficult to change if a unit of logic in the middle of the hierarchy has to be altered. In some cases using composition over inheritance is preferable. For example, an entity called `PayableEmployee` had been inserted into the `Employee` hierarchy (Figure 3-2).

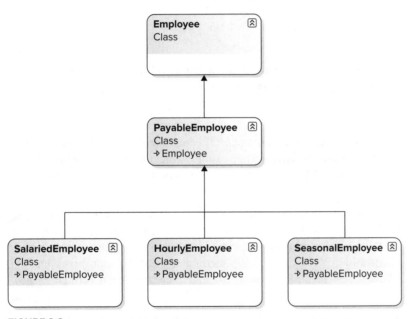

FIGURE 3-2

In this hierarchy, the logic that computes employee's payroll is encapsulated in the `PayableEmployee` class. But what happens if the likely event that the business decides to pay each employee type based on a different algorithm? Should more classes be introduced into the class hierarchy? That would solve the problem at hand, but what if there was logic in the payment algorithm that could be partially shared between the classes? Do you then add yet another layer of inheritance to account for this? Before long the class hierarchy, even for something as simple as this example would become hopelessly complicated.

A better strategy here would be to use composition. Instead of putting the logic to pay employees in a class in the Employee hierarchy, I will define a standardized interface to a payroll computation module called `IEmployeePayrollService`. The `Employee` class will include a protected member variable that can hold a class that implements the `IEmployeePayrollService` interface (Figure 3-3).

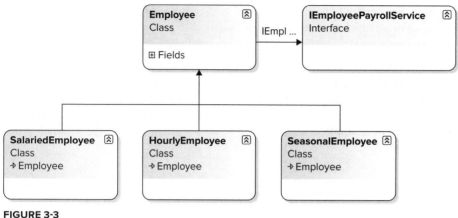

FIGURE 3-3

Now each employee can consume any type of class to calculate payroll they need, provided that it implement the standardized employee payroll service interface.

Polymorphism

Polymorphism may be the most misunderstood tenet of OOP. *Polymorphism* is the concept that although two classes may share the same behavior, they can implement that behavior in very different ways. Polymorphism is somewhat related to inheritance and the relationships between classes that it creates.

For example, in the Employee example just discussed, the Hourly, Salary, and Seasonal employee classes may all inherit from the Employee base class an abstract method called ComputePay. (An *abstract member* is a member where the interface is declared in the base, but the derived class must provide its own implementation.) The ComputePay method can call the appropriate method or methods on the class's instance of the IEmployeePayrollService interface described in the previous section on Inheritance

Although the interface for this method would be identical across all three derived classes, the means they use to determine the employee's pay are very different. Salary employees would have a set number based on their salary. Hourly and seasonal employees would have an hourly rate that is multiplied by the number of hours they worked in the last pay period. However, in our example, hourly workers receive time and a half for overtime, but seasonal workers do not. Each has the ComputePay method, and each one returns a dollar amount for the employee's paycheck, but they use different means to arrive at that number.

The real power of polymorphism is realized when you consider that any class derived from the Employee base class can be treated as an employee regardless of its actual concrete implementation. When payday arrives at the company used in our example, the payroll system needs to issue checks for all employees. With polymorphism the system simply needs to iterate through the list of active employees and call ComputePay on each one. It doesn't need to know what type of employee it's computing the paycheck amount for; the concrete type has the specific implementation it needs. The application simply must collect the number that the method returns.

Without polymorphism, the system would have to do one of two things. The first alternative would be to sort all the employees into three groups (Salary, Hourly, and Seasonal) and process each group in its own unique manner. The other alternative would be to loop through all the active employees, and for each employee a decision would have to be made to determine how to pay that employee. Either of these alternatives results in additional code that not only makes the process slower, but also makes it more complicated and introduces more points of failure. With polymorphism you let the computer do the work for you. An example of this can be found in the section "Replace Conditional with Polymorphism."

For example, I have the hierarchy of animals shown in Figure 3-4:

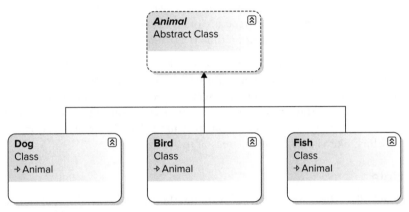

FIGURE 3-4

In addition to all being animals, each of these animals is able to move. But they all move in different ways; dogs run, birds fly, and fish swim. Because they all inherit from Animal, I can reference each sub-type (dogs, birds and fish) as animals. But what if I want to make these animals move? Would the best approach be to implement a Run method on Dog, a Fly method on Bird and a Swim method on Fish? This may seem intuitive, but it creates some severe limitations. Let's say I had a reference in my code to some type of Animal. How would I make it move? Which method do I call? To answer that question I would first have to determine what specific type of Animal I'm dealing with. This is inefficient and defeats the purpose of having an animal hierarchy.

A better approach would be to create an abstract method on the Animal class called Move. Each animal that inherits from hierarchy would then create an implementation of this method and provide its specific method of moving. In this case, I don't need to know what specific type of Animal I have, I know I can call the Move method and the animal will move appropriately.

The SOLID Principles

In the early 2000s, Robert "Uncle Bob" Martin introduced a series of five principles for developing software with OOP that were designed to lead to higher-quality systems that were easier to maintain. These SOLID Principles became a sort of map for developers in both designing new applications and refactoring existing code bases.

The Single Responsibility Principle

The Single Responsibility Principle (SRP) states that each method or class should have one and only one reason to change. This means by extension that each method or class should do one thing or have a single responsibility. Of all the SOLID Principles, this is the one that most developers feel they completely understand. Ironically, it's also probably the most commonly violated principle.

Let's revisit the `Employee` example from the preceding section. Each of the three employee subclasses (`Hourly`, `Salary`, and `Seasonal`) has a `ComputeVacationTime` method. This may seem logical; an employee works and accrues vacation time. The employee goes on vacation and uses vacation time. But think for a moment about the other things in the `Employee` classes. Employee biographical information is stored in those classes. There are now two identified possible reasons for those classes to change: a change to the type or structure of an employee's biographical information, or a change in how an employee's vacation time is calculated.

According to the SRP, one of these pieces of information needs to be moved. In this case, I believe the biographical information should stay, because that information defines an employee. The vacation time calculation should be extracted to a domain service, because the means of computing an employee's vacation time is not something that defines the employee for our purposes. In the end you would have an `Employee` class, which now has only one reason to change, and a Vacation Time Calculation Service, which likewise has only one reason to change.

The Open/Close Principle

The Open/Close Principle (OCP) is the concept that software (methods, classes, and so on) should be open for extension but closed for modification. If this sounds very similar to the OOP tenet of inheritance, it should. They are closely related. In fact, in .NET the Open/Close Principle relies on inheritance.

The point of the OCP is that, as a developer, occasionally either you are supplied with base classes or you produce a framework of base classes for another developer to use. Consumers should not be able to use those base classes; they are closed for modification. This is necessary because other consumers may rely on the functionality that is provided by that base class. Allowing consumers to change these base classes can have a ripple effect that reaches into the far corners of not only your application, but also applications across the Enterprise. Another issue is that at some point the consumer probably will receive an upgraded version of the base class. Before the consumer can upgrade, she must find a way to handle the customizations she's created inside the previous version of the base class.

The question then becomes, "Well, I need to change something about how this base class works. What should I do?" The answer comes in the other half of the OCP; the base class should be open for extension. In this case extension refers to creating a derived class that inherits from the base class and that can extend or override the base class functionality to provide the specific functionality that the consumer needs. This allows the consumer to use a modified version of the class while not impacting other consumers of the class. It also makes it easier for the consumer to use upgraded versions of the base class in the future, because she is unconcerned with her modifications being lost.

The Liskov Substitution Principle

What inheritance is to the OCP, polymorphism is to the Liskov Substitution Principle (LSP). The LSP states that an object used in your application should be replaceable by the super class without breaking the application. This is also commonly called *design by contract.*

If you'll recall the earlier polymorphism example, the ComputePay method used a list of type Employee in which Employee was a base type (the super type). The classes Salary, Hourly, and Seasonal all inherited from Employee and therefore were subtypes of Employee.

According to the LSP, even though you've declared your list as being a list of Employee, you can still populate it with concrete instances of Salary, Hourly, and Seasonal. By virtue of inheritance, they all support the same contract (public set of methods, or API that Employee declares. The application can iterate through the list and call methods that are defined on Employee on the items in your list without knowing or caring specifically what type they are. If they support the contact, the call is legal.

The Interface Segregation Principle

Up until now I've used class-based inheritance in my examples and haven't talked much about interfaces. To review, an *interface* is simply a contract you define (in code) that your class agrees to implement. This agreement requires your class to supply an implementation of every method that interface defines. How the method is implemented is up to the class, so long as it honors the contract by supporting the definition in the interface. Interfaces are a very powerful tool in .NET; they support inheritance and polymorphism the same way classes do.

The Interface Segregation Principle (ISP) states that clients should not be forced to rely on interfaces they do not use. For example, a banking system may have a service that evaluates applications for credit. For the sake of argument, assume that this service handles not only secured credit (car and boat loans, mortgages) but also unsecured credit (credit cards, letters of credit, equity credit lines). If you are developing a client to help finance specialists at car dealerships get car loans for their customers, you really don't care about anything else on this service except the methods to apply for car loans. Without the ISP, your application must know about these other methods.

While this doesn't seem like a problem initially, at best it creates additional complexity for your application, because the API you are now developing against has many more methods than are needed. This can lead to confusion and potentially errors from calling the wrong method. It's also possible that a part of the API that your application doesn't use could change, which would necessitate a change on your end. Now you are incurring maintenance costs on your application for functionality you don't use, want, or even care about. This situation also represents a security risk. This application is specifically for car loans. What happens if an unscrupulous developer takes advantage of this bloated API to allow other types of credit to be secured from the application? Such a problem goes beyond broken or unmaintainable code.

The solution is to create several smaller, more granular interfaces for this service that are specific to the client's needs. In the case of this sample application, an interface specifically for car loans would be appropriate. Your application can access the same class with the same implementation, but this time it uses a specific interface with a subset of the methods on the actual service. This reduces your complexity, insulates your application from changes in other sections of the API, and helps close the security hole.

 Applying the ISP in your code does not *mean that the service is completely secure. Good coding practices to ensure proper authentication and authorization should still be used.*

The Dependency Inversion Principle

In a perfect world there would be no coupling or binding of components in an application. Also, developers would be able to change anything they wanted without having to worry about causing defects or (my favorite euphemism) "unintended side effects" elsewhere in the application. Sadly, we do not live in a perfect world. Therefore, our components need to bind to each other or couple at some point to form an actual application.

The Dependency Inversion Principle (DIP) states that code should depend on abstractions, not concrete implementations, and that those abstractions should not depend on details; the details should depend on the abstractions. Your classes may rely on other classes to perform their work (an Employee service may rely on a data access component to save and retrieve employees from a data store). However, they should not rely on a specific concrete implementation of that class, just an abstraction of it. This means that your Employee service would not know (or care) what specific data access component is being used — only that its abstraction, or code contract (or interface), supports the methods needed to save and retrieve an employee.

Clearly, this concept makes your system much more flexible. If your classes care only that the components they use support a specific contract and not a specific type, you can change the functionality of these low-level services quickly and easily with minimal impact on the rest of the system. In Chapter 6 you'll see how this also allows you to mock these dependencies for testing. At some point you need to provide a concrete implementation of this low-level service to your class for it to do its work. The most common way of doing this, especially for practitioners of TDD in .NET, is the Dependency Injection (DI) pattern. DI patterns are covered in detail in Chapter 6.

CODE SMELLS

Again, no code is perfect. This is a fact of life. But developers who practice TDD still strive to make their code as good as possible. A key skill to help you do that is the ability to evaluate code and to quickly and easily identify common potential trouble spots without having to run the application. These common problems are called *code smells*.

What Is a Code Smell?

Over the many years that applications have been developed, developers have always needed to solve a common recurring series of problems in code. These problems eventually found a series of common, widely known, widely used solutions. These solutions became known as *patterns*. As a corollary, over the many years that applications have been developed, developers have always made many common recurring mistakes. These mistakes, and the problems they tend to cause, are called *antipatterns*. *Code smells* are simply a collection of commonly known and widely found code-based antipatterns. This section demonstrates a few of the more common code smells. The next section focuses on some common steps to correct them.

Duplicate Code and Similar Classes

Consider the following code:

```
public class WidgetService
{
    private const double PricePerWidget = 1.5;

    public double GetQuoteForWidgets(int quantity)
    {
        return PricePerWidget*quantity;
    }

    public string PlaceOrderForWidgets(int quantity)
    {
        var invoice = new Invoice
                    {
                            TotalPrice = PricePerWidget*quantity
                    };
        return invoice.InvoiceNumber;
    }
}
```

This simple WidgetService provides a quote for a specific number of widgets and creates an invoice when a client places an order. However, this code has a major flaw. If you look at the GetQuoteForWidgets and PlaceOrderForWidgets methods, you'll see that the functionality for determining the total cost for an order of widgets is duplicated (X = PricePerWidget multiplied by quantity).

This is a clear violation of the SRP: Someone has taken the logic that is to be used for the same purpose and repeated it in this application. Suppose a new business requirement is introduced to change how the price of an order of widgets is calculated. The developer would have to make sure he located and updated every place in the code where this logic exists, and then he would have to adequately regression-test all those code paths.

This code smell is not confined to duplicate code in the same class. For example:

```
public class WidgetService
{
    private const double PricePerWidget = 1.5;

    public string PlaceOrderForWidgets(int quantity)
    {
        var invoice = new Invoice
                    {
```

```
                        TotalPrice = PricePerWidget*quantity*1.15
                  };
            return invoice.InvoiceNumber;
    }
}

public class DoDadService
{
    private const double PricePerDoDad = 2.25;

    public string PlaceOrderForDoDad(int quantity)
    {
        var invoice = new Invoice
                {
                        TotalPrice = PricePerDoDad*quantity*1.15
                };
            return invoice.InvoiceNumber;
    }
}
```

The business has expanded and now also offers DoDads for sale. To accommodate this new line of business, the development staff has created a DoDadService. Looking at the methods for PlaceOrderForWidgets and PlaceOrderForDoDad, you can see that they are almost identical. This represents another duplication of code, this time across classes, which can lead to maintenance and quality issues down the road.

Big Classes and Big Methods

Bigger is not better. Here's a case in point:

```
public string PlaceOrderForWidgets(int quantity, string customerNumber)
{
    var invoice = new Invoice
                {
                        InvoiceNumber = Guid.NewGuid().ToString(),
                        TotalPrice = PricePerWidget*quantity,
                        Quantity = quantity
                };

    var customer = _customerService.GetCustomer(customerNumber);
    invoice.CustomerName = customer.CustomerName;
    invoice.CustomerAddress = customer.CustomerAddress;
    invoice.CustomerBillingInformation = customer.CustomerBillingInformation;

    double tax;
    switch (invoice.CustomerAddress.State.ToUpper())
    {
        case "OH":
            tax = invoice.TotalPrice*.15;
            break;
        case "MI":
            tax = invoice.TotalPrice*.22;
            break;
```

```
        case "NV":
            tax = invoice.TotalPrice*.05;
            break;
        default:
            tax = 0.0;
            break;
    }

    var shippingPrice = invoice.TotalPrice * .1;
    invoice.TotalPrice += shippingPrice;
     invoice.TotalPrice += tax;

    var paymentAuthorizationCode = _paymentProcessingService.ProcessPayment(
        invoice.TotalPrice,
        customer.CustomerBillingInformation);
    invoice.Approved = ! string.IsNullOrEmpty(paymentAuthorizationCode);
    _invoiceService.Post(invoice);
    return invoice.InvoiceNumber;
}
```

This code has many issues — the most obvious being how long it is. When I see a method this long, the first thing I look for are violations of the SRP. In this case I can see at least five different business functions. This method creates an invoice, associates the invoice with a customer, determines tax based on the customers state, determines shipping costs, and authorizes payment. This means that there are at least five different reasons that this method might have to change. This is unacceptable.

Another common problem with long methods is that they tend to be complex and difficult to follow. Any veteran ASP.NET developer probably has a story about the Page_Load method that was hundreds of lines long and had complex logic branching to try to accommodate all possible states that the page could be rendered in. I have seen some that had over 1,400 lines of code. That's one method, not an entire class! These methods got so big the developers were forced to put regions in them to help keep track of the individual parts of the method. Regions are another code smell due to the face that they obfuscate the code you are working on and are an indication that your class or method is too long and unfocused.

These long methods and large classes are usually a major source of trouble in an application. They are difficult to maintain and almost impossible to completely understand, and their sheer size makes them a breeding ground for bugs. Keep your classes and methods small and nimble. I would rather have an application with 100 small classes than 15 that have thousands of lines of code. Smaller is easier to maintain, easier to understand, and easier to work with.

Comments

A controversial view, although one I believe in, is that unless you're writing device drivers, or some other "down to the metal" code, comments in code are a code smell. The fact is that although most comments are created with the best of intentions, they end up adding no value to your code. They are out of date almost as soon as they are written. They are usually inaccurate, which can cause real damage when a developer takes them at their word and uses that knowledge to make changes to a code base. In the end, comments are simply line noise. For everything comments are supposed to do, another tool or technique does it better.

In terms of comments designed to make the code understandable, the solution is to simply make the code more comprehensible. Don't obfuscate your code with meaningless names and overly complicated control structures. Well-written code should be clean and easy to follow. Comments become a crutch to justify sloppy code.

In terms of tracking who changed what in a code base, source control systems do a much better job than comments do. Source control systems, such as Team Foundation Server, Subversion, and Git, can track commits developers make to a repository and what was in that commit better than expecting a developer to leave a comment. Developers often forget to leave a comment. A source control system never forgets. In this case the tool is already doing the work, so why ask developers to duplicate it, especially when you know they won't do it as well as the tool does?

Source control systems also keep a historical record of code. I've seen many developers comment out large sections of code they are not using instead of simply deleting it on the off chance they may need it later. If you're not using the code, delete it. It adds no value, and you removed it for a reason. If you do need that code later, you can easily retrieve it from your source control system.

Comment headers on classes or methods, sometimes referred to as "Triple Slash Comments" are no exception to this. Many developers start these with the best of intentions, but the result is always the same. The comment is soon inaccurate and incomplete. Developers who read them take them at face value and as a result make decisions based on bad information, which causes a great deal of damage to a code base. The blocks of comments also generate a large amount of line noise which only serves to distract developers from the code. In the end, if your methods and class are short, focused and well written, these comment blocks are completely unnecessary.

Bad Names

A key component of disposing of comments in your code is banishing bad names for variables, methods, and classes. Everything in your application should have a meaningful and descriptive name.

Consider this method:

```
public double GetValue(int a, int b)
{
    var answer = (a*a)*b*P;
    return answer;
}
```

This method is a commonly known mathematical formula. But what is it? The method name gives you no clue, and the variables and constant P provide no help either. If you had to guess, what would you say? (The answer is given later in the chapter.)

It may seem like a small detail, but a bad name for a variable, method, or class in your code can create a large amount of complexity. Short, nondescriptive names serve only to obfuscate your code, many times from yourself. This method may seem to make sense today, but look at it again in a month. Do you think you'll be able to remember what the parameter a represents? If you don't, what chance does anyone else on your team have? I talk more about good naming in the section "Rename Variables, Fields, Methods, and Classes."

Feature Envy

Let's revisit the code from the big classes, big methods example:

```csharp
public string PlaceOrderForWidgets(int quantity, string customerNumber)
{
    var invoice = new Invoice
                    {
                        InvoiceNumber = Guid.NewGuid().ToString(),
                        TotalPrice = PricePerWidget*quantity,
                        Quantity = quantity
                    };

    var customer = _customerService.GetCustomer(customerNumber);
    invoice.CustomerName = customer.CustomerName;
    invoice.CustomerAddress = customer.CustomerAddress;
    invoice.CustomerBillingInformation = customer.CustomerBillingInformation;

    if (customer.LoyaltyProgram == "Super Adamantium Deluxe")
    {
        invoice.TotalPrice = invoice.TotalPrice*.85;
    }

    double tax;
    switch (invoice.CustomerAddress.State.ToUpper())
    {
        case "OH":
            tax = invoice.TotalPrice*.15;
            break;
        case "MI":
            tax = invoice.TotalPrice*.22;
            break;
        case "NV":
            tax = invoice.TotalPrice*.05;
            break;
        default:
            tax = 0.0;
            break;
    }

    var shippingPrice = invoice.TotalPrice * .1;
    invoice.TotalPrice += shippingPrice;
    invoice.TotalPrice += tax;

    var paymentAuthorizationCode = _paymentProcessingService.ProcessPayment(
        invoice.TotalPrice,
        customer.CustomerBillingInformation);
    invoice.Approved = ! string.IsNullOrEmpty(paymentAuthorizationCode);
    _invoiceService.Post(invoice);
    return invoice.InvoiceNumber;
}
```

In addition to the previously mentioned length of this method, this code has another problem: It uses a property or method from the Invoice class on almost every line. A class that uses too many methods of another class is said to suffer from feature envy. In this case the PlaceOrderForWidgets method is clearly envious of the Invoice class. In situations like this, you see functionality that clearly wants to exist somewhere else, be it another class, method, or module. A chief problem that arises from feature envy is brittle code. By relying so much on the Invoice class, the developer has made this method dependent on it. Changes to Invoice could easily mean changes to this method. This method's dependency on the Invoice class needs to be reduced. I'll show you how to fix this problem in the section "Extract Methods."

Too Much If/Switch

At their core, applications are designed to evaluate data and execute some sort of functionality based on that evaluation. The most common control structures for doing this are the If Then Else structure and the Switch Case structure. It's certainly not uncommon to make liberal use of these in an application, but consider this method:

```
public double CalculatePrice(int quantity, string cutomerState,
    string customerStatus)
{
    var basePrice = quantity*PricePerWidget;
    switch (cutomerState)
    {
        case "OH":
            if (quantity >= 1000 && quantity < 9999)
            {
                basePrice = basePrice*.95;
            }
            else if(quantity >= 10000)
            {
                basePrice = basePrice*.90;
            }
            break;
        case "MI":
            switch (customerStatus)
            {
                case "Premier":
                    basePrice = basePrice*.85;
                    break;
                case "Preffered":
                    basePrice = basePrice*90;
                    break;
                case "Standard":
                    basePrice = basePrice*.95;
                    break;
            }
            break;
        default:
            if (quantity > 10000)
            {
                basePrice = basePrice*.95;
```

```
            }
            break;
        }

    return basePrice;
}
```

The high number of evaluations (If and Switch blocks) in this code introduce quite a bit of complexity and decrease the code's readability. Even if the simple code in this example revealed a defect it could be difficult to easily diagnose and correct. In reality, the pricing algorithm for a real product would likely be far more complicated. As an added problem, this method spits in the eye of the SRP: This method contains three different pricing algorithms. This complexity and brittleness can be reduced by limiting the number of If and Switch blocks in your methods. You'll examine how to fix this code in the section "Extract Methods."

Try/Catch Bloat

Handling exceptions is a very important task in application development. A standing rule for my development team is that a user should never encounter an unhandled exception. This does not mean that every line of code should be placed in a Try block — only blocks of code in which something exceptional could happen. An exhaustive list of these things is outside the scope of this book. Some common tasks that should occur in a Try/Catch block are connecting to or interacting with a database, working with a file, and calling a web service.

Much like If and Switch blocks, it's easy to get carried away with what gets placed inside a Try/Catch block:

```
public Customer GetCustomer(string customerId)
{
    try
    {
        var command = new SqlCommand();
        var reader = command.ExecuteReader();
        var customer = new Customer();
        while (reader.Read())
        {
            customer.CustomerId = customerId;
            customer.CustomerName = reader["CustomerName"].ToString();
            customer.CustomerStatus = reader["CustomerState"].ToString();
            customer.LoyaltyProgram = reader["CustomerLoyaltyProgram"].ToString();
        }
        return customer;
    }
    catch (Exception exception)
    {
        _logger.LogException(exception);
        var customer = new Customer {CustomerStatus = "unknown"};
        return customer;
    }
}
```

Best practices for using ADO.NET aside, you can see that this method suffers from some of the same problems as the previous example. For starters, not only does this method contain code to create and execute the command to retrieve the customer from the database, but it also contains code to handle an exception that may be thrown. Albeit subtle, this violates the SRP on several levels.

The code in the `Try` block is doing two separate tasks: creating the ADO.NET command to get the customer from the database, and then mapping the data from the reader to a customer object. This might seem like one task, but it really represents two reasons to change. If the stored procedure used to get the customer were to have its input parameters changed, the code to build the command would have to change. If the data structure of either the customer dataset being returned from the stored procedure or the customer class itself changed, that would be another reason.

The `Catch` block contains another violation of SRP. The method contains code to handle an exception that may result from the call to the database. This is a reason to change. The current algorithm for handling exceptions that arise when retrieving a customer is to log the exception and then return a customer object with a status of "unknown." Tomorrow the procedure could be completely different. This represents another reason that this method would have to change.

Widespread violations of SRP aside, the bloat in the `Try`/`Catch` block makes this method a bit long and introduces some unnecessary layers of complexity. According to the SRP, the mechanics of a `Try`/`Catch` block (calling a unit of work, catching an exception that is thrown) is enough of a reason to change in and of itself and should not be mixed with business or other infrastructure logic. This method will be fixed in the section "Extract Methods."

TYPICAL REFACTORING

To review, code smells are a series of commonly known coding antipatterns. Because they are commonly known, and widespread, developers have been able to develop some common and well-known ways of dealing with and fixing these code smells. These are called refactoring patterns. This section focuses on some of the more common refactoring patterns and explains how and when to apply them to your code.

Extract Classes or Interfaces

There are many reasons why you may want to split a class into smaller, more focused classes or have a series of more granular interfaces extracted from it. If a class is very large, it is probably doing too many things. If a class violates the SRP, it is a candidate to be split. If there is a design or technical reason that the class must remain in one piece, or the class is small but is still doing too many different things, extracting interfaces is a good alternative. Another good time to consider extracting interfaces from a class is when the client cares about only a portion of the class's public interface. Consider the following class:

```
public class InvoiceService
{
    public string CreateInvoice(Invoice invoice) {...}

    public string ProcessPayment(Invoice invoice, double amount) {...}
```

```
        public double GetAmountOwed(Invoice invoice) {...}

        public double GetTotalAmountInvoicedLastFY(Customer customer) {...}

        public double GetTotalAmountPaidLastFY(Customer customer) {...}
    }
```

Although this may not be considered a large class, it does perform several related, yet separate functions that are used by different parts of the system. The CreateInvoice method could be used by an order placement system or e-commerce website when a customer places an order. ProcessPayment and GetAmountOwed might be consumed by an accounts receivable or customer service system. GetTotalAmountInvoicedLastFY and GetTotalAmountPaidLastFY might be used by an accounting or end-of-year reporting service. Size of the class aside, clearly the individual consumers of this class don't need to know about methods they don't use. In this case, it would make sense to refactor this class by extracting its interfaces:

```
    public interface IInvoiceCreatingService
    {
        string CreateInvoice(Invoice invoice);
    }

    public interface IInvoicePaymentService
    {
        string ProcessPayment(Invoice invoice, double amount);
        double GetAmountOwed(Invoice invoice);
    }

    public interface IInvoiceReportingService
    {
        double GetTotalAmountInvoicedLastFY(Customer customer);
        double GetTotalAmountPaidLastFY(Customer customer);
    }

    public class InvoiceService : IInvoiceCreatingService, IInvoicePaymentService,
        IInvoiceReportingService
    {
        public string CreateInvoice(Invoice invoice) {...}

        public string ProcessPayment(Invoice invoice, double amount) {...}

        public double GetAmountOwed(Invoice invoice) {...}

        public double GetTotalAmountInvoicedLastFY(Customer customer) {...}

        public double GetTotalAmountPaidLastFY(Customer customer) {...}
    }
```

This refactor doesn't move any functionality out of the class, but it does change how clients consume it. Instead of having a concrete class with several methods the client doesn't care about, and in some cases shouldn't have access to, this refactor has an instance of a class that it knows supports the interface it cares about. The concrete implementation could be anything; it doesn't matter. So long as the code contract, by way of the interface, is supported, the client can use the object as expected.

Extract Methods

Let's take another look at the `PlaceOrderForWidgets` example from the earlier "Big Classes and Big Methods" section:

```
public string PlaceOrderForWidgets(int quantity, string customerNumber)
{
    var invoice = new Invoice
                    {
                        InvoiceNumber = Guid.NewGuid().ToString(),
                        TotalPrice = PricePerWidget*quantity,
                        Quantity = quantity
                    };

    var customer = _customerService.GetCustomer(customerNumber);
    invoice.CustomerName = customer.CustomerName;
    invoice.CustomerAddress = customer.CustomerAddress;
    invoice.CustomerBillingInformation = customer.CustomerBillingInformation;

    double tax;
    switch (invoice.CustomerAddress.State.ToUpper())
    {
        case "OH":
            tax = invoice.TotalPrice*.15;
            break;
        case "MI":
            tax = invoice.TotalPrice*.22;
            break;
        case "NV":
            tax = invoice.TotalPrice*.05;
            break;
        default:
            tax = 0.0;
            break;
    }

    var shippingPrice = invoice.TotalPrice * .1;
    invoice.TotalPrice += shippingPrice;
    invoice.TotalPrice += tax;

    var paymentAuthorizationCode = _paymentProcessingService.ProcessPayment(
        invoice.TotalPrice,
        customer.CustomerBillingInformation);
    invoice.Approved = ! string.IsNullOrEmpty(paymentAuthorizationCode);
    _invoiceService.Post(invoice);
    return invoice.InvoiceNumber;
}
```

As mentioned, this method violates the SRP by performing five different tasks. This can be corrected by identifying and isolating specific tasks in the method and extracting them to another method.

The most obvious piece of functionality that can be extracted, although it appears midway through the class, is the code that calculates the tax on the order. This code can be pulled out to a method called `CalculateTaxForInvoice`, which is called from the `PlaceOrderForWidgets` method:

```
public string PlaceOrderForWidgets(int quantity, string customerNumber)
{
    var invoice = new Invoice
                    {
                        InvoiceNumber = Guid.NewGuid().ToString(),
                        TotalPrice = PricePerWidget*quantity,
                        Quantity = quantity
                    };

    var customer = _customerService.GetCustomer(customerNumber);
    invoice.CustomerName = customer.CustomerName;
    invoice.CustomerAddress = customer.CustomerAddress;
    invoice.CustomerBillingInformation = customer.CustomerBillingInformation;

    var tax = CalculateTaxForInvoice(invoice);

    var shippingPrice = invoice.TotalPrice * .1;
    invoice.TotalPrice += shippingPrice;
    invoice.TotalPrice += tax;

    var paymentAuthorizationCode = _paymentProcessingService.ProcessPayment(
        invoice.TotalPrice,
        customer.CustomerBillingInformation);
    invoice.Approved = ! string.IsNullOrEmpty(paymentAuthorizationCode);
    _invoiceService.Post(invoice);
    return invoice.InvoiceNumber;
}

private double CalculateTaxForInvoice(Invoice invoice)
{
    double tax;
    switch (invoice.CustomerAddress.State.ToUpper())
    {
        case "OH":
            tax = invoice.TotalPrice*.15;
            break;
        case "MI":
            tax = invoice.TotalPrice*.22;
            break;
        case "NV":
            tax = invoice.TotalPrice*.05;
            break;
        default:
            tax = 0.0;
            break;
    }
    return tax;
}
```

Already this method is starting to look much better! It's shorter and easier to read. Abstracting the functionality to calculate tax to the `CalculateTaxForInvoice` method has removed one responsibility from the `PlaceOrderForWidgets` code. The tax still gets calculated; it's just happening somewhere else. You can tell by the specific method name where it is happening, but you don't need to look at the code that calculates tax every time you look at this method — only when you need to do something with how tax is calculated.

Another piece of responsibility that can be extracted is the code that creates and populates the `Invoice` object. Although an invoice is integral to placing an order for widgets, it is a separate and distinct task (a subtask, really) and should be pulled out. Think of it this way: The process to place an order for widgets may change, but that may not necessitate a change to how an invoice is created. Similarly, the company may enter another line of business at some point that requires a change to the `Invoice` class. The process of ordering widgets does not change (the new field is not used for widget orders), but the code in the `PlaceOrderForWidgets` method may be required to change to accommodate the change in `Invoice`.

Before this method can be extracted, a change must be made elsewhere in the method. Examine the code that gets `paymentAuthorizationCode`:

```
var paymentAuthorizationCode = _paymentProcessingService.ProcessPayment(
    invoice.TotalPrice, customer.CustomerBillingInformation);
```

The code that creates the invoice needs a `Customer` object. The only other place in this method where `Customer` is used is this line of code. Examination reveals that the method simply needs `CustomerBillingInformation` to get payment approval. This is already being gathered by the code that creates the invoice:

```
invoice.CustomerBillingInformation = customer.CustomerBillingInformation;
```

This data is not being changed anywhere else in this method. So does it have to come from the customer object specifically? In some applications, particularly if multiple threads are executing, it may. For this application it doesn't. So the first step is to change the code that calls the `ProcessPayment` method:

```
var paymentAuthorizationCode = _paymentProcessingService.ProcessPayment(
    invoice.TotalPrice, invoice.CustomerBillingInformation);
```

Now that that's done, extracting the invoice-creating functionality is a trivial matter, as you can see from my finished methods here:

```
public string PlaceOrderForWidgets(int quantity, string customerNumber)
{
    var invoice = GetInvoice(quantity, customerNumber);
    var tax = CalculateTaxForInvoice(invoice);

    var shippingPrice = invoice.TotalPrice * .1;
    invoice.TotalPrice += shippingPrice;
    invoice.TotalPrice += tax;

    var paymentAuthorizationCode = _paymentProcessingService.ProcessPayment(
        invoice.TotalPrice, invoice.CustomerBillingInformation);
```

```
        invoice.Approved = ! string.IsNullOrEmpty(paymentAuthorizationCode);
        _invoiceService.Post(invoice);
        return invoice.InvoiceNumber;
    }

    private Invoice GetInvoice(int quantity, string customerNumber)
    {
        var invoice = new Invoice
                        {
                            InvoiceNumber = Guid.NewGuid().ToString(),
                            TotalPrice = PricePerWidget*quantity,
                            Quantity = quantity
                        };

        var customer = _customerService.GetCustomer(customerNumber);
        invoice.CustomerName = customer.CustomerName;
        invoice.CustomerAddress = customer.CustomerAddress;
        invoice.CustomerBillingInformation = customer.CustomerBillingInformation;
        return invoice;
    }
```

The new method GetInvoice is not perfect by any means (in real life I would reorder some statements to make it even shorter and easier to read), but it's a big step beyond what was there before. Turning your attention to the PlaceOrderForWidgets method, it's clear that after extracting only two units of functionality, this method is much more readable, less complicated, and easier to maintain.

In practice I would continue refactoring this method to extract the shipping price computation, total price computation, payment authorization functionality, and approval functionality. After those methods were extracted, I might find more groups of functionality that could be extracted. Or perhaps I would find that the methods I pulled out of PlaceOrderForWidgets still violated the SRP, so I would extract methods from them.

Let's look again at the example from the section "Try/Catch Bloat":

```
public Customer GetCustomer(string customerId)
{
    try
    {
        var command = new SqlCommand();
        var reader = command.ExecuteReader();
        var customer = new Customer();
        while (reader.Read())
        {
            customer.CustomerId = customerId;
            customer.CustomerName = reader["CustomerName"].ToString();
            customer.CustomerStatus = reader["CustomerState"].ToString();
            customer.LoyaltyProgram = reader["CustomerLoyaltyProgram"].ToString();
        }
        return customer;
    }
    catch (Exception exception)
    {
```

```
        _logger.LogException(exception);
        var customer = new Customer {CustomerStatus = "unknown"};
        return customer;
    }
}
```

As mentioned, having the business code in the `Try/Catch` block is a violation of the SRP. Extracting the methods in each block to external methods makes this method simpler and easier to understand:

```
public Customer GetCustomer(string customerId)
{
    try
    {
        return GetCustomerFromDataStore(customerId);
    }
    catch (Exception exception)
    {
        return HandleDataStoreExceptionWhenRetrievingCustomer(exception);
    }
}

private static Customer GetCustomerFromDataStore(string customerId)
{
    var command = new SqlCommand();
    var reader = command.ExecuteReader();
    var customer = new Customer();
    while (reader.Read())
    {
        customer.CustomerId = customerId;
        customer.CustomerName = reader["CustomerName"].ToString();
        customer.CustomerStatus = reader["CustomerState"].ToString();
        customer.LoyaltyProgram = reader["CustomerLoyaltyProgram"].ToString();
    }
    return customer;
}

private Customer
    HandleDataStoreExceptionWhenRetrievingCustomer(Exception exception)
{
    _logger.LogException(exception);
    var customer = new Customer { CustomerStatus = "unknown" };
    return customer;
}
```

Like the previous example, some method extraction could be done here. It's important to remember that method extraction is an iterative process. You should always be on the lookout for functionality that violates the SRP and that should be on its own.

Rename Variables, Fields, Methods, and Classes

Let's review the code sample from the section "Bad Names":

```
public double GetValue(int a, int b)
{
```

```
        var answer = (a*a)*b*P;
        return answer;
}
```

That was several pages ago. Have you figured out what it is yet?

Let's look at the same method, but this time with a well-named variable and a descriptive method name:

```
public double GetVolumeOfACylinder(int radius, int height)
{
    var volumeOfACylinder = (radius*radius)*height*Pi;
    return volumeOfACylinder;
}
```

It's now clear what this method does. Even if it did not have the descriptive method name, or the variable name `volumeOfACylinder`, you could deduce from the code used to perform the calculation that this code determines the volume of a cylinder. This is a simple example, but with a little care taken toward naming, you can make your code much clearer and easier to understand.

Names should be clear, deliberate, and written in common, everyday language. Try not to use acronyms unless they are well known in your company, your business, or software development in general. Don't be afraid of long names. A long, descriptive name is much more desirable than a short name that gives no clue as to its intent. Visual Studio, like most modern development environments, provides some form of autocomplete. Use it. Don't let "That name is too long" be an excuse for poor naming.

Encapsulate Fields

Classes use member variables to track and maintain their internal state. Per the encapsulation rule, these member variables are scoped as private and are not directly accessible to external clients. This is a protective measure to ensure that the class's runtime state does not get corrupted.

Sometimes clients need access to fields on a class. For example, in the `Widget` class shown here, the model number is clearly something that the clients of this class will need to be able to access:

```
public class Widget
{
    private object _internalWidgetState;
    public string _widgetModelNumber;
}
```

On the surface, and naming issues aside, this seems like perfectly reasonable code. But what's to stop a client from changing the value of _widgetModelNumber? It's declared as public, which means that any external object can change that member variable; nothing can be done to prevent it.

A better way to handle situations like this is to encapsulate that member variable in a field (sometimes called a property or "getter and setter"):

```
public class Widget
{
    private object _internalWidgetState;
    public string ModelNumber { get; private set; }
}
```

For starters, the name `ModelNumber` is nicer and falls in line with more naming standards than `_widgetModelNumber`. But the real power of a field is that although `ModelNumber` is still accessible externally, it's in a read-only state. The set is scoped as private, which means that only the `Widget` object itself can set that value.

Replace Conditional with Polymorphism

In the following example, you have been asked to write software to dispatch fueling trucks to various locations for a variety of vehicles. To know how much fuel to send, you need to know how much fuel is currently in the tank of each vehicle. This application supports three types of vehicles, as demonstrated by the following classes:

```
public class Car : Vehicle
{
    public int AmountOfFuelNeededToFillTank()
    {
        return 12;
    }
}

public class Airplane : Vehicle
{
    public int AmountOfFuelNeededToFillLeftFuelTank()
    {
        return 3;
    }

    public int AmountOfFuelNeededToFillRightFuelTank()
    {
        return 4;
    }
}

public class Boat : Vehicle
{
    public int AmountOfFuelNeededToFillFrontFuelTank()
    {
        return 8;
    }

    public int AmountOfFuelNeededToFillRearFuelTank()
    {
        return 10;
    }
}
```

The application must look at each vehicle on a fuel truck's route to determine how much fuel to load onto the truck. The code to do this could look something like this:

```
public class FuelingStation
{
    public int AddFuelToTruck(List<Vehicle> vehiclesOnRoute)
```

```
        {
            var amountOfFuelToLoadOnTruck = 0;
            foreach (var vehicle in vehiclesOnRoute)
            {
                if (vehicle is Car)
                {
                    amountOfFuelToLoadOnTruck += ((Car) vehicle)
                        .AmountOfFuelNeededToFillTank();
                }
                else if(vehicle is Airplane)
                {
                    amountOfFuelToLoadOnTruck +=
                        ((Airplane) vehicle).AmountOfFuelNeededToFillLeftFuelTank();
                    amountOfFuelToLoadOnTruck +=
                        ((Airplane) vehicle).AmountOfFuelNeededToFillRightFuelTank();
                }
                else if(vehicle is Boat)
                {
                    amountOfFuelToLoadOnTruck +=
                        ((Boat) vehicle).AmountOfFuelNeededToFillFrontFuelTank();
                    amountOfFuelToLoadOnTruck +=
                        ((Boat) vehicle).AmountOfFuelNeededToFillRearFuelTank();
                }
            }
            return amountOfFuelToLoadOnTruck;
        }
    }
```

Each vehicle on the fuel truck's route is represented by a vehicle in the `vehiclesOnRoute` list. To determine how much fuel to send, the code must iterate through the list and add up the space needed to fill the tanks from each vehicle. For `Car` this is pretty straightforward; a car (usually) has one fuel tank. Airplanes have two (one on each wing) that can be drained at different rates. Boats can have forward and rear tanks that also can have differing amounts of fuel. Therefore, the logic to get the amount of fuel needed for each vehicle type is different.

The code in the `AddFuelToTruck` method tries to handle this by determining which specific concrete vehicle type it is looking at in each iteration of the loop and then casting `vehicle` to the specific type so that it can call the methods specific to that type to get the fuel information.

Not only is all this casting inefficient, but the `AddFuelToTruck` method also is forced into a position of having to know specifics about each vehicle type that it really shouldn't know or care about. If a new vehicle type is added, or a change is made to an existing vehicle type, this method has to change. This is another violation of the SRP.

This method can be refactored to remove the need for this intimate knowledge of the vehicle types by using polymorphism. First, an interface called `IFuelable` is created:

```
public interface IFuelable
{
    int GetTotalAmountOfFuelNeededForVehicle();
}
```

Because good naming standards have been used, it's pretty clear that the one and only method on the IFuelable interface, GetTotalAmountOfFuelNeededForVehicle, returns the total amount of fuel that needs to be added to the vehicle to fill the tanks. The next step is to implement the interface on the Vehicle classes:

```
public class Car : Vehicle, IFuelable
{
    public int GetTotalAmountOfFuelNeededForVehicle()
    {
        return AmountOfFuelNeededToFillTank();
    }
}

public class Airplane : Vehicle, IFuelable
{
    public int GetTotalAmountOfFuelNeededForVehicle()
    {
        return AmountOfFuelNeededToFillLeftFuelTank() +
            AmountOfFuelNeededToFillRightFuelTank();
    }
}

public class Boat : Vehicle, IFuelable
{
    public int GetTotalAmountOfFuelNeededForVehicle()
    {
        return AmountOfFuelNeededToFillFrontFuelTank() +
            AmountOfFuelNeededToFillRearFuelTank();
    }
}
```

For the sake of clarity, I removed the AmoutOfFuelNeeded... methods from this listing, but they are still in the code. The addition of the IFuelable interface to the declaration forced me to add the GetTotalAmountOfFuelNeededForVehicle to each vehicle class. This allows the developer to encapsulate the algorithm for computing the amount of fuel needed to completely fill the vehicle on each vehicle type, where it belongs. When the AddFuelToTruck method is refactored to take advantage of this interface, it becomes much shorter, more efficient, and easier to read:

```
public int AddFuelToTruck(List<IFuelable> vehiclesOnRoute)
{
    var amountOfFuelToLoadOnTruck = 0;
    foreach (var vehicle in vehiclesOnRoute)
    {
        amountOfFuelToLoadOnTruck +=
            vehicle.GetTotalAmountOfFuelNeededForVehicle();
    }
    return amountOfFuelToLoadOnTruck;
}
```

Additionally, the need for the AddFuelToTruck method to know the total amount of fuel needed for each vehicle disappears, and it can focus on simply adding up how much fuel needs to be loaded.

By using the features of LINQ built into .NET, this could be refactored into an even smaller method:

```
public int AddFuelToTruck(List<IFuelable> vehiclesOnRoute)
{
    return vehiclesOnRoute
        .Sum(vehicle => vehicle.GetTotalAmountOfFuelNeededForVehicle());
}
```

Due to the use of polymorphism, this method can now take advantage of the `Sum` method on the `List` object to be even shorter and easier to read.

Allow Type Inference

Most languages on the .NET platform are statically typed. This means that the developer must declare each variable and method as being of a specific type. C# 3 introduced the concept of type inference to .NET. This simply means that although C# is still a statically typed language, developers can allow the compiler to determine what type a variable should be based on how it is initialized. To be clear, this type inference does *not* happen at runtime; if the compiler can't determine the type when the application is compiled, it generates an error.

Type inference is done in C# using the `var` keyword. Instead of declaring your variable as being of a specific type, you declare it as a `var`:

```
Customer declaredAsCustomer = new Customer(); //declared with a specific type
var typeInferredCustomer = new Customer();    //declared using the var keyword
```

Both `declaredAsCustomer` and `typeInferredCustomer` are instances of the `Customer` class and behave and can be used in the exact same way. The difference is that you don't have to specifically tell the compiler that `typeInferredCustomer` is a `Customer` object.

The benefit of the `var` keyword is that it generates code that can be more readable; some developers view the simple declaration of a variable as line noise. The `var` keyword minimizes this. Refactoring can be easier with variables declared using `var`, because the compiler determines what type the variable should be declared as. If a developer changes how a variable is initialized, the compiler fixes the variable declaration automatically.

Use of the `var` keyword is controversial. Some developers think it is a bad practice, because it obfuscates what type you are working with. This can be true, but I would suggest that this is a problem only in situations with long methods and violations of the SRP. If developers keep the rest of their code clean, the use of the `var` keyword should not be a burden.

SUMMARY

Developers never write perfect code the first time. In practice, trying to write the "perfect method" the first time through is a mistake. Strive to get your application working and your tests passing. With a suite of unit tests that validate your code, you can refactor fearlessly.

Refactoring is to code what editing is to a book or article. Be merciless with your code. Refactor it to increase maintainability. Refactor to make your code more testable. Refactor it to ensure that it obeys the three tenets of OOP: encapsulation, inheritance, and polymorphism. Refactor to make sure you are abiding by the SOLID Principles: Single Responsibility, Open/Closed, Liskov Substitution, Interface Segregation, and Dependency Inversion. All these things not only increase the quality of your code, but also sharpen your skills as a developer and make you a better practitioner of TDD.

Code smells are antipatterns in code. Learn to identify them. Familiarize yourself with refactoring patterns to be able to quickly and easily deal with these code smells. Be sure to use your unit tests to verify that you have not broken the code's business functionality with your refactoring.

Finally, continue to study the tenets of OOP and the SOLID Principles. These concepts are not destinations; they are journeys. You'll always have opportunities to improve how you write code. Don't stop learning.

Test-Driven Development: Let the Tests Be Your Guide

As mentioned in Chapter 3, the aspect of TDD that developers seem to struggle with most is the idea that you should use tests to drive your initial development. For years developers have thought of tests as a way to validate their code when it was complete and ready for delivery. Tests were used in a work flow that took a set of requirements, turned those requirements into working code, and then verified the code using tests.

The problem with this paradigm is that it delays testing until the end of the process. Even the smallest application will have some defects. Without tests you lose the ability to quickly and easily determine where in the code the defect is occurring. It also becomes very difficult to design and write unit tests around existing code, because testability probably was not a priority when the code was written. Refactoring is difficult, because you have no quick and easy way to verify that your refactored code still works the way you intended.

The easiest way to solve this problem is to turn the entire process upside down. In this chapter you will see how writing tests, based on the business requirements of your application before the first line of code is written, can ensure that all the code you write is exercised by a test. Practicing test-first development can also help ensure that you are only writing code that your application needs to carry out its assigned tasks; you will not have the burden of managing code that does not contribute in a constructive way to your application.

The work flow in TDD is often described as "Red, Green, Refactor." This describes a series of steps that starts with a failing test, the developer then writes just enough code to make the test pass, and works to improve that code. In the section called "Red-Green-Refactor," you'll see the importance of these steps and how following them leads to lean, efficient code that satisfies the needs of the business with fewer defects.

IT STARTS WITH THE TEST

The first D in TDD stands for "driven." This means that in your practice of TDD, you must let the tests drive your development. This seems like a simple enough concept. However, when developers who are new to TDD start trying to work in a test-driven manner, they tend to fall back into their old, comfortable routines.

Most traditional development work flows start with requirements gathering. The business managers sit down, usually with a project manager and an architect, and sketch the broad strokes of a system. This process goes through several iterations in which the design is refined and details are expanded. Finally, a set of specifications for either a new application or a change to an existing one is produced.

For development teams or developers who don't practice TDD, the next step is to write the code. As a developer, you use specifications derived from the business requirements to define entities, service classes, and application work flows. At this point the system's quality depends on the developer's understanding of the technical specifications and business requirements as written. When you are done (or you have reached a point that represents your concept of "done"), you send the application to QA for testing. Invariably, QA finds defects in the feature.

Now it becomes your job to correct the defects. Without unit tests to help locate and diagnose the defect, most developers turn to the debugger, placing breakpoints in code where they think the defect could be happening. This is sometimes called the "shotgun approach." It's unfocused and inefficient. If an application has many layers of services and abstractions, you may have to spend a lot of time looking through all of them to find the source of the problem. The end result is that you spend more time locating the defect than actually fixing the code. This is not a very efficient use of your development time.

To add insult to injury, it becomes much harder to write unit tests for code when no forethought has been given to the concept of testability. TDD forces you to think about how you are designing and building your software to make it flexible and loosely coupled. Many developers who don't practice TDD think they are writing loosely coupled and flexible software. But when they don't have some external element keeping them honest (in this case, the unit tests), developers tend to find ways to cut corners. This is natural, because developers have been trained to "Optimize, optimize, optimize!" for years; they haven't been taught to think about maintainability.

In the end this process results in you spending an incredible amount of time to fix even a trivial defect. If you had some built-in way to determine where the defect was coming from, it would save quite a bit of time. Better yet, if you had some automated way of ensuring that your code reflected the business requirements and technical specifications, the defect may never have happened in the first place.

Practitioners of TDD still start with a set of business requirements. The place where TDD deviates from traditional development is the next step. Before you write a single line of code for a feature (including creating a new class to contain that code), you write a unit test based on the current requirement you are working on.

Unit tests are derived from the business requirements and technical specifications. Because of this, the unit tests become living, executable representations of the requirements and specifications. They cease to be something in a document that is quickly forgotten by the developers. They become runnable code that you can use to verify that you are creating the functionality intended by the business. These requirements become tangible things that you, as the developer, can interact with.

After a unit test that represents the requirements and specifications that have been created, you can begin writing code. Your goal at this point is to write the simplest and smallest amount of code to make the test pass. Don't worry if the code feels incomplete or unfinished; if it meets the current unit test, which has been derived from a requirement, it's complete.

As a corollary, don't write code that you do not have a unit test for. Don't worry about writing code to accommodate requirements that might or even probably will be found; requirements don't exist until they've been documented and had a test created for them. No code gets written unless a test requires it to exist.

As you build functionality for a requirement, you will likely uncover other parts of the application that need to be designed and built. This is especially common if you are working in an Agile-based methodology. In most of these methodologies a high-level architecture may be defined, but a big, detailed, up-front design phase does not occur. Detailed design is deferred until a feature or requirement is actually scheduled. This keeps development teams from incurring the overhead of doing a detailed design for features and functionality that never actually get scheduled for development.

When these new subsystems and other pieces of functionality emerge, make sure that you are creating tests for those pieces of code as well. For example, you may be assigned a feature that reads "Retrieve a `Person` object by Person ID." To implement this test, you might first create a Person business domain service, perhaps called `PersonService`. This service would represent the mechanism through which the constituent parts of the application would get a person by Person ID. The objective of `PersonService` is to provide a Person object based on a set of business rules. However, according to the SRP, it would not actually be responsible for retrieving the Person data from the database. One reason for the `PersonService` to change would be the business rules around how a person can be retrieved (for example, instead of Person ID, a `Person` should be retrieved by some other field on the database table.) Another reason for the `PersonService` to change would be how the data is actually retrieved from the data store (for example, initially the `Person` data is stored in a database, but at some point is relocated to a data store behind a web service).

To accommodate the needed separation of concerns, you could create a `PersonRepository` class that takes care of the mechanics of getting the data that represents a person from the database. This new class's only reason to change is if the way a person is retrieved from a database changes.

The business rules around creating a person are in the `PersonService`, so `PersonRepository` needs to worry only about data access.

This new class represents a new test that needs to be written. Remember that unit tests are isolated to the specific class and method they are testing. This means that your tests for `PersonService` should not be responsible for verifying the functionality of `PersonRepository`. In fact, the specific instance of `PersonService` that is used by the unit test should not use a concrete instance specifically of `PersonRepository`. It should use a mock object that implements the same interface as `PersonRepository`. (Mocking is covered in detail in Chapter 5.)

This means that in addition to the unit tests for `PersonService`, you must also write unit tests for `PersonRepository`. Since you are only working on `PersonService` right now, you need to define only the interface for `PersonRepository` and the method that will get a person from the data store by Person ID. Since you'll be using a mock of `PersonRepository` for the `PersonService`, the database-specific functionality isn't needed to make the test for `PersonService` pass.

After the tests for `PersonService` pass, it's time to turn your attention to `PersonRepository`. Your requirement is that `PersonRepository` should be able to get person data from a database based on a Person ID. Your task is to write just enough code to return the person data given a specific Person ID. Remember that unit tests for repository classes are just like unit tests for any other class; they need to be able to be isolated from their specific dependencies. Most database persistence frameworks provide a mechanism to mock the data context and allow you to write isolated unit tests for your repositories. Consult your framework's documentation for specific details.

Once the unit tests for both `PersonService` and `PersonRepository` are complete, the next step is to integrate them. In this case you want your tests to break boundaries; your test should call methods on a concrete instance of `PersonService`, which should in turn call methods on a concrete instance of `PersonRepository`, which should access a data store that has person data in it. The point of writing integration tests is to ensure that your `PersonService` and `PersonRepository` classes work together. It's not uncommon to create two components in isolation, only to find that they don't support each other. By integrating small pieces of the application early on, you can ensure that the components you are building now will be able to be combined into a larger application later.

RED, GREEN, REFACTOR

TDD has many colloquialisms and anagrams. You've already read about OOP, SOLID, and DRY. These three are all very important not only to TDD, but also to good software development practices in general. But if one saying, phrase, or mantra sums up the core beliefs of TDD, it's *red, green, refactor*. It reminds you of the TDD work flow of requirements flowing into tests, which then flow into code. It also sets the expectation that refactoring will occur. Developers and managers who are unfamiliar with TDD often hear the word *refactor* and assume it means to fix what wasn't done right the first time. This perception of what refactoring means is simply not true. Writing code is an iterative process. Refactoring is the continued refinement of your code to make it the most simple, readable, and best it can be.

The Three Phases of TDD

Red, green, refactor defines the work flow that developers follow when practicing TDD. As illustrated earlier, the sequence of steps taken in writing code is important. When followed, this order of steps (requirements, test, code) helps ensure that you have tests for the code you are writing and that you are writing only code that you have a test for.

The term *gold plating* refers to the addition of functionality to an application that was not requested by the user or the business but that still costs money to develop and maintain. The functionality being added may seem like a good idea. But functionality that is unneeded and unused, but that requires resources to create and maintain, is wasteful. The requirements define the system's features and functionality, not the whims of developers.

The Red Phase

When starting with TDD, most developers ask, "How can I write a test for something that doesn't exist?" In fact, many of your tests will be for classes or methods that don't currently exist. This means that your test won't even compile, which is essentially the same as having a failing test. That's OK; remember that you are letting the tests drive the need for the code to exist.

After you create your first test, the next step is one or more support actions. Early in the development of your application, the next thing you do could be creating a project in your Visual Studio solution. If so, you'll need to add a reference to the new project from your test project.

Maybe you already have the project and it's referenced from your test project. Then your next step may be creating a new interface for a service that your unit test requires. Your test won't compile, so it fails until you create this interface. The unit test probably still won't compile at this point; without a concrete implementation of your service, you get a compiler error. Therefore, you need to create a concrete implementation for this new service.

Or maybe the interface and service already exist, but no method exists for the test you are writing. By writing the test first, and being the first consumer of this method, you'll have some insight into how developers will work with this service. Without TDD, developers often create public interfaces for their service in a manner that makes it easy for them, without any thought about how the interface will be consumed. Although the API may make sense to you as you are writing the service, it may be very difficult for the consumer of the service to understand and use. By using your own interface to write tests, you can experience what it's like for consumers of your service to use the service. This helps you define interfaces that are simple to use and easy to understand for your end users.

The last obvious permutation is that you already have an interface and a class, and the method you are testing already exists, but you are testing a new requirement for that method. This test will fail as well, because you haven't written any code to make it pass. In this case the next step is to write code to make the new test pass while not causing the existing tests to fail.

In any case, when you first write your test, for whatever reason, it will fail. Either it won't compile, or the test will compile and run but will fail due to not getting an expected result from the method under test. You are currently in the red phase. Your goal now is to move into the green phase.

The Green Phase

If your test is failing, you are in the red phase. The key to getting to the green phase is to write just enough code to make your new test pass while not causing any of the other tests to fail. The concept of writing "just enough" code to make a test pass is another philosophical hurdle that developers new to TDD sometimes struggle to get over.

For example, suppose you have a requirement that makes it necessary to add a new method to an existing service. The rest of the requirement states that, given an input value of 61, the new method should return false. Many developers who do not practice TDD would agree that the following code example would be the least amount of code necessary to make the test pass:

```
public bool MyMethod(int inputParameter)
{
    if (inputParameter == 61)
    {
        return false;
    }
    return true;
}
```

It's perfectly reasonable to assume that this is what the method should do, but this is not the least amount of code to make the test pass. The requirement and test do not state anything about a condition to make the method return true; the code only says that for situations in which inputParameter equals 61, it should return false. The code shown here may in fact look like what the final version of this method should be. But until a test is created to verify a situation in which a value of true is returned, you shouldn't assume anything.

The following code illustrates the absolute minimum amount of code needed to make the test pass:

```
public bool MyMethod(int inputParameter)
{
    return false;
}
```

Looking at this implementation, it may seem incomplete. It certainly looks unfinished; the method expects a value for inputParameter but doesn't use it. The point of this exercise is to ensure that you are writing *just enough* code to make the test pass, and thus complete the business requirement. If the only current documented business requirement is that method return false when the value of inputParameter is false, then the previous example *does* meet the business requirement. As more requirements for this feature or functionality are fleshed out, more tests will be created. These additional tests will cause you to expand on the functionality of this method. As this method grows, it may be appropriate to add more branches to the if statement. On the other hand a more complex algorithm may be needed. The point is to not introduce complexity to your code until and unless you need to.

As soon as enough code has been created to make the tests pass, you're ready to enter the refactoring phase.

The Refactoring Phase

Until now the goal has been just to get the unit tests to pass. Notice that so far you haven't worried about maintainability, readability, or overall code quality. Now that you've created some unit tests that validate the business requirements, it's time to turn your attention to bringing these three attributes to your code. This practice is called *refactoring*.

Whether practicing TDD or not, developers always find the need to tweak and tinker with their code. Essentially this is what happens when you refactor code. The benefit of refactoring with TDD is that you have a suite of unit tests to validate that your code still meets the business requirements. Periodically examine your business code and your unit tests, and look for opportunities to enhance them by refactoring. Refactor code by making small changes and then using the unit tests to validate that the refactored code still works. So long as the tests pass, your code is correct.

Starting Again

You now have a unit test that passes. You have a method that contains the simplest and shortest code necessary to make the test pass. You've also had an opportunity to refactor that code to ensure that it's readable and maintainable. The next step is to do it again.

If you think back to the code sample in the preceding section, the least amount of code to satisfy the test was to simply return false. Although this is valid to make the test pass and satisfy the current test, it probably is incomplete from a business standpoint. As development continues, more requirements and features will be scheduled for development. These requirements and features translate into new tests. The complete set of these tests — your test suite — reflects all the business functionality expected of the application. This creates a triangulation of tests that ensures, so long as the tests all pass, that the application meets the needs of the business.

An important point to remember when practicing TDD is that your code, and the test results it generates, is only as good as your tests. I've talked about refactoring code, but don't be afraid to refactor your unit tests as well. If a test no longer reflects the requirements, refactor them. If you find a gap in your test, refactor it. If you find that your test misrepresents a requirement, refactor it. Keep your tests clean and maintained. They are just as important to your application as any other piece of code.

A REFACTORING EXAMPLE

Suppose that one of your friends is developing a tic-tac-toe game. He has created the front end that allows users to manage turns and to pick the square in which to place their mark. For this example, he has asked you to create a service that he can use to determine if either player has won by placing his or her mark in three adjacent squares to form a row horizontally, vertically, or diagonally.

By way of requirements, your friend tells you that he plans to represent the game board by creating a 3-by-3 multidimensional array of `char` data types, with the x-axis representing horizontal rows and the y-axis representing vertical columns. This array will be passed into the method you will write as the input parameter. Your friend wants the library to return the mark of the winning player (an X or an O) or a space character if neither player wins.

> *To follow along with the example shown here, download the code from* www
> .wrox.com.

The First Feature

For this task you create a blank solution in Visual Studio called
TicTacToe. To that solution you add a class library called TicTacToe
.UnitTests that contains a class called GameWinnerServiceTests
(which makes the fully qualified name of this class TicTacToe
.UnitTests.GameWinnerServiceTests). You also add a reference to
NUnit, which will serve as your unit test framework (see Figure 4-1).

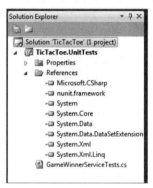

FIGURE 4-1

The first feature your friend asks you to implement states that if no
player has three in a row (horizontally, vertically, or diagonally), no one
wins, and your method should return an empty character. Your first
test is relatively easy. You pass in an empty array (no player has three
in a row) and expect back an empty character (the expected response to
neither player's having three in a row):

*Available for
download on
Wrox.com*

```
[TestFixture]
public class GameWinnerServiceTests
{
    [Test]
    public void NeitherPlayerHasThreeInARow()
    {
        const char expected = ' ';
        var gameBoard = new char[3,3] { {' ', ' ', ' '},
                                        {' ', ' ', ' '},
                                        {' ', ' ', ' '}};
        var actual = gameWinnerService.Validate(gameBoard);
        Assert.AreEqual(expected, actual);
    }
}
```

GameWinnerServiceTests.cs

Right away you'll notice that the code is trying to call the Validate method on the variable
_gameWinnerService, which you haven't declared yet. Since you need an instance of the
GameWinnerService you are creating, go ahead and declare that variable (I've left out the class
declaration for the GameWinnerService test class for clarity):

*Available for
download on
Wrox.com*

```
[Test]
public void NeitherPlayerHasThreeInARow()
{
    IGameWinnerService gameWinnerService;
    const char expected = ' ';
    var gameBoard = new char[3,3] { {' ', ' ', ' '},
```

```
                               {' ', ' ', ' '},
                               {' ', ' ', ' '} };
    var actual = gameWinnerService.Validate(gameBoard);
    Assert.AreEqual(expected, actual);
}
```

GameWinnerServiceTests.cs

As it stands, this test still won't pass, because `IGameWinnerService`
has not been defined. Before this test existed, you didn't need
`IGameWinnerService`, so it had no reason to exist. There is now
a test that requires `IGameWinnerService` to be defined, so that's
your next step. You start by creating a new class library in your
solution called `TicTacToe.Services` and renaming the `Class1.cs`
file it creates `GameWinnerService.cs`. But don't allow Visual
Studio to rename the class inside the file, because you'll just delete
it (see Figure 4-2).

In the `GameWinnerService.cs` file you delete the declaration
for `Class1` and replace it with the declaration for the
`IGameWinnerService` interface:

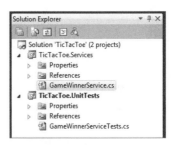

FIGURE 4-2

Available for download on Wrox.com

```
namespace TicTacToe.Services
{
    public interface IGameWinnerService
    {
    }
}
```

GameWinnerService.cs

Returning to the unit test, you need to add a reference in your `TicTacToe.UnitTests` class library
to your new `TicTacToe.Services` class library. Once you've added this reference, your declaration
of `gameWinnerService` as a type of `IGameWinnerService` no longer causes a compiler error.
However, because this interface has no methods yet, your call to `gameWinnerService.Validate`
does cause a compiler error. Therefore, your next step is to add a declaration of the `Validate`
method to the `IGameWinnerService` interface:

Available for download on Wrox.com

```
public interface IGameWinnerService
{
    char Validate(char[,] gameBoard);
}
```

GameWinnerService.cs

When this is done, your code still doesn't compile. Right now, you're attempting to use
`gameWinnerService` without creating a concrete instance. The next step in making the test pass
is creating a concrete instance of a class that supports the `IGameWinnerService` interface. In

the `GameWinnerService.cs` file, create a class called `GameWinnerService` that implements the `IGameWinnerService` interface:

```
public class GameWinnerService : IGameWinnerService
{
    public char Validate(char[,] gameBoard)
    {
        throw new NotImplementedException();
    }
}
```

GameWinnerService.cs

Strictly speaking, this method has no implementation. In fact, it throws an exception stating that fact. But that's OK; you're writing just enough code to get to the next step. When you add code to your unit test in the `NeitherPlayerHasThreeInARow` method to create a concrete instance of `GameWinnerService` and assign it to the `gameWinnerService` variable, the application compiles. Right now that's all you care about.

Add code to the `NeitherPlayerHasThreeInARow` method to instantiate a concrete instance of `GameWinnerService`:

```
[Test]
public void NeitherPlayerHasThreeInARow()
{
    IGameWinnerService gameWinnerService;
    gameWinnerService = new GameWinnerService();
    const char expected = ' ';
    var gameBoard = new char[3,3] { {' ', ' ', ' '},
                                    {' ', ' ', ' '},
                                    {' ', ' ', ' '} };
    var actual = gameWinnerService.Validate(gameBoard);
    Assert.AreEqual(expected, actual);
}
```

GameWinnerServiceTests.cs

The code compiles. When you run your test, (as expected) it fails because the `Validate` method is not implemented, as shown in Figure 4-3.

FIGURE 4-3

Making the First Test Pass

Again, this is okay. You need to see the test fail for many reasons. You need to make sure your test really tests something; a test that never fails doesn't really test your code. Although at this stage it's unlikely, you need to verify that you haven't written too much code. You also need to make sure that you're not re-creating functionality. If your test passes now, without your having to write any more code, there's a good chance you could be duplicating work. Since a goal is to keep your code as DRY as possible, you need to make sure you're not reimplementing something that already exists.

Now it's time to start thinking about moving into the green phase. Your goal now is to write just enough code to make the test pass. It turns out this is pretty easy to do:

```
public char Validate(char[,] gameBoard)
{
    return ' ';
}
```

GameWinnerService.cs

Looking at this code, you might think, "That's not how the rules of tic-tac-toe work," and you would be right. But your current requirement isn't to implement all the rules of tic-tac-toe — only the rule that if neither player has three squares in a row, no one wins. The requirement says nothing about conditions that should return a winner, or about having symbols for either player on the game board. Those requirements do not exist yet. As evidenced by the passing test (shown in Figure 4-4), this implementation of the `Validate` method meets that requirement.

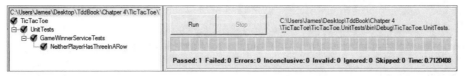

FIGURE 4-4

The current test passes. Because nothing in either the business code (`GameWinnerService`) or the unit test (`GameWinnerServiceTests`) needs refactoring, you move on to the next business requirement.

The Second Feature

The second feature states that if a player's symbol appears in all three cells in the top horizontal row, the player's symbol should be returned as the winning symbol. Here's the unit test for this requirement:

```
[Test]
public void PlayerWithAllSpacesInTopRowIsWinner()
{
    IGameWinnerService gameWinnerService;
    gameWinnerService = new GameWinnerService();
```

```
        const char expected = 'X';
        var gameBoard = new char[3, 3]
            { {expected, expected, expected},
              {' ', ' ', ' '},
              {' ', ' ', ' '} };
        var actual = gameWinnerService.Validate(gameBoard);
        Assert.AreEqual(expected.ToString(),
            actual.ToString());
    }
```

GameWinnerServiceTests.cs

This is very similar to the previous test. It constructs a multidimensional array to serve as your game board and passes it as a parameter to the `Validate` method of the `GameWinnerService` instance `gameWinnerService`. The difference is that this time you populate the top row, and the value of the variable `expected`, with the value `'X'`, which is what you are using as the symbol for your player. When this test calls the `Validate` method, it expects to get a `char` with a value of `'X'` as the return value from `Validate`. When you run this test, it does not pass, as shown in Figure 4-5.

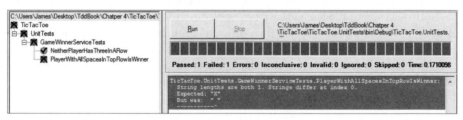

FIGURE 4-5

Your next step is to implement just enough functionality to make this test pass:

```
public char Validate(char[,] gameBoard)
{
    var columnOneChar = gameBoard[0, 0];
    var columnTwoChar = gameBoard[0, 1];
    var columnThreeChar = gameBoard[0, 2];
    if (columnOneChar == columnTwoChar &&
        columnTwoChar == columnThreeChar)
    {
        return columnOneChar;
    }
    return ' ';
}
```

GameWinnerService.cs

Again, this is not necessarily the most efficient or complete logic for a tic-tac-toe game; it is simply what is needed to make your test pass. In this case all you care about is ensuring that if the same symbol appears across the top row, that symbol is returned from the method. As shown in Figure 4-6, this test passes.

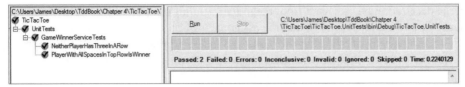

FIGURE 4-6

Before moving on to the next test, let's look at the unit tests now in the `GameWinnerServiceTests` class:

Available for
download on
Wrox.com

```
[TestFixture]
public class GameWinnerServiceTests
{
    [Test]
    public void NeitherPlayerHasThreeInARow()
    {
        IGameWinnerService gameWinnerService;
        gameWinnerService = new GameWinnerService();
        const char expected = ' ';
        var gameBoard = new char[3,3] { {' ', ' ', ' '},
                                        {' ', ' ', ' '},
                                        {' ', ' ', ' '} };
        var actual = gameWinnerService.Validate(gameBoard);
        Assert.AreEqual(expected, actual);
    }

    [Test]
    public void PlayerWithAllSpacesInTopRowIsWinner()
    {
        IGameWinnerService gameWinnerService;
        gameWinnerService = new GameWinnerService();
        const char expected = 'X';
        var gameBoard = new char[3, 3] { {expected, expected, expected},
                                         {' ', ' ', ' '},
                                         {' ', ' ', ' '} };
        var actual = gameWinnerService.Validate(gameBoard);
        Assert.AreEqual(expected.ToString(), actual.ToString());
    }
}
```

GameWinnerServiceTests.cs

Refactoring the Unit Tests

You can see that even with just two tests written, it's time to refactor the unit test code a bit. For starters, both tests use an instance of the `GameWinnerService`. Since the tests use the exact same concrete implementation of this class, and access it through the same abstract interface, you can remove the declarations of `IGameWinnerService` from the individual tests and make it a member variable:

Available for
download on
Wrox.com

```
IGameWinnerService _gameWinnerService;
```

GameWinnerServiceTests.cs

Not only can the declaration be extracted from the individual unit tests, so can the creation of the concrete instance of `GameWinnerService` and the assignment of that object to `_gameWinnerService`. You do this by creating a setup method for the `GameWinnerServiceTests` class and adding the code to create the concrete instance of `GameWinnerService`:

```
[SetUp]
public void SetupUnitTests()
{
    _gameWinnerService = new GameWinnerService();
}
```

GameWinnerServiceTests.cs

At this point you run the unit tests to ensure that your refactoring hasn't broken anything, as shown in Figure 4-7.

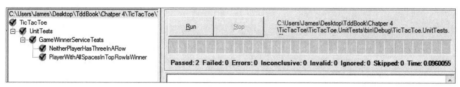

FIGURE 4-7

The tests are already looking quite a bit DRYer, but one other data construct is used in both unit tests — the game board. That can easily be extracted to a member variable as well:

```
private char[,] _gameBoard;
```

GameWinnerServiceTests.cs

As with the extraction of `_gameWinnerService`, the creation of the concrete instance of the `_gameBoard` member variable can be moved out of the individual unit tests and put in the `SetupUnitTests` method:

```
[SetUp]
public void SetupUnitTests()
{
    _gameWinnerService = new GameWinnerService();
    _gameBoard = new char[3, 3]
        {
            {' ', ' ', ' '},
            {' ', ' ', ' '},
            {' ', ' ', ' '}
        };
}
```

GameWinnerServiceTests.cs

Now that these changes have been made, you run the unit tests again to make sure they are still working as before (see Figure 4-8).

FIGURE 4-8

The Third Feature

With the refactoring of the unit tests complete, it's time to start on the third feature The new requirement states that if a player has his character in all three rows of the first column, his symbol should be returned from the `Validate` method, indicating that he has won. This is very similar to the requirement for the last test, as you can see from the code for the unit test that exercises this requirement:

```
[Test]
public void PlayerWithAllSpacesInFirstColumnIsWinner()
{
    const char expected = 'X';
    for (var columnIndex = 0; columnIndex < 3; columnIndex++)
    {
        _gameBoard[columnIndex, 0] = expected;
    }
    var actual = _gameWinnerService.Validate(_gameBoard);
    Assert.AreEqual(expected.ToString(), actual.ToString());
}
```

GameWinnerServiceTests.cs

Running the test shows that it fails, as shown in Figure 4-9.

FIGURE 4-9

As with the previous failing test, you write just enough code in the `Validate` method to make this test pass:

```
public char Validate(char[,] gameBoard)
{
    var columnOneChar = gameBoard[0, 0];
```

```
        var columnTwoChar = gameBoard[0, 1];
        var columnThreeChar = gameBoard[0, 2];
        if (columnOneChar == columnTwoChar && columnTwoChar == columnThreeChar)
        {
            return columnOneChar;
        }

        var rowTwoChar = gameBoard[1, 0];
        var rowThreeChar = gameBoard[2, 0];
        if (columnOneChar == rowTwoChar && rowTwoChar == rowThreeChar)
        {
            return columnOneChar;
        }
        return ' ';
    }
```

GameWinnerService.cs

Running the tests shows that this code was enough not only to make your new test pass, but also to keep the other two passing (see Figure 4-10).

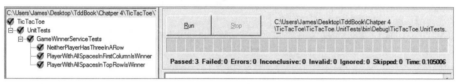

FIGURE 4-10

Refactoring the Business Code

Before going on to the next requirement, you want to do a little more refactoring. This time you turn your attention to the `Validate` method in the `GameWinnerService` class:

```
public char Validate(char[,] gameBoard)
{
    var columnOneChar = gameBoard[0, 0];
    var columnTwoChar = gameBoard[0, 1];
    var columnThreeChar = gameBoard[0, 2];
    if (columnOneChar == columnTwoChar &&
        columnTwoChar == columnThreeChar)
    {
        return columnOneChar;
    }

    var rowTwoChar = gameBoard[1, 0];
    var rowThreeChar = gameBoard[2, 0];
    if (columnOneChar == rowTwoChar &&
        rowTwoChar == rowThreeChar)
    {
        return columnOneChar;
```

```
        }
        return ' ';
    }
```

You may notice two things pretty quickly when looking at this method: It's a bit long, and it violates the Single Responsibility Principle (SRP). It's not unusual to find that these two code smells usually appear together. In this case both problems can be fixed with the same set of refactoring steps. Begin by looking at the first violation of the SRP.

This method does three things. It checks for three in a row in the top row, it checks for three in a row in the first column, and it checks for neither of the first two conditions. The first thing you want to do is extract to a separate method the code that checks the first row:

Available for download on Wrox.com

```
private static char CheckForThreeInARowInHorizontalRow(char[,] gameBoard)
{
    var columnOneChar = gameBoard[0, 0];
    var columnTwoChar = gameBoard[0, 1];
    var columnThreeChar = gameBoard[0, 2];
    if (columnOneChar == columnTwoChar && columnTwoChar == columnThreeChar)
    {
        return columnOneChar;
    }
    return ' ';
}
```

The code in the `Validate` method that invokes this method should now look like this:

Available for download on Wrox.com

```
public char Validate(char[,] gameBoard)
{
    var currentWinningSymbol = ' ';
    currentWinningSymbol = CheckForThreeInARowInHorizontalRow(gameBoard);

    var rowOneChar = gameBoard[0, 0];
    var rowTwoChar = gameBoard[1, 0];
    var rowThreeChar = gameBoard[2, 0];
    if (rowOneChar == rowTwoChar && rowTwoChar == rowThreeChar)
    {
        currentWinningSymbol = rowOneChar;
    }

    return currentWinningSymbol;
}
```

As you can see, you needed to make some significant changes to the logic of the `Validate` method, but the method already looks much better. The logic is more straightforward, the method is easier to read, and it's easier to understand what's going on. You now need to run the unit tests to verify that you haven't changed (broken) any of the external behavior of the `Validate` method. (See Figure 4-11.)

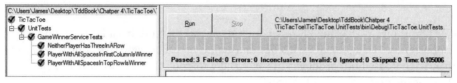

FIGURE 4-11

The tests all pass, which means the refactoring performed on the `Validate` method was successful. Next you extract to a method the code that checks for three in a row in the first vertical column, just as you did with the code for three in a row in a horizontal row:

```
private static char CheckForThreeInARowInVerticalColumn(char[,] gameBoard)
{
    var rowOneChar = gameBoard[0, 0];
    var rowTwoChar = gameBoard[1, 0];
    var rowThreeChar = gameBoard[2, 0];
    if (rowOneChar == rowTwoChar &&
        rowTwoChar == rowThreeChar)
    {
        return rowOneChar;
    }
    return ' ';
}
```

GameWinnerService.cs

After you refactor the code in the `Validate` method to accommodate the extraction of the code that checks for three in a row in the first column, the `Validate` method looks like this:

```
public char Validate(char[,] gameBoard)
{
    var currentWinningSymbol = ' ';
    currentWinningSymbol = CheckForThreeInARowInHorizontalRow(gameBoard);
    currentWinningSymbol = CheckForThreeInARowInVerticalColumn(gameBoard);
    return currentWinningSymbol;
}
```

GameWinnerService.cs

This code may look correct, but running the unit tests reveals that it changes the external functionality of (breaks) the `Validate` method, as shown in Figure 4-12.

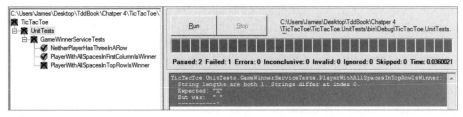

FIGURE 4-12

Correcting Refactoring Defects

Taking another look at the code, it appears that if the `CheckForThreeInARowInHorizontalRow` method returns a winning symbol, it is overwritten by the call to `CheckForThreeInARowInVerticalColumn`. This method returns an empty character because, in that test case, neither player has three in a row in the first vertical column.

The value of unit tests when refactoring should be made clear by this example. You can spot a bug in your code immediately, and because you made only a few small changes, it's easy to determine where the code broke and why. You could engage in refactoring in the first place due to the security that unit tests provide. You don't have to worry about changes causing bugs to appear in code without your knowledge. Your unit tests give you a clear picture of the health of the entire code base.

Before you proceed to the next feature, you need to fix this bug by adding code to the `Validate` method to see if the call to `CheckForThreeInARowInHorizontalRow` returns a winning symbol. If it does, you immediately return from the `Validate` method and don't even bother to call the `CheckForThreeInARowInVerticalColumn` method:

Available for download on Wrox.com

```
public char Validate(char[,] gameBoard)
{
    var currentWinningSymbol = ' ';
    currentWinningSymbol = CheckForThreeInARowInHorizontalRow(gameBoard);
    if (currentWinningSymbol != ' ')
        return currentWinningSymbol;
    currentWinningSymbol = CheckForThreeInARowInVerticalColumn(gameBoard);
    return currentWinningSymbol;
}
```

GameWinnerService.cs

Running the unit tests assures you that these changes fix the failing test and don't break the other two tests, as shown in Figure 4-13.

FIGURE 4-13

Before extracting to their own methods the logic that checked for matches in the first row and first column, there was only one place where this code used the literal value of an empty character (' '). In that case it was fine to have it in the code, because you used it only once. Now you'll be using it in four different places and three different methods. It's time to extract the literal value from the code and declare it as a private constant:

```
private const char SymbolForNoWinner = ' ';
```

GameWinnerService.cs

You can now replace all uses of the literal value in the code for the GameWinnerService class with this new constant:

```
private const char SymbolForNoWinner = ' ';
```

GameWinnerService.cs

If sometime in the future you need to change the value you're using to indicate that there is no winner, you have to change it in only one place, not four.

You need to change one last thing before moving on. The current version of the Validate method looks like this:

```
public char Validate(char[,] gameBoard)
{
    var currentWinningSymbol = SymbolForNoWinner;
    currentWinningSymbol = CheckForThreeInARowInHorizontalRow(gameBoard);
    if (currentWinningSymbol != SymbolForNoWinner)
        return currentWinningSymbol;
    currentWinningSymbol = CheckForThreeInARowInVerticalColumn(gameBoard);
    return currentWinningSymbol;
}
```

GameWinnerService.cs

There is no need to assign currentWinningSymbol a default value, because you overwrite that value anyway. In fact, you can declare currentWinningSymbol and assign it to the return value of CheckForThreeInARowInHorizontalRow on a single line of code:

```
public char Validate(char[,] gameBoard)
{
    var currentWinningSymbol = CheckForThreeInARowInHorizontalRow(gameBoard);
    if (currentWinningSymbol != SymbolForNoWinner)
        return currentWinningSymbol;
    currentWinningSymbol = CheckForThreeInARowInVerticalColumn(gameBoard);
    return currentWinningSymbol;
}
```

GameWinnerService.cs

This removes an unnecessary line of code. This may not seem like much, unless you consider that in Chapter 3 I pointed out that the more lines of code you write, the more chances you give yourself to write the wrong code. By eliminating an unneeded line of code, you reduce the chance that the `Validate` method has a bug.

The Fourth Feature

Now that the refactoring is done, it's time to move on to the next feature. The new requirement states that if a user has three in a row diagonally, starting in the upper-left corner, going through the center, and finishing in the lower-right corner, he or she is the winner. The unit test for this requirement looks like this:

```
[Test]
public void PlayerWithThreeInARowDiagonallyDownAndToRightIsWinner()
{
    const char expected = 'X';
    for (var cellIndex = 0; cellIndex < 3; cellIndex++)
    {
        _gameBoard[cellIndex, cellIndex] = expected;
    }
    var actual = _gameWinnerService.Validate(_gameBoard);
    Assert.AreEqual(expected.ToString(), actual.ToString());
}
```

GameWinnerServiceTests.cs

Running this new unit test reveals that it does not pass, as shown in Figure 4-14.

FIGURE 4-14

As with the three previous unit tests, your next task is to write just enough code to make this test pass. Because you refactored the `Validate` method, you know that checking for a winner with three in a row diagonally would be a new reason for the `Validate` method to change. Start by creating a private method called `CheckForThreeInARowDiagonally`, which you can call from the `Validate` method:

```
private static char CheckForThreeInARowDiagonally(char[,] gameBoard)
{
    var cellOneChar = gameBoard[0, 0];
    var cellTwoChar = gameBoard[1, 1];
    var cellThreeChar = gameBoard[2, 2];
```

```
        if (cellOneChar == cellTwoChar &&
            cellTwoChar == cellThreeChar)
        {
            return cellOneChar;
        }
        return SymbolForNoWinner;
    }
```

GameWinnerService.cs

Now you just need to call this new method from the `Validate` method:

```
public char Validate(char[,] gameBoard)
{
    var currentWinningSymbol = CheckForThreeInARowInHorizontalRow(gameBoard);
    if (currentWinningSymbol != SymbolForNoWinner)
        return currentWinningSymbol;
    currentWinningSymbol = CheckForThreeInARowInVerticalColumn(gameBoard);
    if (currentWinningSymbol != SymbolForNoWinner)
        return currentWinningSymbol;
    currentWinningSymbol = CheckForThreeInARowDiagonally(gameBoard);
    return currentWinningSymbol;
}
```

GameWinnerService.cs

Running the unit tests shows that not only does the new test pass, but all the other unit tests still pass as well (see Figure 4-15).

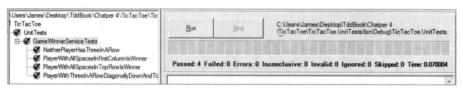

FIGURE 4-15

The `GameWinnerService` is by no means complete at this point. This project will be available for download from the Wrox website at `www.wrox.com`. I urge you to download it and practice the work flow you've learned in this chapter, as well as the refactoring skills from Chapter 3, and complete `GameWinnerService` on your own. It's a great way to practice and get used to the TDD work flow of "red, green, refactor."

SUMMARY

Developers who practice TDD use several frameworks and tools you may not yet be familiar with. But a more difficult hurdle to get over than learning new tools and frameworks may be changing how you think about and approach writing software. Writing a test before you write the code you are testing may not seem natural at first, so you may need to spend some time unlearning what you know about writing code.

The mantra of "red, green, refactor" defines the work flow for practicing TDD. Write your test first, even if it won't compile. Write just enough code to make that test pass. Don't worry if it's not pretty or you don't feel you've covered all the bases the business will care about; that's not your priority right now. Just worry about the requirement in front of you at this moment. If your tests meet the current business requirements and they pass, you're done. Once you have written enough code to complete the business functionality, refactor your code to make it readable and maintainable.

Remember that tests are part of your code base too. Your code will be only as good as your tests are. Don't just test the "happy path." Make sure you triangulate your tests to expose weaknesses in your code. Treat your tests as if they were part of your business logic; do not let code rot set in.

Download the tic-tac-toe `GameWinnerService` example from this chapter and complete it. Come up with your own feature to define game rules. Write tests and then add to the `GameWinnerService` to make those tests pass. Constantly refactor your business code and your unit tests to keep them lean and focused.

Mocking External Resources

WHAT'S IN THIS CHAPTER?

➤ Why statically binding components creates brittle systems

➤ How the dependency injection pattern can help you by dynamically binding these components

➤ How a dependency injection framework can help you manage the dependencies within your application

➤ How to effectively mock your application's data access code with the repository pattern

Most applications you'll write as a business application developer are composed of various components (some you'll create; others will come from a third party) that are combined to perform a task. Sometimes these components represent external resources, such as a database, a web service, a file system, or even a physical device. These external resources are required by the components in your application, yet you still need to be able to test the components in isolation, away from the external resources. Developers practicing TDD do this by providing stand-ins for these external resources at runtime. These stand-ins are called *mocks*.

To use mocks, and to truly isolate the individual components under test, you need an alternative to statically binding the individual components. The dependency injection pattern can be used to inject the concrete implementations of these components at runtime or during testing. Dependency injection frameworks help you manage the web of dependencies and ensure that the correct concrete implementation is provided based on the context your component is being used in.

THE DEPENDENCY INJECTION PATTERN

In a traditional application designed with OOP, you create service and entity classes to abstract real-world processes and entities. An application is then composed of these various service and entity classes. This composition creates dependencies between the classes in your applications. The most obvious way to express and manage these dependencies is to statically create them in code as part of your class's initialization process. (This example can be found in the `Before` folder in the downloaded code sample on www.wrox.com.)

```
public class BusinessService
{
    private readonly string _databaseConnectionString =
ConfigurationManager.ConnectionStrings["MyConnectionString"].ConnectionString;
    private readonly string _webServiceAddress =
        ConfigurationManager.AppSettings["MyWebServiceAddress"];
    private readonly LoggingDataSink _loggingDataSink;

    private DataAccessComponent _dataAccessComponent;
    private WebServiceProxy _webServiceProxy;
    private LoggingComponent _loggingComponent;

    public BusinessService()
    {
        _loggingDataSink = new LoggingDataSink();
        _loggingComponent = new LoggingComponent(_loggingDataSink);
        _webServiceProxy = new WebServiceProxy(_webServiceAddress);
        _dataAccessComponent = new DataAccessComponent(_databaseConnectionString);
    }
}
```

BusinessService.cs

Several problems occur when this method is used to handle dependencies between classes. The most obvious problem is that this code is statically bound to the specific concrete implementations you used when writing this class. There is no way to change the concrete object used in these dependencies without opening the code. This static binding also makes it impossible to substitute mock objects for any of the dependencies, which makes isolating any of the code in this class's methods for unit testing out of the question.

This point is further complicated by the fact that none of these dependencies are contract-based. Instead, they rely on specific definitions of classes. Relying on concrete classes instead of abstract interfaces limits your ability to swap out these services. To open this class for alteration (by definition of the Open/Close Principle [OCP]), you must be careful to replace the dependencies with classes that support the same API or be prepared to make significant changes to this class.

The last major problem with this approach is that `BusinessService` class is required to know far too much about the classes it's dependent on simply to create concrete instances of them. It must know that `DataAccessComponent` requires a connection string, that `WebServiceProxy` requires a service address, and that `LoggingComponent` requires a data sink for its messages. This violates the SRP, because the knowledge to create these classes must surely exist elsewhere in the application. In fact, you can be assured that the same exact code is replicated anywhere in the application that these dependency classes are used. This means that if any of these classes change this class, potentially many more have to change as well.

The dependency injection pattern provides a framework that allows you to provide concrete instances of dependency objects to a class when that class is created. The easiest and most common way of injecting these dependencies is by passing them into an object as constructor arguments. Taking the previous example and refactoring it to the dependency injection pattern would yield a class that looks like this. (This example can be found in the After folder in the downloaded code sample on www.wrox.com.)

```csharp
public class BusinessService
{
    private IDataAccessComponent _dataAccessComponent;
    private IWebServiceProxy _webServiceProxy;
    private ILoggingComponent _loggingComponent;

    public BusinessService(IDataAccessComponent dataAccessComponent,
                           IWebServiceProxy webServiceProxy,
                           ILoggingComponent loggingComponent)
    {
        _loggingComponent = loggingComponent;
        _webServiceProxy = webServiceProxy;
        _dataAccessComponent = dataAccessComponent;
    }
}
```

BusinessService.cs

Implementing the dependency injection pattern has already done a lot to make the BusinessService easier to understand and maintain. Limiting dependencies is still important. A class with too many constructor arguments is a code smell in and of itself, but the dependency injection patterns have made it much easier to manage the dependencies that this class does have.

Aside from the improved readability and maintainability of BusinessService, you can now inject whatever implementations of the dependencies you like when you invoke this class, provided that they implement the prescribed interface. You can provide different implementations of these based on rules or configuration values. This is very helpful in situations where you might want the instance of this application in your QA environment to use a test database or web service and to switch to the production instances of these resources when the application is promoted to production. The major advantage for you as a TDD developer is that mocked instances of these services can be injected into this class for testing. This allows you to provide stand-in implementations that provide canned responses and enables you to isolate the code in this class for testing.

Working with a Dependency Injection Framework

The previous example showed how the dependencies for a class can be injected using constructor arguments, which created a cleaner implementation of BusinessService. But the logic to create the concrete implementations of these dependency objects didn't just disappear; it has to be moved somewhere else in the code base. But where?

Many OOP developers are familiar with one or more factory patterns such as factory, abstract factory, builder and prototype. These are all derivatives of a basic pattern for creating classes in an application. Essentially all factory patterns describe a means of getting an instance of an object that implements a specified interface. The requestor knows only which interface it requires. The factory can determine which particular class to give the requestor based on which interface is requested, and on any configuration settings or context-based rules the factory developer provides.

The factory pattern is very useful for abstracting the logic and details needed to create dependency objects so that they do not have to appear in an application's business domain code. A problem arises with large applications, however. As more and more services and dependencies are added to the application, the task of managing and maintaining the factories becomes quite difficult and time-consuming.

Dependency injection (DI) frameworks give developers an alternative to the traditional factory patterns. They allow you to quickly and easily define the dependencies within a system and the rules for creating the appropriate concrete objects based on those dependencies. These rules and settings can be used to build an entire tree of classes, relieving you of needing to know what your dependencies are dependent on. In short, a DI framework does all the work of a factory class with much less work on your part. The examples in this book use the Ninject DI framework, version 2.1.0.91 developed by Nate Kohari and available for download at www.ninject.org.

The following code revisits the example from the previous section. I've already changed the declared types for DataAccessComponent, WebServiceProxy, and LoggingComponent to the appropriate interfaces and added an interface ILoggingDataSink to the LoggingDataSink class. I've also deleted all code lines that threw a NotImplementedException:

```
public class BusinessService
{
    private readonly string _databaseConnectionString =
        ConfigurationManager
            .ConnectionStrings["MyConnectionString"].ConnectionString;
    private readonly string _webServiceAddress =
        ConfigurationManager.AppSettings["MyWebServiceAddress"];
    private readonly ILoggingDataSink _loggingDataSink;

    private DataAccessComponent _dataAccessComponent;
    private WebServiceProxy _webServiceProxy;
    private LoggingComponent _loggingComponent;

    public BusinessService()
    {
        _loggingDataSink = new LoggingDataSink();
        _loggingComponent = new LoggingComponent(_loggingDataSink);
        _webServiceProxy = new WebServiceProxy(_webServiceAddress);
        _dataAccessComponent = new DataAccessComponent(_databaseConnectionString);
    }
}
```

BusinessService.cs

Interfaces are very important in harnessing the power of dependency injection. By declaring my member variables as interfaces above, I'm implicitly stating that I don't care what the specific concrete implementation of each service is, I only care that it implements the interface that it's being declared as. This enables me to delegate the task of determining what my specific concrete type should be to my dependency injection framework. The dependency injection framework then becomes the sole storehouse of the rules and logic to determine which concrete instance to use when. The use of interfaces helps to make this possible.

This example shows you how to use the Ninject DI framework to take care of the dependencies and their creation. To use Ninject, you must add a reference to the Ninject framework assembly (`Ninject.dll`) to your project, as shown in Figure 5-1.

Ninject needs a class to store the rules it uses to create the concrete instances of your dependencies. These classes are called modules. The next step is to create a new class to hold the rules for the `BusinessApplication.Core` project. I'll call it `CoreModule`. In order to be used by Ninject, this class must inherit from `NinjectModule` and provide an implementation for the `Load` method:

FIGURE 5-1

Available for
download on
Wrox.com

```csharp
public class CoreModule : NinjectModule
{
    public override void Load()
    {
        throw new NotImplementedException();
    }
}
```

CoreModule.cs

By providing a concrete implementation for the abstract class `NinjectModule`, `CoreModule` can give Ninject the information it needs to build concrete classes based on requests from consumers. The overridden `Load` method is where you define the rules for creating your classes. Start with an easy one: `LoggingDataSink`:

Available for
download on
Wrox.com

```csharp
public override void Load()
{
    Bind<ILoggingDataSink>().To<LoggingDataSink>();
}
```

CoreModule.cs

I chose `LoggingDataSink` for this first example because it takes no input parameters and is actually used as an input parameter for one of my other concrete classes. This example uses the `Bind` command from Ninject to specify that any requests to Ninject for a class that implements the `ILoggingDataSink` interface should return a concrete instance of `LoggingDataSink`, which is specified with the `To` extension method.

The next binding to create is the binding for `LoggingComponent`. The syntax to create this binding is exactly the same as the binding for `LoggingDataSink`:

```
public override void Load()
{
    Bind<ILoggingDataSink>().To<LoggingDataSink>();
    Bind<ILoggingComponent>().To<LoggingComponent>();
}
```

CoreModule.cs

Remember, `LoggingComponent` takes an instance of `ILoggingDataSink` as a constructor parameter. But you'll notice that the example does not specify a rule in Ninject that shows how this relationship is structured or how `LoggingComponent` gets the correct concrete instance of `ILoggingDataSink`. The benefit of a DI framework is that you don't have to specify this. Ninject can examine `LoggingComponent` and see that it has one constructor. It also can see that this constructor takes a parameter of type `ILoggingDataSink`. Since Ninject has a rule for how `ILoggingDataSink` gets created, it can infer that when creating an instance of `LoggingComponent`, it also needs to create an instance of a class that implements `ILoggingDataSink` (in this case, `LoggingDataSink`) and pass it to `LoggingComponent` as a constructor parameter. You don't need to do anything else; you get this functionality for free. This functionality extends through however many layers are needed. For example, if `LoggingDataSink` had a constructor argument that Ninject could satisfy (meaning that Ninject has the information it needs to create an object that conforms to the constructor parameter), Ninject would take care of that creation as well. You do not need to do anything else other than specify additional rules.

`DataAccessComponent` is a little more complicated than `LoggingComponent`. It has a dependency and takes a constructor parameter, but for `DataAccessComponent` this parameter is a string from the application's configuration file, not another class.

There will always be situations in which a class requires something as a constructor parameter that Ninject cannot provide. The connection string that is pulled from the application configuration file for `DataAccessComponent` falls into this category. To handle instantiation logic that is more complicated than simply mapping an interface to a class, Ninject lets you create providers for specific interfaces.

A provider is simply a class that allows you to abstract complex creational logic from the code in your module. To create a provider, you create a class and inherit from the abstract `Provider` class that ships with Ninject:

```
public class DataAccessComponentProvider : Provider<IDataAccessComponent>
{
    protected override IDataAccessComponent CreateInstance(IContext context)
    {
        throw new NotImplementedException();
    }
}
```

CoreModule.cs

The generic type provided to the provider base is the interface that this provider will be bound to — in this case, `IDataAccessComponent`. You need to provide an implementation for the `CreateInstance` method that returns an instance of a class that implements the `IDataAccessComponent` interface. In the case of the sample application, this is an instance of the `DataAccessComponent` to which you provide the connection string value from the application's configuration file:

```
protected override IDataAccessComponent CreateInstance(IContext context)
{
    var databaseConnectionString =
        ConfigurationManager
        .ConnectionStrings["MyConnectionString"].ConnectionString;
    return new DataAccessComponent(databaseConnectionString);
}
```

CoreModule.cs

The code to retrieve the connection string from the application's configuration file and return an instance of `DataAccessComponent` is simple and easy to understand. Placing this code in its own provider class enables you to abstract the `DataAccessComponent` creation logic from the simpler rules listed in the `Load` method of `CoreModule`. You now need to add a reference to the `Load` method of the `CoreModule` class to enable Ninject to know how to create a `DataAccessComponent` when an `IDataAccessComponent` is requested:

```
public override void Load()
{
    Bind<ILoggingDataSink>().To<LoggingDataSink>();
    Bind<ILoggingComponent>().To<LoggingComponent>();
    Bind<IDataAccessComponent>().ToProvider(new DataAccessComponentProvider());
}
```

CoreModule.cs

That's all you need. When you request an instance of `IDataAccessComponent` from Ninject, you are provided with a properly created `DataAccessComponent`.

The code to create a provider for my `WebServiceProxy` is almost identical:

```
public class WebServiceProxyComponentProvider : Provider<IWebServiceProxy>
{
    protected override IWebServiceProxy CreateInstance(IContext context)
    {
        var webServiceAddress = ConfigurationManager.AppSettings
            ["MyWebServiceAddress"];
        return new WebServiceProxy(webServiceAddress);
    }
}
```

CoreModule.cs

The change to `CoreModule` to inform Ninject about this new provider is just as simple as the change to add `DataAccessComponentProvider`:

```
public override void Load()
{
    Bind<ILoggingDataSink>().To<LoggingDataSink>();
    Bind<ILoggingComponent>().To<LoggingComponent>();
    Bind<IDataAccessComponent>().ToProvider(new DataAccessComponentProvider());
    Bind<IWebServiceProxy>().ToProvider(new WebServiceProxyComponentProvider());
}
```

CoreModule.cs

With `CoreModule` complete, you can refactor the `BusinessService` class to remove the logic needed to create the dependency objects:

```
public class BusinessService
{
    private ILoggingComponent _loggingComponent;
    private IWebServiceProxy _webServiceProxy;
    private IDataAccessComponent _dataAccessComponent;

    public BusinessService(ILoggingComponent loggingComponent
        IWebServiceProxy webServiceProxy,
        IDataAccessComponent dataAccessComponent)
    {
        _loggingComponent = loggingComponent;
        _webServiceProxy = webServiceProxy;
        _dataAccessComponent = dataAccessComponent;
    }
}
```

BusinessService.cs

This implementation of `BusinessService` is much cleaner than the previous version. Removing the logic necessary to create and maintain the dependency objects prevents you from violating the SRP, because only one place in this code would need to change if the routine to create these dependency objects changed. The `BusinessService` class also no longer needs to care how these objects get created; it's satisfied that the objects it's receiving implement that proper interface. That's good enough.

So, how do you create an instance of `BusinessService`? When using a DI framework, you can't "new-up" objects like you're used to:

```
var businessService = new BusinessService();
```

Without constructor parameters, this will not compile. Instead, you need to ask Ninject for an instance of `BusinessService`. Most DI frameworks provide a sort of repository class that enables you to request objects from the framework. In Ninject this repository is called the kernel. To demonstrate requesting an object from the kernel, you'll create a unit test. The first step is to create a project to contain the unit tests, as shown in Figure 5-2.

In addition to the `nunit.framework` assembly, you add a reference to the Ninject assembly that you need to create your kernel. The kernel is the instance of the Ninject `StandardKernel` class that you will create to be your interface to the Ninject framework. You will ask this instance of the `StandardKernel` for classes by calling the Get method and specifying what interface you need an instance of. The `StandardKernel` uses the rules provided during its construction to determine what concrete instance should be returned, and return a fully completed object graph to the calling method.

Next you create a unit test to test getting an instance of `BusinessService` from the Ninject kernel:

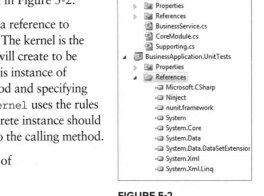

FIGURE 5-2

```
[TestFixture]
public class BusinessServiceTests
{
    [Test]
    public void ShouldBeAbleToGetBusinessServiceFromNinject()
    {
        BusinessService actual;

        Assert.IsNotNull(actual);
    }
}
```

BusinessServiceTests.cs

Attempting to run this test fails, because the code does not compile at this point, as shown in Figure 5-3.

FIGURE 5-3

To make this test runnable, you need to request an object to assign to `actual` from the Ninject kernel. To use the Ninject classes you need to add a `using` statement for the Ninject assembly to the beginning of your unit test:

```
using Ninject;
```

BusinessServiceTests.cs

Now you need to add code to your unit test to create an instance of the Ninject kernel and request an instance of `BusinessService` from it:

```
[Test]
public void ShouldBeAbleToGetBusinessServiceFromNinject()
{
    BusinessService actual;
    var kernel = new StandardKernel(new CoreModule());
    actual = kernel.Get<BusinessService>();

    Assert.IsNotNull(actual);
}
```

BusinessServiceTests.cs

When creating an instance of Ninject's `StandardKernel`, you need to provide it with an instance of `CoreModule`. This is how Ninject is made aware of the rules and steps needed to create objects. In the example here, `StandardKernel` takes only one module (`CoreModule`) as its rule set. In this example this is fine, because only one library (`BusinessApplication.Core`) is being worked with. But what if you had several assemblies? You could make one master module that has the creation rules for everything in your solution, but this is not a good idea. It requires whatever project the master module is placed in to know far too much about the other projects and assemblies. It also limits the reuse of the components in this solution. If you have a component in library B, but its creation rules are contained in a module in library A, you are now dependent on library A and all its dependencies. To solve this problem, create one module for every project in your solution that provides the creational rules for only the classes and interfaces in that library. This means that the libraries are less dependent on each other and reuse is much easier.

The constructor for `StandardKernel` has an override that takes an array of modules. This allows you to create a single kernel for your application (in practice, this kernel should be a singleton) that has all the information necessary to create anything you need anywhere in the application. The syntax to create a kernel like this is simple:

```
var kernel = new StandardKernel(new ModuleA(),
              new ModuleB(),
              new ModuleC());
```

Running the tests shows that an issue still exists, as shown in Figure 5-4.

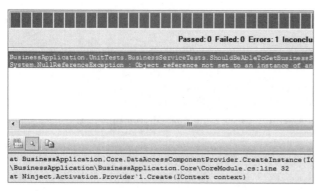

FIGURE 5-4

The stack trace tells you that line 32 in the `CoreModule.cs` file has an issue:

```
var databaseConnectionString =
    ConfigurationManager
    .ConnectionStrings["MyConnectionString"].ConnectionString;
```

CoreModules.cs

When a unit test requires information from application configuration files (`web.config` or `app.config`), it needs its own instance of this file. It doesn't matter if this file is added to the Visual Studio project the test appears in or is copied from another project. It cannot access a configuration file from another project. To resolve this, you can add an `app.config` file to the `BusinessApplication.UnitTests` project and populate it with a sample connection string:

```xml
<?xml version="1.0" encoding="utf-8" ?>
<configuration>
    <connectionStrings>
        <add name="MyConnectionString" connectionString="Sample Configuration"/>
    </connectionStrings>
</configuration>
```

app.config

Now when you run the test, Ninject has created an instance of `BusinessService`, with all its dependent objects, as shown in Figure 5-5.

FIGURE 5-5

Earlier, when you created `CoreModule`, rules for creating `BusinessService` were left unspecified. Since you asked Ninject for an instance of a specific concrete class and not an object to satisfy an interface, Ninject simply used the rules it had for the classes `BusinessService` is dependent on and returned a concrete instance of the `BusinessService` class. The examples in `CoreModule` showed binding an interface to a concrete class, but you can also bind concrete classes to classes:

```
Bind<BusinessService>().To<BusinessService>();
```

When binding a class to itself, Ninject provides a shortcut in its syntax:

```
Bind<BusinessService>().ToSelf();
```

Of course, if you were to create an `IBusinessService` interface and have `BusinessService` implement this interface, you could bind the two and have your test request an instance of `IBusinessService` from the Ninject kernel:

```
IBusinessService actual;
var kernel = new StandardKernel(new CoreModule());
actual = kernel.Get<IBusinessService>();
```

The remaining examples in this book use Ninject extensively and demonstrate many more features of the framework.

ABSTRACTING THE DATA ACCESS LAYER

Most business applications use some sort of data store. It could be a traditional Database Management System (DBMS), a text or binary file, a web service, or some other mechanism for persisting data. Data manipulation and persistence are the focus of most of what you will do as a business developer. But when writing unit tests, it's important that you isolate code being tested, even code that needs to be involved in accessing data. The repository pattern lets you abstract the components of your application that are responsible for accessing external data stores from your business logic and thus create isolated tests for that business logic.

Moving the Database Concerns Out of the Business Code

When .NET 1.0 was released, it featured an update to Microsoft's ActiveX Data Object (ADO) framework called ADO.NET. ADO.NET was not simply a .NET port of ADO; it added many features designed to allow developers to quickly and easily work with classes and objects. As such, early users of ADO.NET adopted a "smart object" architecture in which each class was given the ability to be self-persisting. More often than not this included embedding quite a bit of ADO.NET code within the class itself using either data readers or datasets to retrieve and store data to the database.

Although this did create a code base where developers could quickly and easily develop these self-persisting objects, it caused many other issues. Having the data access logic distributed throughout the application created many maintenance problems, because changes to how one class was to be handled by the database rarely stayed isolated to that class. Because of this, no single point of failure could be built around database access. Changes and defects in how data access was accomplished sometimes required extensive renovation of the application code base.

This also raised issues in systems with complex relationships between classes. In some situations a class couldn't properly instantiate itself without also instantiating several subobjects. This created a problem similar to the issues in the previous section, where the logic and rules around how specific concrete objects are created became fragmented and spread throughout the application. It was impossible not to violate the SRP and have a working system in these cases.

Finally, this pattern made writing isolated unit testing a nightmare, if it was possible at all. The tightly embedded ADO.NET code could not be quickly or easily decoupled from the business logic. This made providing mock objects for these database connection points difficult, if not impossible.

Isolating Data with the Repository Pattern

Eventually developers decided that although smart objects could be helpful, it was a bigger benefit to move the data access logic away from the business entities. Doing so created a decoupling that allowed the business development to proceed and evolve independently from data access and data store development. This independence meant that the back-end data store could change, sometimes in dramatic ways, and the business domain logic and entities were insulated from these changes. This loose coupling made it easier for developers to write isolated unit tests for their business logic.

In short, the repository pattern states that all data access will be encapsulated into a repository object, which the business domain classes will use to perform any and all persistence work (see Figure 5-6).

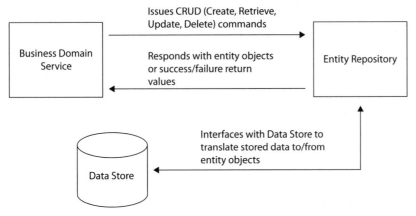

FIGURE 5-6

Repositories create a shim between the business domain and the data store. The repository encapsulates the knowledge of how the data is stored in a flattened format and how that data is translated from this flat form to an entity object. Each entity should have its own repository. However, repositories for different types should have similar interfaces and a common base class to help the data access code remain DRY and to make learning how to work with the repository easier.

Repositories can be used with any number of data access techniques, including ADO.NET, web services, and flat file storage. Many object relational mapper (ORM) frameworks make creating repositories easy. In systems when frameworks such as Entity Framework or nHibernate are used to manage persistence, it's possible to write a single repository that takes an entity type as a generic type and offloads the type-specific work to the framework. Check your ORM's documentation for more information.

Injecting the Repository

You can make some additions to the solution from the previous example by creating a `Person` entity.

```csharp
public class Person
{
    public int Id { get; set; }
    public string FirstName { get; set; }
    public string LastName { get; set; }
}
```

Person.cs

A `PersonService` class serves as the business domain class that works with `Person` objects from a standpoint of enforcing business rules and using `Person` in business work flows. Here is the interface for `PersonService`:

```
public interface IPersonService
{
    Person GetPerson (int personId);
}
```

PersonService.cs

`PersonService` uses an instance of `PersonRepository` for data persistence. This example implements only the `GetPerson` method, and instead of using a database back end, it uses an `IList` member variable to hold `Person` data:

```
public interface IPersonRepository
{
    Person GetPerson(int personId);
}

public class PersonRepository : IPersonRepository
{
    private readonly IList<Person> _personList;

    public Person GetPerson(int personId)
    {
        return _personList.Where(person = person.Id == personId).FirstOrDefault();
    }

    public PersonRepository()
    {
        _personList = new List<Person>
                        {
                            new Person {Id = 1, FirstName = "John",
                                        LastName = "Doe"},
                            new Person {Id = 2, FirstName = "Richard",
                                        LastName = "Roe"},
                            new Person {Id = 1, FirstName = "Amy",
                                        LastName = "Adams"}
                        };
    }
}
```

PersonRepository.cs

Now that pieces of the application in play are defined, you can implement `PersonSevice`:

```
public class PersonService : IPersonService
{
    public PersonService()
    {

    }

    public Person GetPerson (int personId)
    {
        return new Person();
    }
}
```

PersonService.cs

Right now `PersonService` has an empty constructor. You need to inject `PersonRepository` so that `PersonService` has a way to access the data store and change the implementation of the `GetPerson` method:

```
public class PersonService : IPersonService
{
    private readonly IPersonRepository _personRepository;

    public PersonService(IPersonRepository personRepository)
    {
        _personRepository = personRepository;
    }
    public Person GetPerson (int personId)
    {
        return _personRepository.GetPerson(personId);
    }
}
```

PersonService.cs

Finally, you need to define the rules for creating `PersonService` and `PersonRepository` in `CoreModule`:

```
Bind<IPersonRepository>().To<PersonRepository>();
Bind<IPersonService>().To<PersonService>();
```

CoreModule.cs

To verify that everything is wired correctly, you want to write a unit test to verify that you can get an instance of `PersonService` from Ninject and get a `Person` that indicates that `PersonService` could call `PersonRepository`:

```
[TestFixture]
public class PersonServiceTests
{
    [Test]
    public void ShouldBeAbleToCallPersonServiceAndGetPerson()
    {
        var expected = new Person {Id = 1, FirstName = "John", LastName = "Doe"};
        var kernel = new StandardKernel(new CoreModule());
        var personService = kernel.Get<PersonService>();
        var actual = personService.GetPerson(expected.Id);

        Assert.AreEqual(expected.Id, actual.Id);
        Assert.AreEqual(expected.FirstName, actual.FirstName);
        Assert.AreEqual(expected.LastName, actual.LastName);
    }
}
```

PersonServiceTests.cs

Running the unit test and seeing that it passes demonstrates that `PersonService` and `PersonRepository` get created correctly, as shown in Figure 5-7.

FIGURE 5-7

Mocking the Repository

The unit test runs, but a significant problem remains. Because it breaks the boundaries between `PersonService` and `PersonRepository`, it's not truly a unit test. To make this an actual unit test, you need to provide a mocked object to stand in for `PersonRepository` in `PersonService`. This example shows how to create the mock for `PersonRepository` using the Moq framework:

```
var personReposityMock = new Mock<IPersonRepository>();
personRepositoryMock
    .Setup(pr = pr.GetPerson(1))
    .Returns(new Person {Id = 1, FirstName = "Bob", LastName = "Smith"});
var personService = new PersonService(personRepositoryMock.Object);
```

PersonServiceTests.cs

The basics of Moq were covered in Chapter 2, but I'll do a quick review by explaining what I've done here. The first line of this snippet asks the Moq framework to create a mock or stand-in object based on the `IPersonRepository` called `personRepositoryMock`. Right now `personRepositoryMock` is an empty class that implements the `IPersonRepository` interface; it has methods, but they won't actually do anything until an implementation is provided for them.

This is accomplished in the next line by using the `Setup` and `Returns` extension methods in Moq to tell `personRepositoryMock` that when `GetPerson` is called on it with a parameter of 1, it should return the `Person` object described in the `Returns` extension method. Finally, I create an instance of `PersonService` by hand (I'm no longer using Ninject) and inject the mocked version of `PersonRepository` (`personRepositoryMock`) by passing it in as a constructor parameter.

Here's the entire test, with the code to create the mocked version of `PersonRepository`:

```
[Test]
public void ShouldBeAbleToCallPersonServiceAndGetPerson()
{
    var expected = new Person {Id = 1, FirstName = "John", LastName = "Doe"};
    var personRepositoryMock = new Mock<IPersonRepository>();
    personRepositoryMock
        .Setup(pr => pr.GetPerson(1))
        .Returns(new Person {Id = 1, FirstName = "Bob", LastName = "Smith"});
    var personService = new PersonService(personRepositoryMock.Object);
    var actual = personService.GetPerson(expected.Id);

    Assert.AreEqual(expected.Id, actual.Id);
    Assert.AreEqual(expected.FirstName, actual.FirstName);
    Assert.AreEqual(expected.LastName, actual.LastName);
}
```

PersonServiceTests.cs

Notice that in the setup for `personRepositoryMock` the `Person` object does not match expectations. Therefore, the test should fail, as shown in Figure 5-8.

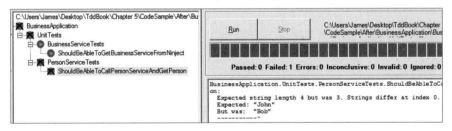

FIGURE 5-8

The failing test, and the message that the first names do not match, demonstrate that this test version of `PersonService` is using the mocked version of `PersonRepository`, not the actual implementation of the class.

SUMMARY

Most applications you will write in your career as a business developer will rely on external resources of some sort. These could be databases, web services, file systems, or even pieces of physical equipment. In spite of this, you still need to ensure that the unit tests you write are isolated to exercise only the specific method you are testing independent of any dependencies. The traditional approach of statically creating these dependencies creates applications that are brittle and difficult to maintain.

The dependency injection pattern allows you to define these dependencies based on interfaces instead of concrete implementations. The concrete implementations of these interfaces can be provided, or injected, into the object at runtime. This enables you to vary the concrete implementation for these dependencies based on the context the object is being used in. At runtime your application can vary the concrete implementation based on the environment (Production, QA, Development). For unit testing you can inject mocked objects to stand in for actual implementations. This allows you to keep your tests isolated and predictable.

Accessing data is a very common requirement for business applications. Many developers have tried embedding the code to perform persistence actions in the actual class definitions themselves. This causes issues with data access code being distributed throughout the application and makes maintenance difficult.

By using the repository pattern, you can isolate this functionality from your business logic. This creates a clean separation between business domain logic and the infrastructure needed to perform persistence. It also makes mocking data access in your unit tests easier, because this code is no longer tightly bound to your business domain code.

PART II
Putting Basics into Action

Starting the Sample Application

WHAT'S IN THIS CHAPTER?

➤ How business requirements drive features that define unit tests

➤ What steps to take before application development begins

➤ How to make decisions about application technologies

➤ How user stories drive agile application development methodologies

➤ Why project organization is important and what to keep in mind when creating your project

Before you write a single line of code for an application, you must complete many tasks. An application is defined by a set of functional business requirements and a set of nonfunctional, technical requirements. The functional requirements describe what the application must do to meet the business's needs. The nonfunctional requirements describe a set of conditions or parameters within which the application must exist. After this information is gathered, functional requirements are used to create user stories, which are decomposed into features that are assigned to developers to be built. Nonfunctional requirements are used to determine the application platform and structure, as well as what frameworks, if any, should be used in the application.

In this chapter you see the various steps and decisions that are necessary before starting to write an application. You'll be given an insight into a working agile implementation. You'll see what decisions are made before the topic of technology is even discussed, and how the proper technology is chosen once those decisions are made. Finally, you'll see how to start your project by creating the basic projects needed for the sample application in a Visual Studio solution.

DEFINING THE PROJECT

Most developers like to write code. In most cases, this is what led us to become developers in the first place. Most developers try to solve a given problem with code. Many developers communicate in code. Some developers even think in code! Given the option, I believe most developers would attempt to do all communicating and problem solving in code. Unfortunately for them, the rest of the business does not communicate, let alone think, in code.

No application gets written without a set of requirements. Even a small application that you might write to keep track of your DVD collection has some sort of requirements-gathering phase, even if it's very informal. Before you can write an application, you need to know what the application is supposed to do. In addition to knowing what the application will do, you must know how the application is to be built and under what conditions it will have to run. All these decisions should be made before development begins.

The business functionality of the application is defined by the business requirements. The technological foundation of the application is defined by the target environment and the choice of technologies used to build the application. In an ideal situation, while the technological choices made should complement the business, the business would not be made to bend to the whim of the chosen technology. Unfortunately, ideal situations are rare. For that reason, it's important to deal with the business needs early on, and let them drive the technological needs.

The target environment defines what resources the application requires to perform its task as well as what limitations the application must work within. The definition of this environment is important to ensure that your application has the necessary resources at deployment, and has been designed and built in such a way that it does not attempt to exceed its means. The choice of technologies used to build the application is important as well. In many cases this will already be decided for you; your company may have standardized on a specific version of .NET and a handful of application frameworks. In other cases you may need to make the case for an inclusion new framework or an upgraded to the latest version of .NET. These factors have a great deal of influence on how an application is designed and built, and the sooner you can make these decisions the better.

Developing the Project Overview

As a business developer, you'll spend most of your time building applications to suit a particular need of the business. It could be an application to streamline or automate an existing process or application to help the company take advantage of a new revenue stream. In any case, a set of high-level requirements must be gathered to identify the application's business needs.

A project overview is a high-level description of the application's business needs. It describes the application's overall purpose, some of the key work flows, and the major user roles and types for the application. This overview is designed to provide the broad strokes of the business requirements. No detailed design or user story creation is done at this point. The idea is to simply identify the large, high-level pieces of the application so that they can be broken down at the next stage.

The next few chapters describe the building of an office supply inventory management system, the code for which will be available on www.wrox.com. I'll call this application OSIM for short. As part of the project overview for OSIM, I have identified the application's major business needs:

➤   The application must keep track of inventory currently in stock.

➤   The application must allow users to add new types of items to the inventory list.

➤   The application must allow users to log replenishments of items into inventory.

➤   The application must allow users to log items being removed from inventory for use.

➤   Users must be authenticated.

Notice that this list doesn't specify how any of these tasks should be done. It doesn't address any technology-specific issues. In fact, you could meet all these business requirements with a notebook kept locked in a filing cabinet. The point of the project overview is not to start solving a business problem using technology. The purpose is to identify the needs while taking an objective and somewhat detached view of the technology that will be used. A pitfall with involving technology at this stage of the project is that the people involved, driven by the developers, will subconsciously try to guide or bend the requirements to a specific technology or solution they already have in mind. This is the opposite of what should be done: The technology should serve the needs of the business, not vice versa.

Defining the Target Environment

Often the needs of the business will impact what the target environment of your application will be. When thinking about the environment that your application will be deployed to, you need to do more than simply consider what operating system the server will run. You need to think about how the application will be used. Will it be a web-based application? Will it run on the user's desktop? Maybe it will run on a mobile platform. Will you need to deploy web services as part of your application?

It's also important to think about how the application will be built, and what sort of infrastructure-based requirements will be levied against it. Does the application have multiple tiers? How many concurrent users do you expect to have at peak times? What kind of response time does the application need to provide? Will the application need to scale? Will it be expected to scale vertically (moving to a more powerful server) or horizontally (deploying the application to more servers) or both? How do those needs affect your application architecture?

The application's target environment should be described in the application's nonfunctional requirements. In some cases a target environment will already be defined, and your application must be designed to fit that mold. In other cases a new environment will be created, but there may be other constraints, such as budget and company hardware and/or software standards. These all need to be taken into account when defining your application's target environment.

For the OSIM application, the target environment will have to accommodate a multitiered application. As part of the technical requirements, the business owner has stated that he wants the application to have a web-based front end, a Windows client-based front end, and a web services interface for external trading partners and various existing Enterprise reporting tools. The tiers will consist of the user interface tier (this includes any application-external web services), a business logic tier, and a data storage tier. Because this is a small, interdepartmental application, you're expecting no more than two to four concurrent users; however, the tiered architecture gives this application room for growth. Based on this, you define your target environment as a Microsoft Windows server running IIS 7 or later (this does not have to be a dedicated server) and Microsoft SQL Server 2008 R2.

Choosing the Application Technology

After a target environment has been defined, you must settle on an application platform. You have many platforms to choose from. J2EE, .NET, Ruby on Rails, and PHP are some of the more popular platforms for creating web applications. The choices you made when defining the target environment will provide some guidance in choosing an application platform, because some server operating systems are better at supporting specific application platforms.

Beyond the operating system, you must consider some other things when choosing an application platform. Does your development staff already have a high degree of knowledge and experience with a specific platform? Do you already have a significant investment in a particular platform? What platform best fits the needs of the application you're building? Finally, you want to choose an application platform that has a future and will continue to be supported going forward.

After you have selected a platform, you still face many decisions. Will your application use an Object Relational Mapper (ORM). If so, which one? Which dependency injection (DI) framework should you use? What about a unit test framework? Which one is best suited to your needs? What about a web framework? The answers to these questions can be arrived at much like the answer to which application platform to use: Find a tool that fits your needs, has good support, and will be there in the future.

The OSIM application will use several frameworks, which are discussed in the section "Choosing the Frameworks." The frameworks I focus on for the purposes of this book are nUnit, nBehave, Moq, and Ninject. The others are listed for illustrative purposes and for a level of completeness. No prior experience with those frameworks is necessary to follow along.

DEFINING THE USER STORIES

In an agile development methodology, user stories define business rules and work flows for the application. These user stories, which are driven by the business's needs, become the application's functional requirements. As user stories are collected, they are decomposed into application features that are assigned to developers, which the developers then use to define their tests, which drive development. For more background on agile methodologies, please refer to the section "A Quick Introduction to Agile Methodologies" in Chapter 1.

Collecting the Stories

User stories are representations of the business requirements for an application. They should describe the expected interactions the business users will have with the application. The act of collecting user stories roughly correlates to the activities described in the section "The Project

Overview" above. Therefore at this point you should be trying to remain technology-agnostic while defining the users' interaction with the system in broad terms.

Gathering the information needed to create these stories and then reengaging with the business to validate them can be one of the most difficult tasks on an application development project. Developers tend to think technology first. Business users are usually not as technologically savvy as the development team. To engage these business users, it's important to communicate with them in a language, setting, and manner that make them comfortable. For that reason, if your team has access to a business analyst (BA), I highly recommend taking advantage of this person's skill in gathering the user stories.

Unfortunately, not all development teams have a BA on staff. In these cases it's up to the architect, lead developer, or even just members of the development team to work with the project manager (PM) to engage the business and define the user stories. The important thing at this stage is to communicate in some manner with the business.

There are many techniques that can be used to communicate with the business and get the needed information to create the user stories. Some techniques are very intrusive, while others are more passive. The three most common (from intrusive to passive) are shadowing, client interviews and joint application design (JAD) sessions.

Client interviews can be helpful because they allow the developer (or PM) to communicate one on one with the business user. A client interview is simply an opportunity to sit down with the business user in a distraction free environment (or as close to distraction free as possible) and ask them questions about the application. These can be one-on-one or in a group interview. Client interviews can be a formal question and answer session, an informal conversation or maybe a demo by the business user of the existing system. In many cases they also give the developer an opportunity to see how the business user currently does his or her job. This can provide invaluable information to the developer when it comes to creating user stories. Client interviews also have the benefit of having relatively low impact on the business users (remember, they have their own jobs to do in addition to helping you derive user stories) and offer much flexibility in terms of scheduling. An issue with relying on client interviews too much is that often you will receive conflicting information from different users. In this case it's important to reengage the business users who provided the conflicting information and try to reach a resolution.

The client interview tends to represent a happy medium when it comes to gathering requirements from users. At one end of the spectrum is shadowing the business users for a period of time. Shadowing simply means following the users for a period of time and observing them perform their work. Shadowing lets you learn a lot about the business problem domain; in many cases a developer can learn things that would never have come up in a client interview. On the other hand, shadowing can be an extreme inconvenience to both the business users and the developer. Furthermore, issues arise when business users must perform actions where a security risk would be created by allowing a developer to shadow them. For example, a nurse works with private patient information and treats patients. Under HIPAA rules, a developer, or anyone else, for that matter, cannot be put in a position where he or she could inadvertently learn private patient information or be privy to a patient's ailment or course of treatment. Shadowing can be used in extreme cases, but be mindful of the disruptions it can cause.

At the other end of the spectrum is the concept of gathering all the business users at once and collecting a set of user stories in one large JAD session. These JAD sessions can be multiday affairs with all the business users or, in the case of large systems, representatives of all business user groups. JAD sessions usually take place offsite to minimize distractions. The benefit of a JAD session is that all the disparate business units are present, so conflicts that would otherwise exist after client interviews or shadowing can be dealt with immediately. This process can also be helpful for business users in terms of understanding the needs of other parts of the business and how those needs relate to their own. JAD sessions can be very disruptive to the business users because they are required to spend perhaps several days working with the development team to derive user stories and not doing their normal jobs. Depending on what those business users do, this may be impractical. A way to alleviate part of this problem is to spread out JAD sessions so that they are not on consecutive days.

The user stories themselves should be descriptions of a user's interaction with the application. An effort should be made to keep the individual user stories as isolated from each other as possible. But in the interest of keeping the user stories short and comprehensible, it's perfectly acceptable to have one user story start where another ends or branches off. Above all, the user stories should be easy for business users and development staff to understand. They should add business value to the system and be something that users can test as soon as the development team has completed the features necessary to satisfy the user story.

The goal of all three approaches is to gather a set of user's stories. For example, a user story for the OSIM application called "Logging in New Inventory of Existing Items" might read like this:

Once the new inventory has been received and counted, an authorized user logs into the OSIM system using the OSIM log in page. Once the user has logged in they select the item "log in new inventory" in the navigation menu. The application takes the user to the add inventory page. The user selects the type of inventory from the item type list and inputs the quantity received in the quantity text box. The user then clicks the "save" button and the inventory count is updated and the page controls cleared out to allow the user to enter more inventory.

If the item type does not exist in the list of item types, a new item type must be added. Refer to the user story "Adding new Item Types." If the user attempts to input a non-numerical value into the quantity field, the application should not allow it. If the user clicks the "save" button, but has not selected an item type from the list or added a quantity that is more than zero, the page should inform the user that the information is invalid and direct them to fix the errors and click save again.

Defining the Product Backlog

In short, the product backlog (PB) is simply a list of work that needs to be done to complete an application. Once user stories are created to define the business requirements, they are decomposed into features that will be assigned to a developer. Some development teams elect to put individual features into a PB. Other teams put whole user stories in the PB and allow the developers to develop the individual features of the user story as they think best. Neither approach is right or wrong. It's a question of what works best for your development team on any given project.

A feature is a unit of work that provides value to the system by satisfying a functional requirement while not violating any nonfunctional requirements. Multiple user stories may refer to the same feature. For example, multiple user stories may mention the user's logging into the application. Creating a log in page may be a feature derived from these user stories, but each user story presumably does not need its own log in page. The log in page feature will satisfy a requirement of each user story that references logging in. There is no need to create a separate feature for each user story.

Another important aspect of a feature is that it can be tested. There should be some way to verify that the feature works correctly without a user's having to run the application in a debugger or run a SQL script to determine if a value in an entity was changed. Certain infrastructure tasks that don't directly influence the user's perception of the system must be performed in an application. As many of these as possible should be done in Iteration Zero (described in the next section).

Users are assigned work from the PB as prioritized by the business with guidance from the PM and architect. In most agile processes, the features in the PB are represented by story or feature cards, which the PM keeps a master list of. Although many tools can be used to maintain PB lists, Microsoft Excel is still the most popular tool for this purpose. Managing the PB is covered in the next section.

THE AGILE DEVELOPMENT PROCESS

All agile processes are different. A variety of branded agile methodologies are available. However, many development shops have found it preferable to use these as starting points, modify the process to suit their particular needs, and then keep any single prepackaged methodology intact. In fact, most branded methodologies encourage this by providing a set of core values and a mechanism known as a retrospective to change the process around these core values. Ultimately, every mature agile process differs in some way to suit the needs of the development staff, Enterprise, or project the methodology is being used in.

Remember that this book is not about agile development. Agile development is discussed here to provide a framework and context for the use of TDD because most agile development methodologies rely heavily on the benefits of TDD.

All agile processes are slightly different, but some common themes and values permeate the agile landscape. A few principles define agile practices. While changing and tweaking agile processes is encouraged, it's generally a good idea not to stray too far from these core principles.

Most agile processes focus on the idea of small, easy-to-manage-and-understand units of work being done in short iterations. These units of work should be focused on a specific, testable feature of the system. The testability aspect is very important. Another core principle in agile is to get software in front of users as quickly and often as possible. If a feature cannot be tested by either a QA tester or a business user, the feature's value is questionable.

Estimating

By their nature, estimates are always wrong. Agile methodologies do not seek to obfuscate or deny this fact; they embrace it. In many older methodologies, the estimates were usually done by a PM or architect. In some cases a lead developer may have been involved, but for the most part the estimate was not done by the people who would actually perform the work. It's difficult enough for most people to accurately estimate their own productivity. Doing so for others is an exercise in futility. Agile methodologies advance the idea that the people doing the work should provide the estimates.

Moreover, as time goes on, those estimates can and should be adjusted based on the growing body of knowledge about the business problem domain and the application itself. In 1981 Barry Boehm developed a concept that would become the basis of a phenomenon known as the Cone of Uncertainty. This concept was first applied to software development by Steve McConnell in his 1997 book *Software Project Survival Guide* (Microsoft Press, ISBN: 9781572316218). The Cone of Uncertainty as it applies to software development states that estimates of work made at the beginning of a project are likely to be inaccurate by a factor of 4. This means that the actual work required to complete a feature could be as little as 25% of the actual estimate or as much as 400% of that estimate. As the project continues, the estimate of work needed to complete the feature becomes more accurate. But it is entirely accurate only when the feature is complete.

For software development teams, this means that the estimate for a given feature made at a project's inception could be off by as much as 400%. In most methodologies these radically inaccurate estimates are baked into a project plan, taken as gospel, and later used as a metric to measure the project's success or failure. In reality, this estimate, especially one done at the beginning of the project, is the developer's best guess based on the information available at that time. In most cases it is incomplete, inaccurate, and likely to change.

A more logical approach is to periodically re-estimate the features in the PB. These new estimates are based on actual knowledge the development team has gained from working in the application for a period of time. While still likely to be inaccurate, these estimates will be closer than the previous estimate. This reassessment allows the PM to refine the project plan and provides a more accurate judgment of whether the development team is on track.

Working in Iterations

The rest of this section describes the agile process I use on my teams. It's important to understand that I did not create this process myself, and it was not created overnight. It's the product of many different developers and development teams (including PMs, BAs, and clients) working on many different projects over the course of several years. The process has grown and evolved with the input of many people and will likely continue to grow beyond the publication of this book. I'm not saying the process described here is the best process for you or your team. It very well may not be. I am a consultant at a company that specializes in custom application development project work for a variety of clients in many different industries with many different project types. This process has been tuned for that purpose. If that does not describe your working environment, this process may not work for you. It's simply one way of working with an agile methodology, and it's provided here as a means to demonstrate what an agile methodology may look like.

Agile preaches short iterations. I prefer to keep my iterations either one or two weeks in duration. The exception to this rule is what I call Iteration Zero. Iteration Zero is the first iteration and usually commences toward the end of the requirements-gathering phase when the major nonfunctional requirements have been gathered and the user stories are being refined. Iteration Zero is my setup iteration. During this time I, or a member of my team, am creating the development environment. This includes setting up any application servers the team will need, as well as setting up the QA environment and configuring the continuous integration (CI) server. Other tasks that are done as part of Iteration Zero include setting up the basic solution and projects in Visual Studio and creating a source control repository to store them in. As part of this process I also reference any third-party assemblies in the appropriate Visual Studio projects. Once the development team has been formed, I make sure that they have the appropriate credentials on any systems they will need access to during development. If I have some basic screen layouts available, I work with a user interface (UI) developer to sprint ahead of the group and create some boilerplate web pages or forms to help the developers get a jump start on their development.

Iteration Zero does not have a set time frame. Sometimes it can take a couple weeks. On smaller projects I can have everything ready in a few hours. The important thing is that I have basic infrastructure and services ready for the development team when Iteration One (the first proper development iteration) begins.

Before the first iteration starts, I and the PM meet with the business owner. This does not mean all the business users; it means the one or two people who are the project's sponsors or stakeholders on the business side. The purpose of this meeting is to plan the work for the next iteration. This meeting will be repeated toward the end of each iteration, except the last one.

The business owner, with suggestions and guidance from the PM and the architect or lead developer, selects the work to be done in the next iteration. The business owner is provided with the number of productive hours that the project team will have for the next iteration. Productive hours are hours the developer spends writing code. I arrive at the number of productive hours for each developer by taking the number of hours in the developer's normal work schedule (for example, if this were a two-week iteration, the developer would normally be working 80 hours) and subtracting hours that I don't expect the developer to be writing code. This could be due to vacation, holidays, meetings, or any other overhead in running the project. Additionally, if the developer is a new developer, or new to the project, I'll take some hours off his productive-hours number to account for the learning curve he will experience.

It's important that clients not equate nonproductive hours with hours that are wasted. In my case, since my business owners are clients, I can explain to them that they are not being billed for holidays or vacation. I also remind them that although the developer's primary purpose is to write code, other tasks on the project that do not involve writing code also are necessary. For developers with learning curve hours, I explain that the business owner is paying less for this resource. It's reasonable to assume that because these developers are less experienced, it will take them longer to complete a task than a more experienced (and expensive) developer.

The business owner is allowed to schedule features or stories only while he has productive hours left to use. For example, if a team has a total of 100 productive hours, and the sum of the features the business owner has already scheduled is 95, they may pick any combination of features still in the PB that does not cause the schedule hours to exceed 100. This means that they may not select features that add up to 6 hours, pushing the total to 101. The developers have been asked to give their best good-faith estimate for the features. It is up to the PM and the technical lead to support their team and hold a hard line on these numbers. Remember, the team is committing to complete all the tasks scheduled for the iteration; don't handicap them by overcommitting them.

What happens more often is that the business owner can't find a permutation of features that equals exactly the number of productive hours. This does not mean that those hours go to waste. Business owners are allowed to select features to place in a "parking lot." This means that they are not really part of the work scheduled for the iteration, but if time is left over, the business owner wants the developers to work on a feature from this parking lot. Features that go in the parking lot should be small and low-priority, because they might not get done in the current iteration (in fact, they can span several iterations). The business owner needs to understand that although the features scheduled for the iteration are commitments for the development team, items placed in the parking lot are not.

My iterations always begin on Monday. Since I like to make my iterations either one or two weeks, it's easier to manage an iteration if it starts on the first day of the week and ends on a Friday. If Monday is a holiday, the iteration still starts on Monday, but I account for the holiday by deducting one day's worth of hours from each developer. On the Friday before the iteration starts, I call a quick meeting (less than 15 minutes) with the development teams and briefly go over what features are scheduled for the next iteration and who they are assigned to. The purpose of this meeting is not to raise or solve problems with the features; it's simply to make everyone aware of what's scheduled for the next iteration and who's been assigned to do what. Problems, issues, or concerns with particular features or stories are discussed after the meeting, allowing those who are not involved to return to work.

Communication Within Your Team

This highlights a key component of this process: individual communication as opposed to group meetings. Most developers dread meetings. They are seen as a waste of time, especially when a dozen people are called in to discuss a topic that they believe really affects only two or three people. A much faster and more efficient way to handle these issues is to encourage the two or three individuals who are interested in or affected by the topic to have an ad hoc conversation and attempt to engage other individuals they deem necessary to the discussion.

An argument can be made that everyone on a team should know what's going on at any given time. However, I don't agree with that. For one thing, even on a small team, it's almost impossible for any one person to know every detail of every user story, feature, nonfunctional requirement, and decision that is made. To expect your development staff to keep all this information in their heads at all times is unreasonable. I have found that a better approach is to have a wiki for the project.

A *wiki* is a user-updateable website that can easily and quickly be used to store information about a project. As groups of developers meet and make decisions, or find solutions to problems, they put their findings and decisions in the wiki. Because the wiki is searchable, other developers on the team can consult it when they have questions or want to understand why certain decisions were made during application development. The combination of small-group discussions and the wiki greatly relieves the need for long, unproductive meetings.

Iteration Zero: Your First Iteration

On the morning of the first day of the iteration, the developer selects an assigned feature or user story to start with. A developer may be assigned more than one feature or story, and the order in which to do them is largely up to that person. During the scheduling process, a good deal of effort is made to try to keep potential bottlenecks to a minimum, but they do occasionally arise. In these cases developers are encouraged to discuss the order in which work will be done to ensure that no one is waiting on someone else for a long period of time. In some cases the developers may choose to pair-program on their features if they are closely related.

After the developer has selected the feature to begin working on, the next step is to read the user story and meet with the BA, PM, or some other subject matter expert (SME) who represents the business on the development team. This role of business advocate on the development team is critical and should not be left unfilled. The developer must meet with this person and go over the feature to ensure that he or she understands the feature or user story from the business's point of view. Many defects in an application arise simply because the developer thought he or she understood the business need, but did not.

When the SME and the developer agree on how the feature or user story should be developed from a business perspective, the developer meets with the architect or lead developer on the project. The purpose of this meeting is for the developer to explain how he or she plans to design and develop the code needed to complete the feature and to ensure that it fits within the larger vision of the application. It's important that an application's code and functionality be consistent, regardless of who wrote the code. The goal of this discussion is to help ensure that consistency.

Testing in Iteration Zero

After the developer meets with the SME and the architect or lead developer and understands the business need behind the feature and how the feature fits into the larger application, he begins development. Using TDD, he starts by writing unit tests for his feature. After the developer has written a unit test, he writes just enough code to make the test pass. If the test passes, the developer continues writing unit tests and then code to make the test pass until he has passing unit tests for all the requirements in the feature. While in this process, the developer should be running the entire suite of unit tests to ensure that his new code has not broken any existing functionality already in the application. Finally, the developer writes integration tests to ensure that the components he has written for his feature integrate correctly with the rest of the application. As soon as all these tests pass, the developer commits his code to the main development branch and marks the feature complete and ready for QA to test.

In my development shop we have a CI server that watches for commits to the main development branch. When a commit occurs, the CI server builds the application and runs all the unit and integration tests. If any unit or integration test fails, the build is marked as failed, and the development team is notified. The top priority when the build fails is fixing the code to get a good build. The team switches priorities and works together to resolve any issues and restore the build to a successful state as quickly as possible.

If the build is successful, the compiled application is deployed to the QA environment. The QA group is notified of what features or defect fixes are in the new build. A QA tester verifies that the feature is complete or correct, or that the defect has been corrected. If the feature is incomplete, or defects are still present, the QA tester notifies the developer of his or her findings.

If the QA tester is satisfied that the feature is complete and correct, or that the defect in question has been fixed, he or she marks the feature as complete, or the defect as closed. The build is promoted to a client QA environment (an environment where the client can access the application). Only the QA tester can mark a feature as complete or a defect as closed. Neither the PM or architect can override the QA decision. If disagreement arises, the involved parties can discuss the matter. However, the QA retains the power to determine what is complete and what is not.

Ending an Iteration

Because my iterations are one or two weeks and they always begin on Monday, I know that Friday is the last day of my iteration. A show-and-tell meeting with the business is scheduled for the Monday or Tuesday after the end of the iteration. This is an opportunity to show the client the work that has been done in the last iteration. It's also a good opportunity for the development team to interact with the business users and gain a better understanding of the business requirements.

This meeting is extremely important to the project's success and should not be skipped. One of the main pillars of agile methodologies is the rapid feedback provided by business users. It's important to make the business users understand that they are not seeing a completed application, but a work in progress. The point of having the business look at this application, even though it is unfinished, is to determine if the development team has correctly translated the business's requirements and needs into the application. In cases where the application does not meet the business's needs, there are two possible outcomes: defects and changes.

Defects are differences between the stated business requirements and the application's behavior. This can be anything as minor as a misspelled label on a web page to a missing step in a business work flow. Defects identified right away are much easier and less expensive to correct than a defect that is found six months later or, worse, after the application has been put into production. Defects that arise from this show-and-tell meeting are always top-priority items; the development team needs to correct these defects before continuing with further development.

Changes are events where the application reflects the business requirements, but the business requirements for some reason are inaccurate. This could be because of a defect in the requirements-gathering phase. It could be due to a change in the business that occurred since the requirements were gathered. It could be a situation where the business didn't take some factor into consideration when creating the business requirements. Whatever the case, these changes should either have new user stories created or cause changes to existing user stories. These new or altered user stories need to be verified and decomposed into features, which then must be estimated. These new user stories and features are added to the PB to be scheduled for a later iteration.

Iterations continue as long as the client or business user has work remaining and the resources to continue development. As a consultant, I find that clients often choose to end development with some features still in the PB. This is because when requirements are gathered for an application, business users, and even some developers, tend to start creating requirements documents that more resemble wish lists than a list of the actual business needs. Many features are nice to have but are not crucial to the application's functionality. Many clients, when asked to schedule these feature and thus commit budget to them, decline to do so. They may not see the value in those features. They may want to defer the feature until their next budget year. They may simply decide that the feature is not worth the money it would require to build. This is OK. The strength of an agile methodology is the ability to focus on what adds value to an application and to make rational and well-informed decisions about the things that do not add value.

CREATING THE PROJECT

You should not take for granted the structure of your solutions and projects in Visual Studio. Organization will set you free, and it's important to make sure that your development assets are organized in a logical and consistent manner. Project organization is the first line of defense for your application architecture, because the project structure helps define and drive the composite parts of the application. The organizational structure of your project should be logical. It should be clear where specific components exist. This clarity helps the developers understand how to partition their components and how to find components in the application that others have created.

Choosing the Frameworks

Software development involves many repetitive tasks. Many of these, although critical to the application's function and success, are not really considered to add business value. Functionality such as data persistence, logging, and dependency injection are all things that applications rely on. But from a business standpoint it doesn't matter how much attention and care you put into writing a data access library, because it doesn't directly solve a business problem. This type of code is called plumbing code, and it was the impetus of the phrase among developers "Don't be a plumber."

For tasks that are repetitive, time-consuming, or difficult to implement, developers have come to rely on frameworks. A framework is a library or set of libraries that you utilize in your application to perform a task that is similar from application to application. For example, most .NET applications use some sort of database. The code that accesses the database and handles data persistence does not add any business value, yet writing this code can take a long time. That's time that the developer could spend writing code that adds business value to the application. Instead of writing the same boilerplate data access code repeatedly, you could use a persistence framework to handle the data persistence chores.

Hundreds of frameworks exist for all sorts of development tasks. Odds are if you find yourself writing the same code to solve the same problem on project after project, a framework can perform that task for you. Frameworks should be used liberally in your application where they make sense. Although frameworks provide a lot of power by automating common tasks, they are generally designed to do one specific thing. Do not ask a logging framework to be a persistence framework; that's not what it was meant to do.

When choosing a framework for your application, you must keep in mind a few points. Does the framework you're looking at provide the functionality you need? This may seem like an obvious question, but many developers have tried to utilize a framework that does something "kind of" like the task they are using it for. Sometimes this is OK; most frameworks are open-source and can be extended or modified to suit your needs. But making sure that the framework's intended class is as close to your need as possible will make this retrofit much easier.

Pick a framework that offers support. Many frameworks are open-source projects. For these open-source frameworks, make sure a large, active community is involved in adding new features, fixing defects, and providing education. If the framework is a third-party tool that you are purchasing, make sure it's from a reputable company that can provide references and offers some sort of online tutorial or support.

Last, consider the learning curve. You may have team members who are familiar with the DI framework structure map. If this is the case, don't insist that they use Ninject. The team already has knowledge in place; use it. If they are unfamiliar with both tools, ask a few senior members of the team to look at each framework and give you their thoughts on which one would be easier for the team to use. Nothing can kill team morale faster than being forced to use a tool they dislike and don't understand.

There are some reasons not to pick a particular framework. If your chief argument for the selection of a framework is "It's new and cool," you might want to reevaluate your decision. New frameworks are often exciting and offer features that their predecessors did not have. And certainly many new frameworks are perfectly fine to use. But you need to make sure that the framework meets an actual need besides relieving your boredom or serving as resume filler.

For development of the OSIM application, I have elected to use .NET 4.0 as my application framework. I will employ these frameworks to aid the development:

- ➤ **ASP.NET MVC** is a web framework for .NET designed to allow web sites to be built using the model/view/controller (MVC) pattern.

- ➤ **Automapper** is an open-source framework that lets you easily map your entity objects that will be used internally in the application to your data transfer objects (DTOs) that will be used by the front ends.

- ➤ **WPF** is a framework for building Microsoft Windows client applications.

- ➤ **WCF** is a framework for building web services in .NET.

- ➤ **Fluent NHibernate** is an ORM that serves as the persistence (data access) layer in the application.

- ➤ **nUnit** is a unit testing framework.

- ➤ **nBehave** is a business-driven development (BDD) naming library that lets you write your tests in a more fluent and business-user-friendly manner.

- ➤ **Moq** is a mocking framework.

- ➤ **Ninject** is a DI framework.

This list includes many non-Microsoft frameworks and tools. The reason for the use of these frameworks here is that despite not being from Microsoft, these frameworks are all extremely popular, and there is a good chance you will encounter them in your practice of TDD. Microsoft has done an excellent job of providing many examples of how these various frameworks integrate together. Few widely known resources exist that address integration of a large group of non-Microsoft frameworks.

Also, while Microsoft has done a good job of creating ORM frameworks (Entity Framework), unit testing frameworks (MS Test), and dependency injection frameworks (Unity), the frameworks I've chosen to use here, and in my everyday development, have benefits over the Microsoft counterparts, and work better in my development shop. If you wish to use the Microsoft counterparts to these frameworks you will have no disadvantage in developing software or practicing TDD. While the examples in this book may not translate one-for-one with the Microsoft frameworks, the concepts still apply.

Defining the Project Structure

This section describes how I structure my Visual Studio projects. Like the methodology described previously, this structure is the product of many developers working over many projects. Our teams would come up with ideas to alleviate issues, try them, and then evaluate the result. It took several projects over a period of years for this structure to get to this level of refinement, and like our methodology, it is still subject to change as needed.

What many developers don't realize is that the project structure really exists in two places: the structure of projects, files, and objects in the Visual Studio solution, and how the project is laid out in the file system. How the project is arranged in the file system is just as important as how your Visual Studio solution is structured, because many files and assets are part of a project but don't necessarily reside in the Visual Studio solution. If you are developing a marketing website with a lot of custom graphics, you may choose not to store these as part of the Visual Studio solution to keep memory usage low. Third-party assemblies can also be a troublesome asset to manage. Laying out all the project files in a consistent manner and having your source code repository mirror that structure makes it easy for developers to find files and other assets. It also helps developers get the application up and running quickly once it has been pulled to the local drive from the source control repository.

Organizing Project Folders

I have a folder on my local hard drive called `DevProjects` where I keep all my applications, be they .NET projects or some other platform. As a consultant I have many clients, and within this `DevProjects` folder I have a subfolder for each client. When starting a new project, I go to that client's subfolder in the `DevProjects` folder and create a folder for the project. When I bind my solution to my source control server, I do so at this project folder level so that all subfolders within it are included and tracked in the source code repository. Within that project folder I always create at least two more subfolders called `src` and `libs`.

The `src` folder contains the source code for the project. This is the folder I will tell Visual Studio to create its project in when the time comes. This folder's structure will be managed via the Visual Studio IDE. I will create folders in my Visual Studio project, and Visual Studio will create the folders on the file system. Anything that is part of the Visual Studio project, meaning that I can access the file or asset via the Visual Studio Solution Explorer, goes in the `src` folder.

The `libs` folder contains all the third-party assemblies and any supporting files they may need. When I need to add a third-party assembly to my Visual Studio project, I first copy it and its needed support files to the `libs` folder. Next, I go to Visual Studio and add a reference to the assembly I just copied to the `libs` folder. Since this project is bound to the source control repository at the project level, everything in this `libs` folder is included and tracked in source control. Because the references to assemblies in Visual Studio projects use relative paths, I know that no matter where on my hard drive this project is located, it will use the assemblies from its `libs` folder.

When a developer pulls the project to a machine for the first time, or even refreshes his current source from the source control repository, he is assured of getting all the third-party assemblies needed to build and run the application. He also knows that he has the exact versions of these assemblies that the application has been designed to work with. The developer no longer has to wonder if he has the correct version of a given framework installed. He also doesn't have to look through his system to find the exact assembly the project is looking for. It's already there. In some cases you will have different projects in different Visual Studio solutions that use different versions of the same framework. By keeping the assemblies grouped with the source code that uses them, you no longer have to worry about your application's using the wrong version of a given framework.

It is true that with this paradigm you have multiple copies of the same assembly. It's also true that the assemblies have to be stored in your version control system. Some developers do not like to do this. I have found, however, that the benefit of keeping the assemblies close to the source code far outweighs the concerns and arguments against keeping multiple copies of these files, or keeping them in the source control repository.

On occasion I create other folders in the project folder. If the project isn't using a document collaboration system (but it should be), I create a `docs` folder to hold project documentation. The advantage of putting the documents there is that they remain close to the code and benefit from the version-control features of the source code control system. If a project is using a desktop database engine (such as Microsoft Access) and isn't using a Database Management System (DBMS), or if I need to include SQL scripts as part of the project, I create a `db` folder to store these assets.

Again, these are two extreme cases. In general your project should use a document collaboration server such as SharePoint to store project documents. If your application uses a DBMS system, the need for a `db` folder is similarly reduced. I resist creating these or any other folders, because the proliferation of folders is generally a sign of bad application development habits.

Creating the Visual Studio Solution

After the folder structure has been created, it's time to create the Visual Studio solution. Again, an organized structure in your Visual Studio solution is important. The projects in your solution ultimately become the individual assemblies in your application. Not partitioning this functionality correctly can leave you with bloated assemblies that have an inappropriate mix of functionality that makes deploying and scaling the application difficult.

I start by creating an empty Visual Studio solution, as shown in Figure 6-1. The reason for this is that when I create my projects I want their names to reflect the namespace the assembly represents. If you allow Visual Studio to create a solution for you when you create a project, the solution's name is derived from the project's name, and you lose some flexibility with how you name your individual projects.

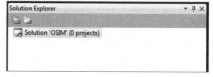

FIGURE 6-1

Good project naming is very important to the organization of your solution. A project name should reflect the namespace it represents and describe what features and functionality the resulting assembly will provide. All applications need a class library that will house the core or business domain services and entities. This is generally the first project I create. In the case of the example for this book, I'm creating a class library called OSIM.Core, although a name such as OSIM.Domain would be acceptable as well. As soon as the project is created, I delete the Class1.cs file that Visual Studio prepopulates the project with, and I create two folders within the project: Entities and DomainServices (see Figure 6-2).

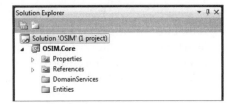

FIGURE 6-2

In addition to keeping the names clear, the project and folder-naming conventions mirror the namespaces. For example, if I were to create a Person class in the Entities folder, that class's fully qualified name would be OSIM.Core.Entities.Person.

One school of thought in TDD says that I should not create this project until I need to. TDD does push the idea of not writing any code until you need it to pass a test. By extension, you could say I shouldn't create that project until I need it, and this would be a valid point. However, on my team, I want the major projects in place so that on the first day of Iteration One, the development team can start writing code immediately. This is a bit of a gray area where the ideas of testing first and being pragmatic can be at odds. In the end you have to evaluate your situation and do what works best for your team and your project.

Speaking of tests, I know that the next two projects I always need in any solution are for my unit tests and my integration tests. I'll create those projects next, as shown in Figure 6-3.

Within my test projects I like to create some structure to keep my tests organized by creating a folder for each project in my solution. Currently I have only the OSIM.Core project, so I'll just create the folders for that project, as shown in Figure 6-4.

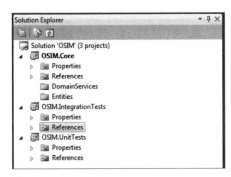

FIGURE 6-3

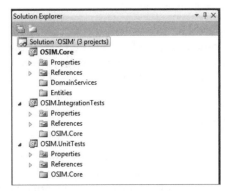

FIGURE 6-4

Based on the current high-level design of the OSIM application, I know that this application will have three front ends: a web-based front end developed on the ASP.NET MVC 2 framework, a

Windows client front end developed using WPF, and a web services interface using WCF. And yes, web services are a front end. They represent an access point for an external user to interact with the application just the same as a web page or a Windows form. The only difference is that instead of a human directly interacting with the interface, the user needs a web service proxy of some sort to use the interface. I'll create the appropriate project types for each of these interfaces, as shown in Figure 6-5.

FIGURE 6-5

Now that I have three more projects in my solution, I should add folders to the test projects for them, as shown in Figure 6-6.

Currently these are all the projects I need for my application based on the initial high-level design. Later in the project I may find that I need other projects for support purposes. When creating these, the first question to ask is "Does this really belong in a separate project?" Many developers talk themselves into creating new projects in the name of granularity. In some cases what results are two assemblies that are so reliant on each other, on their own they provide little to no value. Often errors arise because an attempt is made to deploy an application with one assembly but not the other. If two or more classes really require each other to function, they should not be split into different projects.

FIGURE 6-6

If you truly need to create a separate assembly, make sure your naming convention continues to identify what project this new project is supporting, and how. For example, if you wanted to create a project to contain themes for the Windows client project, a good name would be `OSIM .WinClient.Themes`.

For now, this project structure is complete. I'm sure I'll have to add structural elements as the project progresses, but I don't want to start the application development project by overcomplicating my environment. In general you want to keep your project structure as simple and clean as possible and make changes and additions only if they are needed.

SUMMARY

Many tasks must be completed in an application development project before you start writing code. The first task is to gather the business and technical requirements. In agile methodologies this consists of a high-level project overview that helps you define the application's size and scope. Agile methodologies steer away from the concept of a big up-front design and just seek to get the broad picture. Detailed design is deferred until the user story or feature is scheduled.

After the high-level requirements have been gathered, a target environment must be defined. This environment will help shape the type of application you develop and can help drive out many of the nonfunctional technical requirements. After this environment has been defined, the various application technologies must be selected.

The business requirements are used to create the user stories, which define where the application's business value comes from. User stories should be technology-agnostic and testable. Otherwise, the requirements might be bent to fit the technology, which is the opposite of what your goal should be. These user stories are broken into features that are added to a product backlog and assigned to developers during development project iterations.

When you develop an application using an agile process, your iterations should be short and end with a deliverable to the business. Make sure that the business understands that this is not a complete system, and get feedback on what has been done so far. If there are defects, fix them immediately. If changes are needed, create new user stories and place them in the PB. It is much easier to correct the application during development than during production.

The structure of your application in both the file system and Visual Studio is important. It should be clear, simple, and consistent. Making your structure easy for developers to understand and work with will help keep the project's assets partitioned correctly and make it easier for developers new to the project to understand the architecture and code base.

Implementing the First User Story

Now that the overall scope and high-level design for the office supply inventory management (OSIM) application have been defined, it's time to start constructing the application. As outlined in my agile-based methodology, construction starts with the business owner choosing the user stories or features to be developed in the first iteration. With some guidance from the PM and the application architect, the business owners have decided on the following user story:

A user should be able to add a new type of item to the application.

This is a logical place to start, because this is an inventory management system. To manage inventory (and work with the features that would be provided by the other user stories), the users need to have a list of items in inventory.

To start, you need to break the larger user story into smaller features. Features should be small, simple, isolated, and testable. For the current user story, I've come up with this list of features:

➤ An item type entity and a persistence layer that can store the item entity in the data store

➤ An item type domain service that can provide a list of item types in the data store

➤ A user interface to enable business users to list existing item types and create new ones

This list of features demonstrates the layers and parts of the application needed for a nontechnical business user to verify that this user story is completed. Once this user story is completed, a nontechnical business user will be able to use the application to create new item types and then verify that they were completed correctly by viewing them in the list of item types. The technical staff does not need to be involved. The business user does not need a developer or DBA to run a query on the data store to verify that the item type was in fact created. Working on their own, business users can verify that the user story is complete and working correctly.

Now that the features are defined, you need to determine in what order you'll build them. Applications, like onions, parfaits, and ogres, are built on the idea of layers. Because applications are built in layers, the application construction should start at the core, and layers should be built upon so that each subsequent layer builds on the functionality of the one beneath it. At the core of OSIM, as with most business applications, is the data store. Like most applications, the outermost layer of OSIM is an interface, which could be a web page, Windows client application, or service layer. Therefore, here's the logical progression for development of these features:

1. The item type entity and persistence layer

2. The item type business domain service

3. The front-end user interface that will allow business users to interact with the item type business domain service

TDD is used in this example to build this application, so you need to determine what your first test should be.

THE FIRST TEST

Picking the first test to write for any feature is an important task. It sets the feature's direction and tone. It also ensures that the components and methods needed for the feature are built and layered in the correct order. The first test is usually for the most basic requirement of the feature you are building. As such, it indicates that as you continue development and move to refactoring, you never stray too far from the basics of the functionality that the feature needs to provide.

Choosing the First Test

In choosing the first test to write, you need to be sure that you really understand the user story and the business need behind it. The technological implementation will flow from the business need. In most cases a clear, logical progression determines how the features of each user story should be built. (Generally speaking, each application has a user interface layer of some sort on top of a business domain layer, with a persistence layer that communicates with a data store of some sort at the core. In some larger applications some of these layers are subdivided or use external resources, which can create some split or sublayering.

Regardless of how architecturally complex an application may be, I find it is generally easier to start by building features that are closest to the core of the application and then build out. This enables you to keep the core of the application as simple as possible. The layers built on top of this core have a simple set of APIs to work with, which in turn helps drive their interfaces toward simplicity. With a well-defined core, you can quickly and easily develop new features without duplicating a lot of code.

Some developers choose to start development at the UI layer and work in. There is nothing wrong with this approach per se. As you write the tests for the layer you are currently developing, however, you need to define the API for the layer beneath the current layer and stub it out. This can be a good way to do development, because it creates APIs that are driven more by the consumers of the library based on their needs and less by library developers who think they know what downstream clients need. I use this approach often. The key to success is being able to go back and write the tests for the methods you are creating the stubs for. This is not so much a technology or process issue as it is a discipline issue. After you have developed the discipline needed in TDD, you can certainly try this approach. It can be more efficient for systems that are principally driven by a single UI. In cases where you are focusing on a set of libraries that will be consumed by a wide variety of consumers, I find the bottom-up approach more efficient. In any case, feel free to try both, and do what works best for you.

In the case of the current feature, which is the ability to store an item type to the data store, the first test will be to ensure that a valid item type entity is saved to the data store. This will be validated by ensuring that a valid item type ID number is returned from the persistence layer.

Naming the Test

Unit tests are just methods on classes. Therefore, you can give your test any name that is a valid method name in .NET. However, in keeping with the spirit of TDD, I find it desirable to give my tests names that are meaningful and descriptive. To that end, I borrow a bit from another development methodology: behavior-driven development (BDD).

BDD is an extension to the ideals put forth by TDD. BDD stresses stakeholder involvement in the software development process with both the technical and nontechnical groups. It can be thought of as a sort of agile-based methodology that stresses collaboration across groups. As a matter of course, most teams that practice some sort of agile methodology end up following many of the tenets of BDD. BDD itself is a broad topic and therefore is not covered in detail in this book.

For the unit tests I write, I like to use a BDD style for naming tests. This style stresses complete, descriptive names that are business-user-friendly and attempts to avoid using technical terms. BDD is about making your class, method, and variable names mirror plain English as much as possible.

In my usage of this style I think of the description of my test as a sentence. The class name that contains the test, as well as any base class it implements, should spell out a set of conditions under which the test will run. For the current feature, you start by creating a class that describes the most basic of these preconditions: working with the item type repository. This class will be called `when_working_with_the_item_type_repository` and will be where you put the code that initializes a testable `ItemType` repository. As a result, `when_working_with_the_item_type_repository` will become a base class for all the unit tests that test the `ItemType` repository.

The naming style used here is important. Many developers dislike the idea of using the underscore character in the name of a class or method. When it comes to production code that will be read only by other developers and technical staff, I agree. However, a goal of TDD is to ensure that your tests reflect the business needs, requirements, and rules. Therefore, it's important to involve the nontechnical business users in your coding practices when it comes to writing your unit tests. Most technical staff have years of experience in reading class and method names presented in camel case (such as GetItemsFromDatabaseByCustomerId). They are comfortable with it, and reading these names comes easily. This is not the case with most business users, however. For them, a name with words separated by underscores is easier to read and understand. Because you, on the technical side of the business, are reaching out to the business, it's important that you try to meet them at least halfway. To that end, naming your tests in a manner that is more pleasing and easier for the business to understand is a must. It's also important that names of test classes and methods avoid use of technical terms that business users may not understand.

The base class `when_working_with_the_item_type_repository` will not actually contain a unit test. That is an incomplete description of an executable action. The name indicates that you are working with the item type repository, but it doesn't indicate what you are doing with it. To complete this set of conditions, you need to create a class that inherits from `when_working_with_the_item_type_repository` and that describes, in both name and code, the remainder of the initial condition. The class that inherits from `when_working_with_the_item_type_repository` and that implements the unit test will be called `and_saving_a_valid_item_type`. The name of this class, when taken with the base class it inherits from, clearly defines a starting condition for the test: When working with the item type repository, and saving a valid item, something will happen. That "something" is the name of the unit test method.

When naming your actual unit test method, try to complete the sentence you created with the class name. If you were to describe the point of the test to a business user, you might say something like "When working with the item type repository, and saving a valid item type, a valid item type ID should be returned." Using this model, it's easy to see that the name of the unit test method should be `then_a_valid_item_type_id_should_be_returned`.

Writing the Test

To help me write my tests in a BDD style, I use a framework called NBehave which can be downloaded at nbehave.org. NBehave is a BDD framework for .NET that allows developers to create specifications (business rules written in plain English) and link them to executable test code. This in effect creates a domain-specific language (DSL) that allows nontechnical business users to write tests based on a framework provided by the DSL created with NBehave.

The ability to write and execute these testing DSLs with NBehave is powerful. However, in this book I simply use NBehave to provide syntactic sugar that will help keep my unit tests more readable and manageable in a BDD style. As the example continues throughout this book, I'll point out where I use these syntactic features of NBehave.

With the naming scheme and high-level class layout for the first set of tests in place, you can now start writing them. But before you create test classes for this feature, you have some housekeeping to perform. To use the NBehave framework, you need to add references to the NBehave assemblies. Specifically, you need two: `NBehave.Spec .Framework`, which is the base NBehave assembly, and `NBehave.Spec .NUnit`, which provides syntactic sugar and enables NBehave to work with NUnit. You also need to add a reference to the NUnit assembly `nunit.framework` to enable you to write and run your unit tests, as shown in Figure 7-1.

Next you need to add a `Specification` base class. The `Specification` class in this example was developed by a team I used to work on. It provides a base class for unit tests written in a BDD style. It ensures that all unit test classes derive from the NBehave class `SpecBase` and that all derived classes are marked as unit tests for NUnit. You create the `Specification` class in the `OSIM.UnitTests` project and use this code to define the class:

FIGURE 7-1

```
[TestFixture]
public class Specification : SpecBase
{

}
```

Specification.cs

Now that the setup tasks are complete, you are ready to start writing the unit tests for the feature. First you create a class file to hold the unit tests in the `OSIM.Core` folder of the `OSIM.UnitTests` project and call it **ItemRepositoryTests.cs**, as shown in Figure 7-2.

Remove the class definition for `ItemRepositoryTests` that Visual Studio places in the file so that you are left with a `.cs` file that contains only a namespace definition:

FIGURE 7-2

```
namespace OSIM.UnitTests.OSIM.Core
{

}
```

ItemRepositoryTests.cs

Now you're ready to create your unit test classes. Start with the `when_working_with_the_item_ type_repository` base class:

```
public class when_working_with_the_item_type_repository : Specification
{

}
```

ItemRepositoryTests.cs

Right now this class doesn't do much other than inherit from `Specification` and thus identify itself to NUnit as a class that may contain unit tests. It also inherits the functionality provided by the NBehave SpecBase class. Once you begin writing the test for this example, and others, the common code to set up your test environment is placed in this class, and other test classes inherit from it.

Next, create the class to contain the unit test for the current feature, `and_saving_a_valid_item_type`:

```
public class and_saving_a_valid_item_type :
    when_working_with_the_item_type_repository
{

}
```

ItemRepositoryTests.cs

Generally speaking I keep all the unit tests for a particular class in the same `.cs` file. Many developers prefer to have a one-class-per-file rule. I agree with this practice for production code (although it doesn't extend to interfaces, but more on that later). However, for unit tests I have found it's easier to place all the tests for a particular piece of the application side by side in the same file. For starters, business users seem to find it easier to navigate through tests if they are all located in the same place. This makes sense, because most business users are used to dealing with documents. If they are working on a contract, they don't have each paragraph in a separate file; it's all in one place. That's how business users are conditioned to think about information. In your effort to meet them halfway, consolidating tests into one file is a small price to pay. Additionally, because you plan to have a lot of tests (on many of my projects, the number of unit tests runs into the hundreds or thousands), it's impractical to put each unit test in its own file. Doing this would cause the Solution Explorer in Visual Studio to run very slowly. If you get into a situation where you have a `.cs` file of unit tests that has become too big to manage, look into splitting it along some logical seam. But I always opt to have a few large files rather than many small files for my unit tests.

The next step in constructing this unit test is to create the actual test method `then_a_valid_item_type_id_should_be_returned`. You add that method, with the attribute that defines it as an executable unit test, to the `and_saving_a_valid_item_type` class:

```
public class and_saving_a_valid_item_type :
    when_working_with_the_item_type_repository
{
    [Test]
    public void then_a_valid_item_type_id_should_be_returned()
    {

    }
}
```

ItemRepositoryTests.cs

Now that you have the test classes set up, you can turn your attention to writing the test logic. Every test has three fundamental parts: setting up the starting conditions and environment, executing the code under test, and evaluating the result. Setting up the initial environment may seem to be the first order of business. But remember that a key ideal of TDD is to write only code that is essential, and to not write that code until you need it. The convention is most often applied to the business logic that is written using TDD, but it can and should be applied to the tests you write as well. In this case, the first thing you want to write is the code that calls the feature you are working on.

Having subdivided this test into three tasks (setting up the environment, executing the code under test, evaluating the result), now you need at least three methods — one to perform each of these tasks. You already have the `then_a_valid_item_type_id_should_be_returned` method, and it may seem the logical place to call your code under test and measure the result. But remember that the SOLID Principles, including the Single Responsibility Principle (SRP), also should be applied to your tests, in a pragmatic manner. Therefore, you want to have a method for setting up the context your test will run under, a method for executing the code under test, and a method to evaluate the result.

In keeping with the BDD style of your class and method names being meaningful and nontechnical and creating an almost sentence-like construct for the parts of the test, you want the method that executes the code under test to be as descriptive as possible. However, because this method will be something that presumably appears in almost every test, you need it to be generic as well. Luckily, NBehave provides just the method you need: `Because_of`. In the `and_saving_a_valid_item_type` class, you can create an overridden implementation of this method (the base method appears in the NBehave class `SpecBase`):

```
protected override void Because_of()
{
        base.Because_of();
}
```

ItemRepositoryTests.cs

In most cases you won't need to call the base class version of this method, so the call to the base class's implementation of `Because_of` can be removed. Instead, you want to add code that calls your code under test and saves the result for later evaluation by the `then_a_valid_item_id_should_be_returned` method:

```
protected override void Because_of()
{
    _result = _itemTypeRepository.Save(_testItemType);
}
```

ItemRepositoryTests.cs

You hold the return value in a member variable called `_result`. Keep an instance of your repository that's under test in the `_itemTypeRepository` member variable and pass in an item type that is stored in the `_testItemType` member variable. Currently, the `and_saving_a_valid_item_type` class looks like this:

```
public class and_saving_a_valid_item_type :
    when_working_with_the_item_type_repository
{
    private int _result;
```

```
    private IItemTypeRepository _itemTypeRepository;
    private ItemType _testItemType;

    protected override void Because_of()
    {
        _result = _itemTypeRepository.Save(_testItemType);
    }

    [Test]
    public void then_a_valid_item_type_id_should_be_returned()
    {

    }
}
```

ItemRepositoryTests.cs

Now that you've defined the code to execute the code under test, you can add code to the then_a_
valid_item_type_id_should_be_returned method to evaluate the result that is returned and
stored in the _result member variable:

```
    [Test]
    public void then_a_valid_item_type_id_should_be_returned()
    {
        _result.ShouldEqual(_itemTypeId);
    }
```

ItemRepositoryTests.cs

This demonstrates another example that takes advantage of the syntactic sugar provided by NBehave
to make the unit-testing code more readable by business users. The ShouldEqual method is simply
another way of writing the asserts demonstrated in Chapter 4. In this case, though, instead of
business users having to understand what an assert is and how its syntax works, they can read the
code like a sentence. For example, if you were to read that line of code out loud, you might say
something like "Result should equal item type ID." Compare that with what you would say when
reading an assert from left to right, like a sentence. One is clearly easier to understand than the other.

Attempting to run this test now will fail. In fact, the code won't even compile. This test executes a
method on an interface (IItemTypeRepository) that doesn't exist and is trying to pass in a class
type (ItemType) that also doesn't exist. If you've been following along and writing this code in
Visual Studio, no doubt you are seeing a lot of red right now. The next step is to fix that by creating
some business classes.

The question of in what order to create your business classes is not one that can be quantified and
spelled out in a book. Actually, it depends. In this case, you have an IItemTypeRepository that has
a Save method that takes an object that is of type ItemType as an argument. For the sake of making
development easier in this example when you get to the item type repository, you create ItemType
first so that it exists when the time comes to write the repository code.

In the `OSIM.Core` project is a folder called `Entities`. In that folder, create a class called `ItemType`, as shown in Figure 7-3.

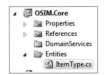

FIGURE 7-3

Right now you don't have any specific requirements about what kind of data should comprise an `ItemType`. But the class `ItemType` has to be persistable (meaning that it can be saved to a database). In order to save an entity to the database, the entity must have a unique ID. This enables the application to find that specific entity in the database later. Therefore, it's reasonable to assume that the `ItemType` class should have a definition for a public property of type `int` called `Id`. As well, Fluent NHibernate (FNH), the Object Relational Mapper (ORM) that will be used to handle data persistence in Chapter 8, requires that this property be declared as virtual, so you need to make that declaration as well. I'll explain why the virtual keyword is needed when I discuss FNH mappings in Chapter 8.

Available for download on Wrox.com

```
public class ItemType
{
    public virtual int Id { get; set; }
}
```

ItemType.cs

Returning to the test, you need to add a `using` statement to the top of the `ItemRepositoryTests`.cs file:

Available for download on Wrox.com

```
using OSIM.Core.Entities;
```

ItemRepositoryTests.cs

The test should now be able to resolve the `ItemType` class. The next step is to create the `IItemTypeRepository` interface. To accomplish this, you need to create a new folder in the OSIM .Core project called `Persistence` as shown in Figure 7-4.

This folder houses the persistence (data access) logic for the OSIM application. You need to create a file to store the `IItemTypeRepository` and the concrete `ItemTypeRepository` classes, so you need to add a new class to the `Persistence` folder in the `OSIM.Core` project called `ItemTypeRepository`, as shown in Figure 7-5.

FIGURE 7-4

FIGURE 7-5

Because you created this as a class, Visual Studio includes a default implementation for you:

```
namespace OSIM.Core.Persistence
{
    public class ItemTypeRepository
    {

    }
}
```

ItemTypeRepository.cs

The SOLID Principles say that when developing code you should concern yourself with contracts and interfaces instead of concrete implementations. In the test you reference the `ItemTypeRepository` from an interface called `IItemTypeRepository`. Therefore, you need to add an interface called `IItemTypeRepository` that the `ItemTypeRepository` class will implement:

```
namespace OSIM.Core.Persistence
{
    public interface IItemTypeRepository
    {

    }

    public class ItemTypeRepository : IItemTypeRepository
    {

    }
}
```

ItemTypeRepository.cs

Notice that the interface and the repository are in the same `.cs` file. This is not a mistake. Conventional wisdom says that these entities should be in separate files. But if an interface is implemented by only a single class, why do they need to be in separate files? I have found that in most cases keeping the interface and the concrete class in the same file makes managing these entities easier and does not limit how I work with the interface or the concrete class. In some situations it makes sense to place the interfaces in separate files. In fact, sometimes the interfaces should be placed in separate projects. But I have found these to be edge cases. If one of these cases does arise, it's a simple matter to move the interface to another file or project. Therefore, you can start from a position of developing for the majority of cases and keep the interface and the concrete class in the same file.

Returning to the `OSIM.UnitTest` project, you can a `using` statement for the `OSIM.Core` `.Persistence` namespace to the `ItemRepositoryTests.cs` file to allow the `and_saving_a_valid_item_type` unit test class to resolve the `IItemRepository` interface. Here are the complete contents of the `ItemRepositoryTest.cs` file:

```
using NBehave.Spec.NUnit;
using NUnit.Framework;
using OSIM.Core.Entities;
using OSIM.Core.Persistence;

namespace OSIM.UnitTests.OSIM.Core
{
    public class when_working_with_the_item_type_repository : Specification
    {

    }

    public class and_saving_a_valid_item_type :
when_working_with_the_item_type_repository
    {
        private int _result;
        private IItemTypeRepository _itemTypeRepository;
        private ItemType _testItemType;
        private int _itemTypeId;

        protected override void Because_of()
        {
            _result = _itemTypeRepository.Save(_testItemType);
        }

        [Test]
        public void then_a_valid_item_type_id_should_be_returned()
        {
            _result.ShouldEqual(_itemTypeId);
        }
    }
}
```

ItemRepositoryTests.cs

The last order of business before you can compile and run this test is to add a Save method
to the IItemRepository interface. This will also create the need to add a Save method to the
ItemRepository class:

```
using System;
using OSIM.Core.Entities;

namespace OSIM.Core.Persistence
{
    public interface IItemTypeRepository
    {
        int Save(ItemType itemType);
    }

    public class ItemTypeRepository : IItemTypeRepository
    {
```

```
public int Save(ItemType itemType)
{
    throw new NotImplementedException();
}
}
}
```

ItemTypeRepository.cs

Currently the implementation of the `Save` method on `ItemRepository` doesn't do anything. That's fine. Remember that the goal right now is to write just enough code to make the test pass. Until now you've been unable to compile the code, so you haven't seen a failing test yet. You don't want to write any code until you know code needs to be written.

Sure enough, compiling and running the test does show that the test currently fails, as shown in Figure 7-6.

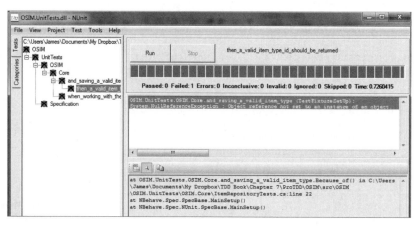

FIGURE 7-6

IMPLEMENTING THE FUNCTIONALITY

Even though it took a while to get there, it is important to see that the test fails. If the test had passed, this could have meant several things. A passing test might indicate that the code does not correctly exercise the requirement or feature that you are currently developing. A failing test is important because it helps confirm that the test correctly references functionality that does not yet exist in the application. A passing test could also show that the requirement you're working on is a duplicate of some sort, or that this particular feature of the current user story was already satisfied by a previous requirement, feature, or user story. In any of these cases, it's important to investigate any test that passes without any application code being written.

Writing the Simplest Thing That Could Possibly Work

Because the test failed, your goal now is to write just enough code to make the test pass. In some cases this is as easy and trivial as writing or changing a single line of code. This is fine.

It's important to meet only the current business requirement and not try to guess what will be needed in the future. It's also important to keep your code as simple as possible. Simple code is less likely to have defects and is easier to maintain in the future.

In this example, the implementation of the feature will end up being a little more involved than just a single line of code. It is still important, even in situations where you know you need to do a lot of work to make a test pass, to work in increments, to test frequently, and to write only code at the instant you need it, not before. Running the test (not just your test, but all the tests) frequently, even when you know it will not pass, ensures that in the act of developing your current feature's functionality you are not breaking features in other parts of the application. Odds are that you will affect other code in the application at some point. This is not always a bad thing and can even be necessary at times. Knowing about it as soon as it happens, especially if it's unexpected and creates a negative impact, will help you understand how your code is interacting with the rest of the application. If the effect on the other feature is unintended, it will be much easier to fix the sooner you know about it, because the list of changes that could have caused the error is relatively short.

According to my results, a null object error occurred on line 22 of the `ItemRepositoryTests.cs` file. The line this turns out to be is the call to `ItemTypeRepository` in the `Because_of` method of the `and_saving_a_valid_item_type` test class:

```
protected override void Because_of()
{
    _result = _itemTypeRepository.Save(_testItemType);
}
```

ItemRepositoryTests.cs

This test fails because although `_itemTypeRepository` has been defined, the variable has not been populated with an object yet. Chapter 2 demonstrated the `Setup` attribute that NUnit provides for setting up some execution context before each test runs. Because this example uses a BDD style of naming and NBehave to provide a framework for BDD-style tests, you have another option. Ultimately, your class inherits from the NBehave class `SpecBase`, which provides a virtual method called `Establish_context`. The `Establish_context` method provides a place to create the context under which your test will run. Because I tend to build my unit test classes as layers of classes that each define a precondition for my test, having a common method that exists in the class hierarchy to create the execution context is convenient. It's also easy to understand for business users to whom I may want to show my test.

To get past this initial failure of the test, you only need to create an object of type `ItemTypeRepository` and store it in the `_itemTypeRepository` member variable:

```
protected override void Establish_context()
{
    base.Establish_context();

    _itemTypeRepository = new ItemTypeRepository();
}
```

ItemRepositoryTests.cs

With that task done, you should run the tests again. In this case the test probably will still fail, but you should stay in the habit of running the tests often. At the very least, run them when you finish each small task along the way to completing your feature, as shown in Figure 7-7.

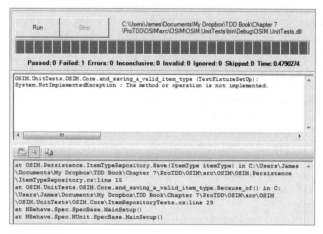

FIGURE 7-7

As expected, the test still fails. But it is failing in a different place and for a different reason. This indicates that you are making progress. The new failure is due to a `System.NotImplementedException` occurring in the `Save` method of `ItemTypeRepository` — specifically, on line 15 of the `ItemTypeRepository.cs` file:

```
public class ItemTypeRepository : IItemTypeRepository
{
    public int Save(ItemType itemType)
    {
        throw new NotImplementedException();
    }
}
```

ItemTypeRepository.cs

I use Resharper by JetBrains (www.jetbrains.com) to augment my Visual Studio development environment. When this method was created by Resharper, it automatically added this implementation that throws the `NotImplementedException` for me. If you are not using Resharper it is still a good idea to create this initial implementation to remind you that the code has not been implemented.

To complete this feature, you need to implement this method. Right now you just want to write the simplest code possible that may work:

```
public class ItemTypeRepository : IItemTypeRepository
{
    public int Save(ItemType itemType)
    {
        return 1;
    }
}
```

ItemTypeRepository.cs

No one can deny that this is the simplest code that may satisfy the needs of the test. Granted, it is unlikely that this single line of code will be the solution to this feature or the user story it is derived from. But based on where you are now in the life cycle of this feature, it is the logical next step. Running the test again yields another failed test, as shown in Figure 7-8.

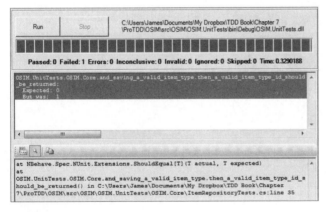

FIGURE 7-8

In this case, the number that is returned from the repository method is not what the test was expecting. It's clear that some more context is needed.

To define the context more completely, you need to tell the test what ItemType Id value it should expect from the call to the Save method on ItemTypeRepository. If I am writing tests to save data to a data store and I am getting an Id number of some sort in return, I like to have my unit test randomly select this number at execution:

```
protected override void Establish_context()
{
    base.Establish_context();

    var randomNumberGenerator = new Random();
    _itemTypeId = randomNumberGenerator.Next(32000);

    _itemTypeRepository = new ItemTypeRepository();
}
```

ItemRepositoryTests.cs

On the surface, you may look at this unit test and think that I have introduced some degree of unpredictability. But this isn't the case. I expect the `Save` method on the `ItemTypeRepository` class to always respond the same way: It should return an ID number for an entity that is being saved to the data store. I have created a situation in which the ID number that gets returned from the `ItemTypeRepository` is different each time the test is run, but remains the same during the scope of each individual execution of this test. Because this determining of a random ID number is done as part of the process that creates the context for the test, it doesn't introduce any unpredictability to the test. I'm simply changing the value of the ID number that gets returned; the steps to return that ID number have not changed. In case this distinction still is not quite clear, I will touch on it later when I demonstrate creating a mocked dependency for `ItemTypeRepository`.

If you run this test again, you will see that it fails, as shown in Figure 7-9.

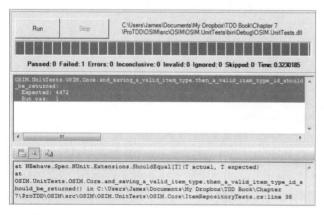

FIGURE 7-9

In this case the test expects 4472 to be returned as the value for the `ItemType Id`. The current implementation of `Save` for the `ItemTypeRepository` class returns 1.

It's time to take the next step in making this test pass. At this stage it is helpful to think about the design of the application. Specifically, it's time to discuss how the data persistence will be implemented.

This application uses the Object Relational Mapper (ORM) framework Fluent NHibernate (FNH) for data persistence. I explained the concept behind ORMs in Chapter 5, and I'll show how it is used to handle data persistence in this example in Chapter 8. The .NET world offers a variety of ORM frameworks to choose from. I chose FNH for this example because it's the framework I am most familiar with. This does not mean that FNH is the best ORM for your project. If you or your team have more experience with an ORM such as Entity Framework, and that tool serves your needs, it's probably the right ORM for you. The examples in this book that use FNH are portable, and you should be able to implement the same practices with any ORM you and your team decide to use.

> *If you're unfamiliar with FNH, don't worry. This example doesn't use any advanced features of the FNH framework. I will also stop and briefly explain the steps in the example that are specific to FNH.*

FNH, like most modern ORMs, encourages the use of the repository pattern discussed in Chapter 5. Because I use FNH frequently, I already have developed a base generic repository that can be used for projects that employ FNH. As with the `Specification` class, I utilize this class on most of my projects. This repository will be included with the code samples that are available for download; however, this example demonstrates how to build a repository from scratch.

FNH provides a `Session` class that handles all interaction with the data store. Calls from the application code to the repository always end with one or more calls to the FNH `Session` object. A `Session` object is created by an instance of the FNH interface type `ISessionFactory`. To use these types in your `ItemTypeRepository`, you need to add references to the `FluentNHibernate` and `NHibernate` assemblies, as shown in Figure 7-10.

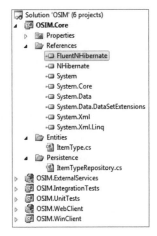

FIGURE 7-10

Before the `ItemTypeRepository` can recognize the classes in the FNH framework, you will need to add a using statement to the ItemTypeRepository.cs file:

```
using NHibernate;
```

ItemTypeRepository.cs

Now you need to add a member variable to the `ItemTypeRepository` class to store the `ISessionFactory` object:

```
public class ItemTypeRepository : IItemTypeRepository
{
    private ISessionFactory _sessionFactory;

    public int Save(ItemType itemType)
    {
        return 1;
    }
}
```

ItemTypeRepository.cs

Finally, you need to add a constructor to the `ItemTypeRepository` class that allows a class that implements `ISessionFactory` to be supplied when `ItemTypeRepository` is created:

```
public ItemTypeRepository(ISessionFactory sessionFactory)
{
    _sessionFactory = sessionFactory;
}
```

ItemTypeRepository.cs

To review, here is a complete listing of the current `ItemTypeRepository` class:

```
public class ItemTypeRepository : IItemTypeRepository
{
    private ISessionFactory _sessionFactory;

    public ItemTypeRepository(ISessionFactory sessionFactory)
    {
        _sessionFactory = sessionFactory;
    }

    public int Save(ItemType itemType)
    {
        return 1;
    }
}
```

ItemTypeRepository.cs

Now is a good time to try to run the tests. Unfortunately, the application no longer compiles. When you created the constructor on `ItemTypeRepository` that allowed clients to inject a value for `ISessionFactory`, you removed the default (no parameter) constructor. To use `ItemTypeRepository`, you need to provide a value for the constructor that implements `ISessionFactory`. Because this is a unit test, and you need to keep the code in `ItemTypeRepository` isolated, you need to provide a mocked object instead of a valid FNH Session Factory.

As you'll recall from Chapter 2, the mocking framework Moq lets you create mock or stub objects to inject into the classes you are testing to ensure that code is isolated from external dependencies. To use the Moq framework, you first need to add a reference to it to the OSIM .UnitTests project, as shown in Figure 7-11.

The next step is to add code to the `Establish_context` method of the `and_saving_a_valid_item_type` class to create a mock object based on the FNH `ISessionFactory` interface:

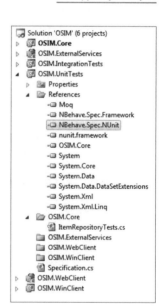

FIGURE 7-11

```
protected override void Establish_context()
{
    base.Establish_context();

    var randomNumberGenerator = new Random();
    _itemTypeId = randomNumberGenerator.Next(32000);
    var sessionFactory = new Mock<ISessionFactory>();

    _itemTypeRepository = new ItemTypeRepository();
}
```

ItemRepositoryTests.cs

You'll notice that Visual Studio indicates that it doesn't have a definition for `ISessionFactory`. This is because the `OSIM.UnitTests` project has no reference for the FNH libraries. They need to be added (see Figure 7-12).

You then need to add a `using` statement to the `ItemRepositoryTests` `.cs` file to include the required FNH namespace:

```
using NHibernate;
```

Now you can use your mocked Session Factory as a constructor parameter for `ItemTypeRepository`:

Available for download on Wrox.com

```
protected override void Establish_context()
{
    base.Establish_context();

    var randomNumberGenerator = new Random();
    _itemTypeId = randomNumberGenerator.Next(32000);
    var sessionFactory = new Mock<ISessionFactory>();

    _itemTypeRepository = new ItemTypeRepository(sessionFactory.Object);
}
```

FIGURE 7-12

ItemRepositoryTests.cs

It's now time to create an implementation of the `Save` method of the `ItemTypeRepository` method that calls the FNH API. As mentioned, all database access with FNH is done through the `Session` class. You get an instance of this `Session` class from an instance of an object that implements the FNH `ISessionFactory` interface. Here's the implementation of the `Save` method in `ItemTypeRepository` that utilizes the `Session` class to save the `ItemType` to the database:

Available for download on Wrox.com

```
public int Save(ItemType itemType)
{
    int id;
    using (var session = _sessionFactory.OpenSession())
    {
        id = (int) session.Save(itemType);
        session.Flush();
    }
    return id;
}
```

ItemTypeRepository.cs

These FNH-specific commands require a bit of explanation if you've never used the FNH framework. The first thing you do is get a `Session` from `SessionFactory`. This is essentially your connection to the database. `SessionFactory` is configured with the information needed to connect to the database when it's created. This topic is covered in more detail in Chapter 8. The first call is to the `Save` method of the `Session` object. This method saves the entity to the database and returns the value of the primary key or ID. Specifying which field in the entity is the ID is done in the mapping, which is covered in Chapter 8. Next you call `Flush` to ensure that any pending operations to the database are complete. When the end of the `using` block is reached, the `Session` is closed.

Running the test again yields another failure, as shown in Figure 7-13.

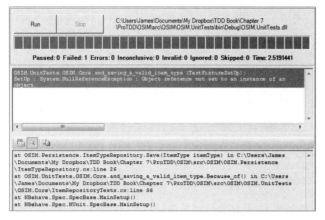

FIGURE 7-13

Line 26 of the `ItemTypeRepository.cs` file is the call to the `Save` method of the `Session` class. `NullReferenceException` tells you that `SessionFactory` returned a null object when the `OpenSession` method was called. This means that you need to add another mock object to the test to stand in for `Session`. You also need to add a stub method for `SessionFactory.OpenSession` that returns the mocked `Session` object:

Available for
download on
Wrox.com

```
protected override void Establish_context()
{
    base.Establish_context();

    var randomNumberGenerator = new Random();
    _itemTypeId = randomNumberGenerator.Next(32000);
    var sessionFactory = new Mock<ISessionFactory>();
    var session = new Mock<ISession>();

    sessionFactory.Setup(sf => sf.OpenSession()).Returns(session.Object);

    _itemTypeRepository = new ItemTypeRepository(sessionFactory.Object);
}
```

ItemRepositoryTests.cs

This syntax should look similar to the code in the section "Moq Basics" in Chapter 2. It instructs the mock that will stand in for `SessionFactory` to return the mock you are creating for `Session` when the `OpenSession` method on the `SessionFactory` object is called. Running the test at this point shows that your work is still not done though (see Figure 7-14).

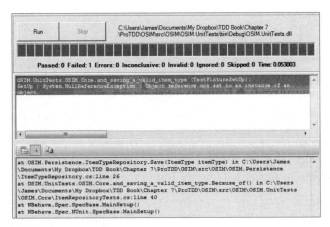

FIGURE 7-14

The final hurdle is supplying the `Session` mock with a stubbed implementation of the `Save` method. In this case you want the `Save` method to return the random `ItemType Id` that you are generating in the `Establish_context` method of the test class:

Available for
download on
Wrox.com

```
session.Setup(s => s.Save(_testItemType)).Returns(_itemTypeId);
```

ItemRepositoryTests.cs

Here's the complete implementation of `Establish_context`:

Available for
download on
Wrox.com

```
protected override void Establish_context()
{
    base.Establish_context();

    var randomNumberGenerator = new Random();
    _itemTypeId = randomNumberGenerator.Next(32000);
    var sessionFactory = new Mock<ISessionFactory>();
    var session = new Mock<ISession>();

    session.Setup(s => s.Save(_testItemType)).Returns(_itemTypeId);
    sessionFactory.Setup(sf => sf.OpenSession()).Returns(session.Object);

    _itemTypeRepository = new ItemTypeRepository(sessionFactory.Object);
}
```

ItemRepositoryTests.cs

Running the Passing Test

As shown in Figure 7-15, the test now passes.

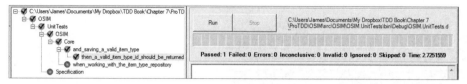

FIGURE 7-15

This passing test means that you are done with this feature. In a work environment you will probably come back later and do some refactoring, but this passing test is proof that the feature is complete based on the requirements and can be integrated into the rest of the codebase.

If you are like most developers I know, you have an urge to fuss over and tinker with code and add things that make it "better." Resist that urge. Adding unrequested functionality, sometimes called "gold plating," tends to cause more problems than it solves. The addition takes time, adds complexity to the codebase, creates maintenance overhead, and can affect the behavior of other areas of the systems that are covered by the requirements. Don't fall into the "Well, the business probably will need it" trap. Until the business specifically asks for additional functionality, it is unneeded. It's not a matter of being lazy; it's a matter of keeping the codebase and the application as simple as possible while providing the business with the functionality it needs. In the current example, a documented business requirement is finished. That requirement has been translated into a unit test. The code satisfies that test. This is the definition of done.

Writing the Next Test

With this test done, it's time to look at the user story or feature again and determine if any more tests need to be written. In this case, you determine that you want to write a test to make sure that if someone tries to save a null object to the database, the repository throws an exception. As with any other feature or requirement, the first step is to write a test. Open the `ItemRepositoryTests.cs` file (if it's not already open) and add a new test class for this base that inherits from the `when_working_with_the_item_type_repository` base class:

```
public class and_saving_an_invalid_item_type :
when_working_with_the_item_type_repository
{

}
```

ItemRepositoryTests.cs

Next you add a method to validate that the result of the test is what you're expecting — in this case, that an `ArgumentNullException` is thrown:

```
public class and_saving_an_invalid_item_type :
when_working_with_the_item_type_repository
{
    private Exception _result;

    [Test]
```

```
public void then_an_argument_null_exception_should_be_raised()
{
    _result.ShouldBeInstanceOfType(typeof(ArgumentNullException));
}
}
```

This code declares _result as type Exception, which is the base type of ArgumentNullException. This is because although you expect the call to ItemTypeRepository to raise an exception, you want to verify the type of exception that is thrown. If you declare _result as the specific type you're looking for (in this case, ArgumentNullException), and something completely different is thrown, such as an exception of type NullReferenceException, your test experiences a runtime error before it can evaluate the result. By declaring _result to be a variable of type Exception, you can store the exception that is thrown regardless of the specific type.

So, how does _result get populated? The previous example used an override implementation of the Because_of method that called the method under test and stored the return output in the _result member variable:

Available for
download on
Wrox.com

```
protected override void Because_of()
{
    _result = _itemTypeRepository.Save(_testItemType);
}
```

In this case, because you need to capture an exception that is thrown when the Save method on the ItemTypeRepository is called, you need to structure your implementation of the Because_of method a little differently. For this test, you want to place the call to Save in a Try/Catch block, and in the Catch section store the exception object in the _result member variable:

Available for
download on
Wrox.com

```
protected override void Because_of()
{
    try
    {
        _itemTypeRepository.Save(null);
    }
    catch (Exception exception)
    {
        _result = exception;
    }
}
```

If you were to try to run this test, you would get a compiler error. The unit test class and_saving_an_invalid_item_type does not have a declaration for the member variable _itemTypeRepository. This member variable was created and instantiated in the previous test as part of the and_saving_a_valid_item_type class. You could do the same thing in the and_saving_an_invalid_item_type class. But you've already written this code once. Although some code duplication in unit tests is acceptable, you still want to keep the unit test code as DRY (don't repeat yourself) as possible. Both the and_saving_a_valid_item_type and and_saving_an_invalid_item_type classes inherit from the when_working_with_the_item_type_repository base class. To reduce the code duplication, move the declaration and code to create the mock for _itemTypeRepository in that base class:

```
public class when_working_with_the_item_type_repository : Specification
{
    protected IItemTypeRepository _itemTypeRepository;

    protected override void Establish_context()
    {
        base.Establish_context();
        _itemTypeRepository = new ItemTypeRepository(sessionFactory.Object);
    }
}
```

ItemRepositoryTests.cs

You remove the declaration of _itemTypeRepository from the and_saving_a_valid_item_type class and from the line that instantiates the instance of ItemTypeRepository:

```
public class and_saving_a_valid_item_type :
when_working_with_the_item_type_repository
{
    private int _result;
    private ItemType _testItemType;
    private int _itemTypeId;

    protected override void Establish_context()
    {
        base.Establish_context();

        var randomNumberGenerator = new Random();
        _itemTypeId = randomNumberGenerator.Next(32000);
        var sessionFactory = new Mock<ISessionFactory>();
        var session = new Mock<ISession>();

        session.Setup(s => s.Save(_testItemType)).Returns(_itemTypeId);
        sessionFactory.Setup(sf => sf.OpenSession()).Returns(session.Object);
    }
}
```

ItemRepositoryTests.cs

You've moved the declaration and instantiation of the mock for ItemTypeRepository, but the ItemTypeRepository mock relies on the mock of SessionFactory, which in turn relies on the mock of Session object. You need to create these as instance variables of the when_working_with_the_item_type_repository class:

```
public class when_working_with_the_item_type_repository : Specification
{
    protected IItemTypeRepository _itemTypeRepository;
    protected Mock<ISessionFactory> _sessionFactory;
    protected Mock<ISession> _session;

    protected override void Establish_context()
    {
        base.Establish_context();

        _sessionFactory = new Mock<ISessionFactory>();
        _session = new Mock<ISession>();

        _itemTypeRepository = new ItemTypeRepository(_sessionFactory.Object);
    }
}
```

ItemRepositoryTests.cs

Next, you need to move the line of code that stubs the `CreateSession` method of the
`SessionFactory` mock from the `Establish_context` method of the `and_saving_a_valid_
item_type` class to the `Establish_context` method of the `when_working_with_the_item_type_
repository` class:

```
protected override void Establish_context()
{
    base.Establish_context();

    _sessionFactory = new Mock<ISessionFactory>();
    _session = new Mock<ISession>();

    _sessionFactory.Setup(sf => sf.OpenSession()).Returns(_session.Object);

    _itemTypeRepository = new ItemTypeRepository(_sessionFactory.Object);
}
```

ItemRepositoryTests.cs

This change leaves the `Establish_context` method of the `and_saving_a_valid_item_type` class
looking like this:

```
protected override void Establish_context()
{
    base.Establish_context();

    var randomNumberGenerator = new Random();
    _itemTypeId = randomNumberGenerator.Next(32000);

    session.Setup(s => s.Save(_testItemType)).Returns(_itemTypeId);
}
```

ItemRepositoryTests.cs

The last change you need to make is to have the `Establish_context` method of the `and_saving_a_valid_item_type` class use the member variable `_session` from the `when_working_with_the_type_repository` class:

```
protected override void Establish_context()
{
    base.Establish_context();

    var randomNumberGenerator = new Random();
    _itemTypeId = randomNumberGenerator.Next(32000);

    _session.Setup(s => s.Save(_testItemType)).Returns(_itemTypeId);
}
```

ItemRepositoryTests.cs

Moving these declarations enables you to reuse quite a bit of code over not only these two tests, but also any additional tests you may need to write. Keeping the `_session` variable as a protected member of the base class `when_working_with_the_item_type_repository` enables you to restub that method individually for each test class you do. The `Establish_context` method in `when_working_with_the_item_type_repository` takes care of stubbing the session factory so that you don't need to tell it to return the mock of `Session` for every test. Because more tests were added to this class, this turns out to be an efficient way of arranging things.

Before you consider the refactoring of the test class finished, you want to rerun the `then_a_valid_item_type_id_should_be_returned` test in the `and_saving_a_valid_item_type` test class, as shown in Figure 7-16.

FIGURE 7-16

The NUnit unit test runner has picked up the new `then_an_argument_null_should_be_raised` unit test. But for now you should be concerned with only the existing `then_a_valid_item_type_id_should_be_returned` test. You should be more concerned about that one right now because you want to make sure that refactoring your unit test classes (`and_saving_a_valid_item_type` and `when_working_with_the_item_type_repository`) hasn't broken the tests in any way. The test passed before refactoring, and if you didn't make any changes to the business code, you can be reasonably sure that you have not broken the test. When refactoring your unit tests, running the existing tests to ensure that they all still pass and that you haven't broken any of them is an important step. Do not skip it!

Because the refactor of the unit test classes is complete for now, you can move on to looking at the new test class (and_saving_an_invalid_item_type) and running this test for the first time (see Figure 7-17).

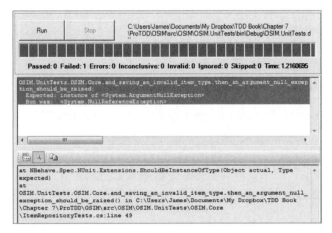

FIGURE 7-17

You get an unexpected exception from the call to Save on the ItemTypeRepository class. This is a great example of why it was important to declare _result broadly as a type Exception and not the more narrowly focused ArgumentNullException. The reason for this failing test is that the mock of the Session class does not have a stub for the method Save that reacts to the value null. Because the mechanics of creating the mocks of the SessionFactory and Session objects are taken care of in the when_working_with_the_item_type_repository class, all you need to do is declare the stub for the Save method:

Available for download on Wrox.com

```
protected override void Establish_context()
{
    base.Establish_context();

    _session.Setup(s => s.Save(null)).Throws(new ArgumentNullException());
}
```

ItemRepositoryTests.cs

With the stubbed Save method set up on the Session object, it's time to run the test again, as shown in Figure 7-18.

FIGURE 7-18

Now that the `Session` mock is throwing the proper exception, the test passes. Here's the complete `ItemRepositoryTests.cs` file:

```csharp
using System;
using Moq;
using NBehave.Spec.NUnit;
using NHibernate;
using NUnit.Framework;
using OSIM.Core.Entities;
using OSIM.Core.Persistence;

namespace OSIM.UnitTests.OSIM.Core
{
    public class when_working_with_the_item_type_repository : Specification
    {
        protected IItemTypeRepository _itemTypeRepository;
        protected Mock<ISessionFactory> _sessionFactory;
        protected Mock<ISession> _session;

        protected override void Establish_context()
        {
            base.Establish_context();

            _sessionFactory = new Mock<ISessionFactory>();
            _session = new Mock<ISession>();

            _sessionFactory.Setup(sf => sf.OpenSession()).Returns(_session.Object);

            _itemTypeRepository = new ItemTypeRepository(_sessionFactory.Object);
        }
    }

    public class and_saving_an_invalid_item_type :
    when_working_with_the_item_type_repository
    {
        private Exception _result;

        protected override void Establish_context()
        {
            base.Establish_context();

            _session.Setup(s => s.Save(null)).Throws(new ArgumentNullException());
        }

        protected override void Because_of()
        {
            try
            {
                _itemTypeRepository.Save(null);
            }
            catch (Exception exception)
            {
                _result = exception;
            }
```

```
        }

        [Test]
        public void then_an_argument_null_exception_should_be_raised()
        {
            _result.ShouldBeInstanceOfType(typeof(ArgumentNullException));
        }
    }

    public class and_saving_a_valid_item_type :
    when_working_with_the_item_type_repository
    {
        private int _result;
        private ItemType _testItemType;
        private int _itemTypeId;

        protected override void Establish_context()
        {
            base.Establish_context();

            var randomNumberGenerator = new Random();
            _itemTypeId = randomNumberGenerator.Next(32000);

            _session.Setup(s => s.Save(_testItemType)).Returns(_itemTypeId);
        }

        protected override void Because_of()
        {
            _result = _itemTypeRepository.Save(_testItemType);
        }

        [Test]
        public void then_a_valid_item_type_id_should_be_returned()
        {
            _result.ShouldEqual(_itemTypeId);
        }
    }
}
```

ItemRepositoryTests.cs

IMPROVING THE CODE BY REFACTORING

When you start writing code using TDD, your only goal is to make the tests pass. Don't worry about writing code that is elegant or functional or pretty. Make sure that you can meet the primary purpose of development: satisfying the needs of the business. The passing tests, which are themselves based on business requirements, indicate that business needs are being met. After the business needs are met, you should think about refactoring.

As stated in Chapter 4, refactoring is the act of improving on existing code to make it more efficient, more readable, and more maintainable without affecting the code's external behavior. Having a suite of passing unit tests allows you to freely refactor your code and know exactly when you've gone beyond the point of having code that satisfies the business. Now is the time to put on your editor hat and take a good, hard look at your code. Is it readable? Can someone new to the team look at your code and quickly understand its function and how the code accomplishes this? Does your code meet the SOLID Principles? Do you have a lot of duplicate code? Are you effectively using interfaces and abstractions? Are your dependencies being injected to keep your coupling loose? Now is the time to address these questions. Work to make your code better, but keep your tests passing.

TRIANGULATION OF TESTS

The "happy path" is always easy to test. If your unit tests stay on the happy path or tests one set of input values that fall within the middle range of the possible inputs, they are not telling you the whole story. Actually, it's worse than that: They lie to you. They tell you that your code satisfies the business needs and have a high degree of quality. This isn't true.

The problem is that all input is evil. When you don't build tests that probe the boundaries of your code and go beyond, you are essentially crossing your fingers and hoping that the users never push the boundaries of your application. Users just want software that works. They don't understand concepts of memory size, out-of-bounds errors, null object exceptions, or the problems that arise from using values that are either higher or lower than the range of values your code expects. And they shouldn't have to; your application should worry about these issues.

When writing unit tests, be sure they explore the boundaries of what your method expects. If your method expects a value between 1 and 10, write a test that passes in 5. Then write tests that pass in 1 and 10. Then write tests that pass in 0 and 11. Make sure that your code knows what to do with the unexpected. That was the point of the `and_saving_an_invalid_item_type` test class and its `then_an_agrument_null_exception_should_be_raised` test. I wanted to make sure that the `ItemTypeRepository` class would be able to handle the case in which a client called the `Save` method with a null object and respond accordingly. Triangulate your tests to ensure the quality of your code.

SUMMARY

The first user story or feature you develop for an application is important. The success of this first unit of work can set the tone and define the project's values. When planning your work, order your features in a logical manner that starts toward the core of your application and builds out. When breaking your user stories into features, be sure to keep them small, isolated, and testable.

When creating your unit tests, use a consistent standard for naming classes, methods, and variables. The names you give them should be meaningful — not only to developers but also to nontechnical business users who may be asked to validate your tests. Investigate BDD naming styles and conventions, and apply this knowledge to naming your classes, methods, and variables.

See your test fail before you write any code. This is important to ensure that your test is testing functionality that does not exist. If your test passes without any code being written, this could mean many things. Perhaps this is a duplicate feature. It could be that the functionality needed was created as a side effect of a previous feature. Another possibility is that your test is not testing the correct functionality. Find the reason; don't just assume that a test that passes in this manner means it's OK to proceed with development.

Write just enough code to make your test pass — no more. When implementing the business code to make your test pass, always try to do the simplest thing that might work. When the test passes, you are done. Do not gold-plate. If a feature, defect, or request for a piece of functionality doesn't appear in the user stories or feature list, do not build it. Wait until it's needed; do not preempt the process.

Be sure to triangulate your tests. Testing the best-case scenario or the "happy path" does nothing to ensure that you are creating quality code. Test the edge cases for your methods: input parameters that are on the boundaries of what is expected, values that fall out of these boundaries, and unexpected values and conditions. Remember, all input is evil.

With a suite of passing tests, you know that your application meets the needs of the business. When those needs are met, work on refactoring your code to make it more optimized, readable, and maintainable. Keep the SOLID Principles in mind, and use them as a guide when refactoring your code. Keep your tests passing, and you'll know that your code still meets the needs of your business.

Finally, look at ORM frameworks such as NHibernate and Entity Framework to help accelerate your development. Offloading your data access functionality to a framework like this can make development faster and less prone to defects.

Integration Testing

➤ How integration tests are different from unit tests and why integration tests are important

➤ Why it's important to start writing and running integration tests early

➤ How to write an automated integration test with NUnit and where the practice deviates from writing unit tests with NUnit

➤ What end-to-end tests are and why they are critical to the success of an application development effort

➤ How to manage the external resources that are used by integration and end-to-end tests

➤ When and how integration and end-to-end tests should be run

The point of unit tests in TDD is to drive the development of discrete components and sections of an application. To that end, it's important to keep the unit tests and the code they exercise isolated from other components or external resources. In fact, tests that test the same unit of functionality should be isolated from each other. This means that these tests can be run in any order or combination and produce the same predictable results. This is necessary to ensure that the application's individual components are being developed in a simple, loosely coupled, and complete manner. The isolation of unit tests also makes it easier to diagnose and correct defects that cause tests to fail.

There comes a time, however, when an application's components must be combined. Ensuring that these various parts come together correctly is the job of integration tests. Integration tests verify that the various components and external resources of the application you are developing work together correctly.

INTEGRATE EARLY; INTEGRATE OFTEN

When using TDD, classes and methods are developed based on tests. Specifically, they are developed based on the idea that the tests mirror the specifications and functional requirements. When you write enough code to make all the tests pass, your class and/or method meets all the specifications and requirements. Other classes, external resources, and other components of the application are mocked and stubbed to allow the code you are testing to be tested in isolation. The kind of testing ensures the quality of the individual classes and components.

Because of this concept of isolation, true TDD unit tests by definition guarantee quality only up to the edge of the current class or method. This results in a series of seams that exist between the classes, components, and external resources used by the application as a whole. These seams are defined by the interfaces provided by the various classes, components, and external resources. Even when an interface seems clear in its intent, problems can still arise when the time comes to join two or more pieces of software to form an application. You should ensure that these dependencies are mocked and stubbed correctly. However, it is still possible for errors and defects to be introduced. Perhaps the input being provided to a method isn't what was expected. Maybe a method's output is not what the consuming class wants. In many scenarios, classes, components, and resources are well designed and have well-written unit tests that all pass. Yet, these classes, components, and external resources don't function as expected when they are linked. Many of these problems can be mitigated with good design and communication. But even in the most optimal situations, integration issues can still arise. Only by testing the integration of these components, classes, and external resources can you be sure that the seams of the application you are developing are solid and dependable.

An integration test is a test designed to target the various seams in an application and ensure that the pieces of the application work together correctly. They are similar to unit tests in that the same automated unit testing framework can (and should) be used to create them. They differ in that unlike unit tests, which use mocks to isolate specific methods and classes under test, integration tests cover all the application code between the method that the integration test was written for, all the way to the lowest level of the system, usually the data store.

As important as integration testing is, many developers are content to leave it until the end of the project. This is a mistake. Many software developers whose experience predates the emergence of TDD (and even many others) can tell you at least one horror story about a long night spent before an application's launch or deployment to QA trying to figure out why two or more components of a larger system simply refused to work together. Clearly, this schism was unanticipated, and in many cases the development team was forced to pull an all-nighter to diagnose and correct the problem. Many times the solution was a patch or shim. I saw one that was literally designed and drawn on the back of a pizza box. These patches and shims (which in most cases were created without any documentation to describe them) usually fixed the symptoms. But what most developers didn't realize, or want to talk about, was that the underlying problem still existed. It was just hiding, waiting for an unsuspecting junior developer who was assigned to maintain the application.

The good news is that it doesn't have to be this way. In fact, it really shouldn't be this way. These late-night hack sessions can easily be avoided if the development team starts automated integration testing early in the project and maintains it throughout the development cycle.

Creating automated integration tests early in the development cycle and running them on a consistent schedule will help you find and fix errors that develop between the seams of the classes, components, and external resources that comprise your application. If an automated integration test fails, you'll know right away that an issue has developed along one of these seams in your application, not in two months during deployment. Running them regularly, say as part of your CI process, will provide you with a short list of suspects when a defect is introduced into the application.

In cases where you are working in brownfield development (you are maintaining, extending, or enhancing an existing application) without existing unit tests, integration tests may be the only option available for automated testing if practices such as dependency injection were not employed in the application design or coding practices up front. On these older projects, particularly if they have large code bases or are already in production, it is usually economically unfeasible to reengineer the code base to introduce the dependency injection that would allow true unit testing. In these cases, remember that any testing (even integration testing) is better than no testing at all.

As you continue to develop and enhance these larger existing applications, you should attempt to introduce the techniques and methods that will make it possible to unit-test sections of the application. A full-scale rewrite of the application may be impossible, but you should work to improve the application from within whenever you can.

WRITING INTEGRATION TESTS

Writing integration tests is similar to writing unit tests. In fact, you will use a lot of the same frameworks to write your integration tests that you use to write your unit tests. The difference is that when you write integration tests, the goal is not necessarily to test the individual units of code. The goal of integration testing is to test the seams between the individual pieces of code. This means that the isolation rule that I talked about previously at length no longer applies. Well, that's not exactly true; the tests are isolated by the seam or seams they are testing, but they interact with several different classes and components — perhaps even an external resource. The goal of integration tests is to make sure that these different components all work together.

In practice, this means that at some point your integration tests will have to interact with some external resources. Your tests could read and write data to a database. Your tests could call a web service. Your tests could interact with files or folders on the hard drive. Because of this, it's important that you have access to an environment with test versions of all these resources over which you can exercise some measure of control. Before each test you need to reset the environment to a consistent pretest state. If you added or changed data in a database, you need to either remove it or put it back the way it was. If you call a web service, you need a test version of that service that responds consistently and correctly based on the input you pass to it. You need to be sure that you can put the file system back in order and undo any changes your tests have caused.

How to Manage the Database

One thing unit tests, integration tests, and end-to-end tests have in common is that they expect their environment to be in a specific state at the beginning. For unit tests this is easy, because the dependency on external resources is removed through dependency injection and mocking. For integration tests and end-to-end tests this is little more complicated, because external resources are an integral part of these tests.

The external resource most commonly used by integration tests and end-to-end tests is a database. The need to have a consistent starting environment for integration and end-to-end tests means that before these tests are run, the data in the database must be placed in a specific state. In the example used in this chapter this is an easy task; the configuration used by Fluent NHibernate for my integration test burns down and rebuilds the database for each test run. The efficiency of this approach is debatable, but you can be assured that your database is always in a consistent state when the test is run.

In cases where you are not using an ORM, or when the burn down/rebuild approach is impractical, you need to build some sort of rollback action into your test to ensure that your tests always run in a consistent environment. This can take a couple different forms. In many cases the logical place and time to perform this database cleanup is during the initialization of the test. This ensures that your environment is always in the correct state to execute your tests.

In some cases it may be easier and more practical to run a reset script or stored procedure at the end of your test. In these cases you want to be sure to structure your test so that this script or procedure runs every time the test is run, regardless of the test's success or failure. In these cases, you would need to run this script as soon as you have retrieved the data you need to validate the test, but before you begin the actual validation. This is because NUnit, and most unit-testing frameworks, end execution of the test on the first failed assertion. This means that if you wait to perform the database cleanup until after all the assertions are complete, the cleanup will not happen if the test fails.

How to Write Integration Tests

In the previous chapter I started developing the core of what will ultimately evolve into the data access layer for the OSIM application. Recall that the current implementation was written only to make the tests (and_saving_an_invalid_item_type.then_an_argument_null_exception_should_ be_raised and and_saving_a_valid_item_type.then_a_valid_item_type_id_should_be_ returned) pass.

These are unit tests and are designed to focus solely on the code in the Save method of a class that implements the IItemTypeRepository interface. This particular implementation of the IItemTypeRepository interface uses Fluent NHibernate to perform its data access. As a result, the Save method is ultimately dependent on an instance of one object that implements Fluent NHibernate's ISessionFactory interface, as well as an instance of an object that implements Fluent NHibernate's ISession interface. To keep the unit tests isolated (ensuring that they test only the code in the Save method of this implementation of IItemTypeRepository) you can pass in mock objects that implement ISessionFactory and ISession interfaces. I will show you how to provide these mocked objects with stubs for methods defined by the interfaces as needed. In the end, the code in the Save method is tested, but I haven't verified that the implementation of IItemTypeRepository can actually save an instance of the ItemType class to the database.

Reviewing the ItemTypeRepository

In truth, `ItemTypeRepository` (the implementation of `IItemTypeRepository`) will not save an instance of the `ItemType` class to the database. By way of review, this is code for the current implementation of `ItemTypeRepository`:

```csharp
using System;
using NHibernate;
using OSIM.Core.Entities;

namespace OSIM.Persistence
{
    public interface IItemTypeRepository
    {
        int Save(ItemType itemType);
        ItemType GetById(int id);
    }

    public class ItemTypeRepository : IItemTypeRepository
    {
        private ISessionFactory _sessionFactory;

        public ItemTypeRepository(ISessionFactory sessionFactory)
        {
            _sessionFactory = sessionFactory;
        }

        public int Save(ItemType itemType)
        {
            int id;
            using (var session = _sessionFactory.OpenSession())
            {
                id = (int) session.Save(itemType);
                session.Flush();
            }
            return id;
        }

        public ItemType GetById(int id)
        {
            using (var session = _sessionFactory.OpenSession())
            {
                return session.Get<ItemType>(id);
            }
        }
    }
}
```

ItemTypeRepository.cs

You may notice that I've added a new method since the preceding chapter. `GetById` enables consumers of `ItemTypeRepository` to retrieve an instance of an `ItemType` by supplying the ID, which is the primary key for the `ItemType` data table in the database. Specifying the primary key for an entity is covered later in this chapter, in the section on Fluent NHibernate mappings. The code to call the Fluent NHibernate session to get an `ItemType` by ID in the code listed above is trivial, so I won't spend time describing it. Fluent NHibernate does have facilities to search for entities by fields other than the primary key, but that is beyond the scope of this book. Please refer to the Fluent NHibernate documentation for details on search criteria.

Right now, `ItemTypeRepository` has only one implementation of a constructor:

```
public ItemTypeRepository(ISessionFactory sessionFactory)
{
    _sessionFactory = sessionFactory;
}
```

ItemTypeRepository.cs

This constructor takes an instance of `ISessionFactory` as the sole parameter. Right now it is being used to pass in the mocked instance of `ISessionFactory`. For the purposes of integration, you need to somehow provide an object that is a working implementation of the `ISessionFactory` interface. You have a variety of ways to provide an implementation of the `ISessionFactory` interface to the `ItemTypeRepository` upon creation. I prefer to use Ninject, which was covered in Chapter 5 to handle class instantiation and dependency resolution. There's no reason you can't use it to provide a correctly created and configured instance of `ISessionFactory` to each `ItemTypeRepository` at the time the `ItemTypeRepository` is created.

FIGURE 8-1

Adding Ninject for Dependency Injection

To use Ninject to create the `ItemTypeRepository` and its dependencies, including an instance of `ISessionFactory`, first you need to create a module class for the `OSIM.IntegrationTests` project. Call this new class `IntegrationTestsModule`, as shown in Figure 8-1.

To use Ninject, you need to add a reference to the Ninject assembly in the `OSIM.IntegrationTests` project, as shown in Figure 8-2.

After you add the Ninject library to the `OSIM.IntegrationTests` project, you can start working on the `IntegrationTestsModule` class. The first step is to add a `using` statement to the `IntegrationTestModule.cs` file for the `OSIM.Core.Persistence` namespace:

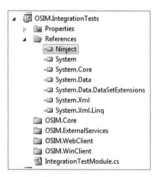

FIGURE 8-2

```
using OSIM.Core.Persistence;
```

IntegrationTestModule.cs

Next you need to add a reference to the NHibernate assembly to the `OSIM.IntegrationTests` project, as shown in Figure 8-3.

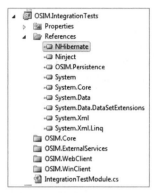

FIGURE 8-3

You also need to add a reference to the NHibernate namespace:

```
using NHibernate;
```

IntegrationTestModule.cs

Last, you need to add a using statement for the Ninject.Modules namespace and change the definition of IntegrationTestModule to inherit from the NinjectModule base class provided by Ninject. After that, the contents of the IntegrationTestModule.cs file should look like this:

```
using NHibernate;
using Ninject.Modules;
using OSIM.Core.Persistence;

namespace OSIM.IntegrationTests
{
    public class IntegrationTestModule : NinjectModule
    {

    }
}
```

IntegrationTestModule.cs

Right now IntegrationTestModule won't compile. NinjectModule has an abstract method called Load that you need to implement:

```
public class IntegrationTestModule : NinjectModule
{
    public override void Load()
    {
        throw new NotImplementedException();
    }
}
```

IntegrationTestModule.cs

The application will compile now, but if you were to try to use the `IntegrationTestModule` to build an instance of `ItemTypeRepository` — or anything, for that matter — a `NotImplementedException` would be thrown. You need to add some binding rules to this module so that it can create an instance of the `ItemTypeRepository` class when Ninject is asked for an instance of `IItemTypeRepository`. The first rule is easy; when Ninject is asked for an instance of `IItemTypeRepository`, an instance of `ItemTypeRepository` should be returned:

```
public override void Load()
{
    Bind<IItemTypeRepository>().To<ItemTypeRepository>();
}
```

IntegrationTestModule.cs

The next step is more complex. You can't just bind an instance of the `SessionFactory` class to the `ISessionFactory` interface. Fluent NHibernate doesn't provide an implementation of a class that implements `ISessionFactory` that you can instantiate in code. You need to invoke the Fluent NHibernate static class `Fluently` by providing it with a set of configuration information that Fluent NHibernate can use to create an instance of an object that implements the `ISessionFactory` interface.

In this example I want to use a Ninject provider. A provider is a class whose job is to create and return an object that implements a specific interface. Providers also enable developers to instantiate objects to define instantiation rules that are more complex than simply stating "If I ask for X, give me Y." The rules for instantiating a configured instance of `ISessionFactory` definitely fall into this category.

The first step is to add a binding rule to the `Load` method of the `IntegrationTestModule` that instructs Ninject to utilize the specified provider when satisfying a request for the interface in question:

```
public override void Load()
{
    Bind<IItemTypeRepository>().To<ItemTypeRepository>();
    Bind<ISessionFactory>().ToProvider
       (new IntegrationTestSessionFactoryProvider());
}
```

IntegrationTestModule.cs

You need to create an instance of `IntegrationTestSessionFactoryProvider`. For the sake of simplicity, you can just create this class in the `IntegrationTestModule.cs` file and place it after the definition of `IntegrationTestModule`. Technically, the `IntegrationTestSessionFactoryProvider` class needs to implement the `IProvider` interface that Ninject provides. But an easier way to build this class than implementing the `IProvider` interface is to inherit from the `Provider<T>` base class, also provided by Ninject. To use this base class, you need to add another `using` statement to the `IntegrationTestModule.cs` file:

```
using Ninject.Activation;
```

IntegrationTestModule.cs

You also need to add a reference to the OSIM.Core project and add a using statement to bring in the namespace where ItemType is located:

```
using OSIM.Core.Entities;
```

IntegrationTestModule.cs

Next, you need to define the IntegrationTestSessionFactoryProvider class:

```
public class IntegrationTestSessionFactoryProvider : Provider<ISessoinFactory>
{
}
```

IntegrationTestModule.cs

The Provider base class defines an abstract method called CreateInstance, for which you need to supply an implementation:

```
public class IntegrationTestSessionFactoryProvider : Provider<ISessionFactory>
{
    protected override ISessionFactory CreateInstance(IContext context)
    {
        throw new NotImplementedException();
    }
}
```

IntegrationTestModule.cs

The IntegrationTestModule will provide Ninject with the rules and information necessary to create instances of your classes and complete object graphs for running integration tests. For production, you want to use Ninject modules that create actual production dependencies. I have included a file in the Persistence folder of the OSIM.Core project with a sample of what a production Ninject module might look like.

Creating the Fluent NHibernate Configuration

You need to call the Fluent NHibernate Fluently static class and provide the necessary configuration information to access a database:

```
public class IntegrationTestSessionFactoryProvider : Provider<ISessionFactory>
{
    protected override ISessionFactory CreateInstance(IContext context)
    {
        var sessionFactory = Fluently.Configure()
            .Database(MsSqlConfiguration.MsSql2008
                .ConnectionString(c => c.Is(ConfigurationManager.AppSettings
                ["localDb"])).ShowSql())
            .Mappings(m => m.FluentMappings.AddFromAssemblyOf<ItemTypeMap>()
```

```
                .ExportTo(@"C:\Temp"))
            .ExposeConfiguration(cfg => new SchemaExport(cfg).Create(true, true))
            .BuildSessionFactory();

        return sessionFactory;
    }
}
```

IntegrationTestModule.cs

This code bears some explanation. As mentioned in Chapter 7, Fluent NHibernate uses an object that implements the `ISession` interface to access the database. This implementation of `ISession` is provided by `ISessionFactory`. To get an instance of an object that implements `ISessionFactory`, you need to use the Fluent NHibernate `Fluently.Configure` API. Luckily, these API calls are all implemented as extension methods, which makes creating this `ISessionFactory` implementation a bit easier.

The process starts by calling the `Fluently.Configure` method. You add a call to the extension method `Database` to the call to `Configure`. The `Database` method tells Fluent NHibernate where the database is located and what kind of DBMS it is using. In this case, I am using an instance of Microsoft SQL Server 2008. The connection string is stored in the AppSettings section of my configuration file under the key `localDb`.

Next you need to tell Fluent NHibernate where the mappings for the entity objects are located. I'll touch on NHibernate mappings later in this chapter, but in this case I'm telling Fluent NHibernate that the mappings are located in the same assembly that the `ItemTypeMap` class is defined in. The `ItemTypeMap` class is the Fluent NHibernate mapping class for the `ItemType` class. This class doesn't exist yet, but it will be created in the `OSIM.Core` project.

The `ExportTo` method instructs Fluent NHibernate to export the mapping information to a file in the Temp directory on the C drive. This file can be very helpful if the object-to-data table mappings that Fluent NHibernate generates are incorrect or are not what you expected.

I use the call to the `ExposeConfiguration` method to destroy and regenerate my database schema, which is managed by the call to the `Create` method of a newly created `SchemaExport` object. This is very helpful for integration tests because object structures often change during development, and having to manually alter the database table to store the data for these classes can be tedious. It also ensures that you are always working with a new, clean database schema instance. This means that you have less work to do with respect to resetting your testing environment. When moving to production, you want to be sure that you remove the call to `ExposeConfiguration`, or you risk dropping your production database. The `ExposeConfiguration` method and the `SchemaExport` classes are very powerful. You should consult the Fluent NHibernate documentation to fully understand their usage beyond this example.

`BuildSchemaFactory` is the final call. It starts the process to create the `ISessionFactory` instance based on the configuration information you have provided.

Because the integration test will store data in a database, you need to create a development database. This project uses Microsoft SQL Server 2008 R2 as the DBMS. Create a database called

OSIM.Dev and accept all the normal defaults for its creation, as shown in Figure 8-4.

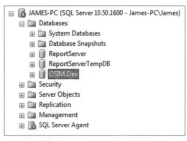

Creating the Fluent NHibernate Mapping

The next step is to create the object-to-data-table mapping for the ItemType class. Fluent NHibernate, like all ORM frameworks, requires a mapping of some sort that instructs the ORM how to translate the public fields in a class to fields in a data table. Traditional NHibernate uses XML files, which can be difficult to understand and prone to defects. Fluent

FIGURE 8-4

NHibernate is an extension to the NHibernate framework that enables developers to create these mappings in C# or VB.NET. This is a major benefit over traditional NHibernate XML mappings. For one thing, most developers are more familiar and comfortable with C# or VB.NET. Working in the language you are more comfortable with and skilled in is always preferable. And because the mapping files are compiled as opposed to being read at runtime, fewer errors occur in Fluent NHibernate mappings.

The location of these mappings is important. Although they are dependent on the entity types in the OSIM application, they are technically part of the persistence layer. For that reason, I like to keep them with the repository and other persistence logic in the OSIM.Core project.

A question you might be asking yourself right now is "Why is he putting the persistence logic in the core domain project?" As developers we're taught to separate out all the pieces of the application into separate assemblies. The reason given for this need for separation is that when a change is made one assembly can easily be swapped in for another. In fact this ad hoc "plug-and-play" ability with assemblies is a bit overstated. In many cases, not matter how much separation and abstraction you introduce into your application code base, changes to one assembly almost always require changes in most, if not all, of the other assemblies.

What does this have to do with keeping the persistence logic in the core domain project? The answer is simplicity. Yes, applications should be architected to keep divergent functions separate, such as data access and presentation. But this, along with all architectural choices comes with a cost. I see the value of keeping my presentation logic separate from my domain services as being greater than the cost (in complexity) that I incur by separating them. For a small departmental application, like the OSIM application in the example, I don't see the benefit of separating the domain services and the persistence logic as outweighing the cost (again, in complexity) that I incur by separating them.

True, this application could be architected to keep the persistence logic in its own separate assembly. But doing this would require other changes in the architecture to remove the potential for circular dependencies. And in large

> *applications, where different components will need to be scaled at different rates, it's important to keep these separate. But most applications are small departmental applications that, even in a large enterprise are only going to be deployed to a handful of users. In these cases, pragmatism wins out. I can always refactor the application if I need to pull the persistence, or any other layer for that matter out into its own assembly.*
>
> *The other argument you'll see is that it makes switching from one persistence framework to another more difficult. I view this as a non-starter; if someone came to me and wanted to do this I would need to have a pretty good reason for this change for me to be supportive. The primary issue being that no matter how separated your persistence layer is from the rest of your application, changing persistence framework isn't as simple as changing the batteries in a remote control; you are going to have to do some major renovation. Not just to accommodate the new API, but to handle changes between the frameworks for things like transactional support and connection pooling. There's an old adage I like to remind my clients and developers when issues like these come up; if it ain't broke, don't fix it!*

You start by creating a folder in the `Persistence` folder of the `OSIM.Core` project called `Mappings`, as shown in Figure 8-5.

Next you create a class in the `Mappings` folder called `ItemTypeMap`, as shown in Figure 8-6.

FIGURE 8-5

FIGURE 8-6

Visual Studio creates a stub class in the `ItemTypeMap.cs` file:

```
namespace OSIM.Core.Persistence.Mappings
{
    public class ItemTypeMap
    {

    }
}
```

ItemTypeMap.cs

To make this a Fluent NHibernate mapping class, you need to add `using` statements for the `OSIM.Core.Entities` namespace (where the declaration of `ItemType` is located) and the `FluentNHibernate.Mapping` namespace (where the definitions of the `FluentNHibernate` mapping classes are located). Then you need to change the declaration of the `ItemTypeMap` class so that it inherits from the `ClassMap<T>` Fluent NHibernate base class. `ClassMap<T>` is a generalized class, and you need to pass in the type that you want this class to be (a map) — in this case, `ItemType` — as the generic type parameter:

```
using FluentNHibernate.Mapping;
using OSIM.Core.Entities;

namespace OSIM.Persistence.Mappings
{
    public class ItemTypeMap : ClassMap<ItemType>
    {

    }
}
```

ItemTypeMap.cs

Fluent NHibernate expects a default constructor in every mapping class that provides the mapping information for the entity that is being mapped by the mapping class. Here's how you add that to `ItemTypeMap`:

```
public class ItemTypeMap : ClassMap<ItemType>
{
    public ItemTypeMap()
    {

    }
}
```

ItemTypeMap.cs

Before you create the mapping for `ItemType`, let's revisit the definition of that class. Here is the current definition of `ItemType`:

```
namespace OSIM.Core.Entities
{
    public class ItemType
    {
        public virtual int Id { get; set; }
    }
}
```

ItemTypeMap.cs

Right now, there's not much to it. In fact, the only field in `ItemType` is the `Id` field, which serves as the entity's primary key. The reason for this somewhat anemic definition is that the current unit tests do not call for any other fields in the definition of ItemType. For the purposes of this example, though, you add a name field, because it makes this example a bit more meaningful:

```
namespace OSIM.Core.Entities
{
    public class ItemType
    {
        public virtual int Id { get; set; }
        public virtual string Name { get; set; }
    }
}
```

ItemTypeMap.cs

At this point, you might be wondering why these fields are declared as virtual. The short explanation is that Fluent NHibernate uses reflection as part of its process when creating data table schemas, and storing and reading data from the database. Without declaring these fields as virtual, Fluent NHibernate wouldn't be able to do its magic.

Inevitably, even if you've been working with Fluent NHibernate for some time, you will occasionally forget about this requirement. A good rule of thumb is that if you get a mapping error that doesn't seem to make sense, first check to make sure that all the public members of the class that you are mapping are declared as virtual members. That usually is the problem.

It's finally time to create the mapping for ItemType. Returning to the ItemTypeMap class, you add the mapping rules for Id and Name to the default constructor for ItemTypeMap:

```
public class ItemTypeMap : ClassMap<ItemType>
{
    public ItemTypeMap()
    {
        Id(x => x.Id);
        Map(x => x.Name);
    }
}
```

ItemTypeMap.cs

Id and Map are the two most commonly used Fluent NHibernate mapping commands. Id specifies in which field or fields in the entity class map to the primary key of the table the data will be stored. The Map command simply tells Fluent NHibernate to map that field in the entity class to a field of the same name and type in the data table. The result of this mapping class is the creation of a table called ItemTypes with two columns: Id (which is the primary key) and Name. There are extensions for things such as relationships and indexes, which will be used later in the project. Also, some complex commands allow you to do things such as store two similar types in the same table and create complex relationships. You can even store data in tables or fields where the name of the table or field in the database does not match the class or field name in the application code. This is all covered in the Fluent NHibernate documentation.

Creating the Integration Test

The next step is to put the connection string for the database in a configuration file. First, you add an `app.config` file to the `OSIM.IntegrationTests` project, as shown in Figure 8-7.

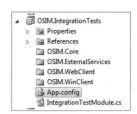

FIGURE 8-7

The reason this file is created in the `OSIM.IntegrationTests` project is because when I run this integration test, the `OSIM.IntegrationTests` assembly becomes the execution context. Therefore, the .NET runtime, via the NUnit test runner, looks for a configuration file for the `OSIM.IntegrationTests` assembly. If it can't find it, a runtime error occurs.

Next you create an `appSettings` section to the `App.config` file and put a key called `localDb` in the `appSettings` section with the connection string for the `OSIM.Dev` database:

```xml
<?xml version="1.0" encoding="utf-8" ?>
<configuration>
  <appSettings>
    <add key="localDb" value="Data Source=JAMES-PC;Initial Catalog=OSIM.Dev;
        Integrated Security=True"/>
  </appSettings>
</configuration>
```

App.config

Now that all the database and ORM work is done, you can finally get around to writing your test. Unlike with unit tests, you don't care so much about seeing the test fail first; in fact, in many cases the test passes right away. This is because although unit tests are designed to drive development (they demonstrate that code needs to be written), the purpose of integration tests is verification. (You already expect the code to exist and work; you just want to verify this expectation.)

If you don't have an `OSIM.Core.Persistence` folder in your `OSIM.IntegrationTests` project yet, go ahead and add one, as shown in Figure 8-8.

Now that you have a location for your `ItemTypeRepository` tests, you create a new `cs` file to store the test classes, as shown in Figure 8-9.

FIGURE 8-8

FIGURE 8-9

Visual Studio creates its normal stub class in the `ItemTypeRepositoryTests.cs` file:

```
namespace OSIM.IntegrationTests.OSIM.Persistence
{
    public class ItemTypeRepositoryTests
    {

    }
}
```

ItemTypeRepositoryTests.cs

Per the BDD naming style employed in this project, change the name of the `ItemTypeRepositoryTests` class to `when_using_the_item_type_repository`, and have it inherit from the `Specification` base class. For this class to compile, you also need to add references to the `OSIM.UnitTests` project as well as the `NBehave.Spec.NUnit` and `NBehave.Spec.Framework` assemblies. You also need to add a `using` statement to bring in the `OSIM.UnitTests` namespace:

```
using OSIM.UnitTests;

namespace OSIM.IntegrationTests.OSIM.Persistence
{
    public class when_using_the_item_type_repository : Specification
    {

    }
}
```

ItemTypeRepositoryTests.cs

Like the `when_working_with_the_item_type_repository` class created for the unit tests in the preceding chapter, this class serves two purposes. Its definition helps you build a BDD-style name for your test that completely and correctly describes the action you're testing. It also provides a base class where you can perform common setup steps that will be needed by all the integration tests for `ItemTypeRepository`. For now, you leave the `when_using_the_item_type_repository` class and build the class that will contain the actual integration test.

Another difference between integration and unit tests is that whereas unit tests should be focused on one step or piece of functionality at a time, it's perfectly acceptable for integration tests to test several steps at once. This current test is a good example. You want to verify that you can write to and read from the database with `ItemTypeRepository`. In an automated test you can't verify that you can read from the database without adding something to it, and you can't verify that you can write to the database without reading back the value to make sure it was saved correctly.

Because of this, the test names of the integration tests, including the one you're about to write for the `ItemTypeRepository`, are a bit less focused than the names of the unit tests. In this case, the name of the test class — `and_attempting_to_save_and_read_a_value_from_a_datastore` — describes both actions you must perform to ensure that `ItemTypeRepository` is working correctly:

```
public class and_attempting_to_save_and_read_a_value_from_the_datastore :
    when_using_the_item_type_repository
{

}
```

ItemTypeRepositoryTests.cs

The test method name describes the expected output of both of these steps:

```
[Test]
public void then_the_item_type_saved_to_the_database_should_equal_the_item_type
_retrieved()
{

}
```

ItemTypeRepositoryTests.cs

Because you haven't referenced the NUnit assembly in the `OSIM.IntegrationTests` project, do that now, as shown in Figure 8-10.

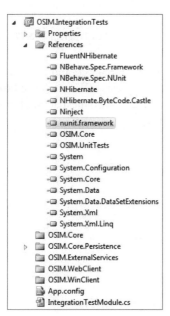

FIGURE 8-10

You also need to add a `using` statement to bring the `NUnit.Framework` namespaces into the `ItemTypeRepositoryTests.cs` file:

```
using NUnit.Framework;
```

ItemTypeRepositoryTests.cs

The list of steps to perform an integration test is a little longer and more involved than the steps to perform a unit test. This is logical, because the integration test covers a wider breadth of application functionality. In essence you know that you want to create and populate an `ItemType` object, store it in the database, retrieve that same item type into a different instance of `ItemType`, and then verify that the fields match. The code for the `then_the_item_type_saved_to_the_database_should_equal_the_item_type_retrieved` method is actually pretty simple. You just want to iterate through the fields on the retrieved (actual) instance of `ItemType` and make sure that the values match the corresponding values on the stored (expected) instance of the `ItemType` object:

```
[Test]
public void
then_the_item_type_saved_to_the_database_should_equal_the_item_type_retrieved()
{
    _result.Id.ShouldEqual(_expected.Id);
    _result.Name.ShouldEqual(_expected.Name);
}
```

ItemTypeRepositoryTests.cs

To complete this code so that it compiles, you need to add declarations of `_expected` and `_result` to the `and_attempting_to_save_and_read_a_value_from_the_datastore` class. You also need to add `using` statements for the `NBehave.Spec.NUnit` and `OSIM.Core.Entities` namespaces. Here is the complete content of the `ItemTypeRepository.cs` file to this point:

```
using NBehave.Spec.NUnit;
using NUnit.Framework;
using OSIM.Core.Entities;
using OSIM.UnitTests;

namespace OSIM.IntegrationTests.OSIM.Persistence
{
    public class when_using_the_item_type_repository : Specification
    {

    }

    public class and_attempting_to_save_and_read_a_value_from_the_datastore :
        when_using_the_item_type_repository
    {
        private ItemType _expected;
        private ItemType _result;

        [Test]
```

```
        public void
then_the_item_type_saved_to_the_database_should_equal_the_item_type_retrieved()
        {
            _result.Id.ShouldEqual(_expected.Id);
            _result.Name.ShouldEqual(_expected.Name);
        }
    }
}
```

The next step I like to take is to write the `Because_of` method for the test. In this case you need to save an instance of the `ItemType` class to the database using the `ItemTypeRepository`. Then, using the same `ItemTypeRepository`, retrieve the same data you just saved to the database (using the `Id` value returned by `ItemTypeRepository`) into a different instance of `ItemType`, which is represented by the `_result` member variable:

```
protected override void Because_of()
{
    var itemTypeId = _itemTypeRepository.Save(_expected);
    _result = _itemTypeRepository.GetById(itemTypeId);
}
```

You also need to add a `using` statement to import the `OSIM.Core.Persistence` namespace:

```
using OSIM.Core.Persistence;
```

All that's left is to write the `Establish_context` method. The first task in the `Establish_context` method is to create an instance of `ItemTypeRepository` and assign it to the `_itemTypeRepository` member variable. Because Ninject is the dependency injection framework in this example, you need to create an instance of Ninject's standard kernel and provide it with an instance of the `IntegrationTestModule` class. It contains the rules for creating an `ItemTypeRepository` for integration testing:

```
private StandardKernel _kernel;

protected override void Establish_context()
{
    base.Establish_context();
    _kernel = new StandardKernel(new IntegrationTestModule());

}
```

To use the Ninject Standard Kernel, you need to add a `using` statement for the `Ninject` namespace:

```
using Ninject;
```

Now you need to ask Ninject for an instance of a class that implements the `IItemTypeRepository` interface. When you instantiated the `StandardKernel` object for the `_kernel` member variable, you provided it with an instance of the `IntegrationTestModule` class. The `IntegrationTestModule` class has all the rules and steps Ninject needs to create an instance of a class that implements the `IItemTypeRepository` interface for purposes of integration testing. You simply need to ask the `_kernel` object for an object that implements the `IItemTypeRepository` interface. Ninject takes care of all the creation steps:

```
protected override void Establish_context()
{
    base.Establish_context();

    _kernel = new StandardKernel(new IntegrationTestModule());
    _itemTypeRepository = _kernel.Get<IItemTypeRepository>();
}
```

Before moving forward, let's stop and take a look at the current code from a pragmatic point of view. The `ItemTypeRepository.cs` file contains the class `when_using_the_item_type_repository`, which `and_attempting_to_save_and_read_a_value_from_the_datastore` inherits. It's reasonable to assume that all classes that perform integration testing for `ItemTypeRepository` will inherit in some way from the `when_using_the_item_type_repository` class. It's also reasonable to assume that most (if not all) classes that perform integration testing on the `ItemTypeRepository` class will need an instance of an object that implements the `IItemTypeRepository` interface that is the same as the other `ItemTypeRepository` test classes. Therefore, it would make sense to move the declaration of the `_kernel` and `_itemTypeRepository` member variables, as well as the code that instantiates them, to the `when_using_the_item_type_repository` base class.

After moving the declarations and creating an `Establish_context` method in the `when_using_the_item_type_repository` class to do this, the `when_using_the_item_type_repository` and `and_attempting_to_save_and_read_a_value_from_the_datastore` classes should look like this:

```
public class when_using_the_item_type_repository : Specification
{
    protected IItemTypeRepository _itemTypeRepository;
    protected StandardKernel _kernel;

    protected override void Establish_context()
    {
        base.Establish_context();

        _kernel = new StandardKernel(new IntegrationTestModule());
```

```
            _itemTypeRepository = _kernel.Get<IItemTypeRepository>();
        }
    }

    public class and_attempting_to_save_and_read_a_value_from_the_datastore :
    when_using_the_item_type_repository
    {
        private ItemType _expected;
        private ItemType _result;

        protected override void Establish_context()
        {
            base.Establish_context();
        }

        protected override void Because_of()
        {
            var itemTypeId = _itemTypeRepository.Save(_expected);
            _result = _itemTypeRepository.GetById(itemTypeId);
        }

        [Test]
        public void then_the_item_type_saved_to_the_database_should_equal_the_item_type
    _retrieved()
        {
            _result.Id.ShouldEqual(_expected.Id);
            _result.Name.ShouldEqual(_expected.Name);
        }
    }
}
```

ItemTypeRepositoryTests.cs

The last order of business before you run this test is to create an instance of the ItemType class for the _expected member variable, which you need to save to the database:

```
protected override void Establish_context()
{
    base.Establish_context();

    _expected = new ItemType {Name = Guid.NewGuid().ToString()};
}
```

ItemTypeRepositoryTests.cs

I like using Guids as string test data. It's easy to get a random value every time. And because it's always a new and different value, I don't have to worry about situations in which old data doesn't get cleaned out of the database for whatever reason, corrupting my test results. Of course, to use a Guid you need to add a using statement for the System namespace (if you don't already have one):

```
using System;
```

ItemTypeRepositoryTests.cs

All that's left is to run the test. As you can see from Figure 8-11, the test passes without your having to write additional code.

FIGURE 8-11

If I want further verification, I simply need to use my favorite database management tool (for this example I'm using SQL Management Studio) and look at the contents of my database and table (see Figure 8-12).

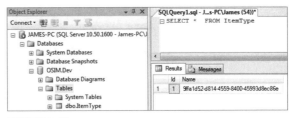

FIGURE 8-12

When I wrote my unit tests, I wrote the tests before I wrote the code. I could certainly have taken that same approach here. In reality, the only code I wrote was code to handle injecting an object that implements `ISessionFactory` into the `ItemTypeRepository` class, the Ninject module to handle the creation of said `ItemTypeRepository` class, and the Fluent NHibernate configuration to connect to the development database. The difference between the three activities I just described and the user stories and features that drive unit tests is that the functionality I needed to implement to make the integration test pass was not code that added business value. It was code that supported the code that adds business value.

That's not to say that this code and this functionality are unimportant. If users can't save their data to a data store and retrieve it later, the application itself is not as usable. But if you are writing an application to process mortgage payments or track inventory of prescription drugs, your business users are far more concerned with the business rules that are implemented in the application than what framework is used to store that information to a database, or what patterns are used to create the objects in the system.

Another reason I tend to write my integration test first is, frankly, habit. In my day job as a consultant, I supervise a lot of developers who are young and inexperienced. Even some of the seasoned veterans have not been exposed to concepts such as ORMs and IOC containers. In my function as a development lead, I want to make sure that these tools and concepts are adhered to. If I simply gave a developer with no experience in IOC containers the task of writing this integration test, they likely would hand-roll an object factory of some sort or, worse, create statically bound member variables. In this case, and in another situation, where integration tests vary from unit tests (at least for me), I want my developers, especially ones who are inexperienced with these new tools and techniques, to keep the usage of these tools and techniques in the front of their minds. When they write unit tests I prefer the opposite; they should only be thinking about meeting the immediate business need identified by the feature or user story. Any other concerns are secondary and can be dealt with via refactoring at the point of integration. When fastening together the pieces of the system, I want my teams to be sure they are using the correct glue.

End-to-End Integration Tests

The purpose of unit tests is to drive development of code by creating executable and automated tests that verify that the application addresses the business need as defined by the features and user stories. The purpose of integration tests is to ensure that the application's various components work together to form a larger application. An end-to-end test verifies that the application addresses all the requirements of a feature or user story and that the functionality is complete and correctly integrated. Unit tests cover a specific unit of business functionality, and integration tests cover the seams between components. End-to-end tests cover the entire system from as close as possible to the front end or user interface all the way through to the back-end data store, web service, or any other external dependencies the application may have.

End-to-end tests are very valuable for a couple of reasons. They verify the complete integration of the application across all layers. They also ensure that the needs of the feature or user story are being met in a more holistic manner.

Like unit and integration tests, end-to-end tests have some unique characteristics of their own. Any given test suite has relatively few end-to-end tests in comparison to the unit tests and integration tests. Unlike unit tests, which cover a specific small-business task, end-to-end tests target complete business work flows. Therefore, whereas a unit test has a very narrow focus, an end-to-end test covers a wide breadth of functionality. Unlike integration tests, end-to-end tests don't care about specific seams. In fact, they should be completely unaware that such seams exist. Most end-to-end tests should start by creating an instance of the closest possible access point to the user interface. If the user interface is something that can be used, such as is the case with ASP.NET MVC applications, applications written in WPF or Silverlight that utilize the MVVM pattern, or WCF/ASMX services, that should be the starting point for the end-to-end test. The end-to-end test then simply allows that object to call functionality that cascades down to the classes in the other layers. The end-to-end test does not care that an `ItemTypeRepository` was used. Its concern is that when a user supplies the correct information and invokes the same code as the Save button on an input form, the data is saved and a proper result is returned.

Keeping Various Types of Tests Apart

The entire test suite for your application will be composed of unit tests, integration tests, and end-to-end tests, and these tests all serve different purposes. Developers should run unit tests frequently. They should run integration tests less frequently, and end-to-end tests even less often. For purposes of managing what tests get run and how often, it's important to keep the various types of tests isolated from each other. To this end, I usually create two testing projects in my Visual Studio solution for each application: a unit test project and an integration test project (which also contains my end-to-end tests). Keeping them in separate projects, and therefore separate assemblies, enables me to have more control over when these tests are run. This will be covered in more detail in the next section.

WHEN AND HOW TO RUN INTEGRATION TESTS

Integration tests, especially end-to-end tests, can take much longer to run than unit tests, due to their need to interact with the application's external dependencies. The need to interact with these external dependencies can also cause issues if two or more developers attempt to run these tests concurrently. For these reasons, integration and end-to-end tests are not, and should not be, run as often as unit tests.

When being run by developers, integration and end-to-end tests should be run when the developers have completed or are close to completing a feature or user story. This is necessary to ensure that you have not introduced any defects into the application's current functionality. Some developers or development teams create a practice that developers need not run integration and end-to-end tests that do not relate to the work, function, or user story that the developer is working on at the time. This can be a fine practice, provided that the application is segmented to make it easy to determine which tests are germane and which tests don't need to be run. At the very least, these tests must be run before you commit any code to the main code repository.

Integration and end-to-end tests should also be run as part of a CI process. One of the purposes of a CI process is to ensure that all the various components and sections of an application integrate and function correctly before the application is released to the QA staff. This ensures that the QA staff does not spend time testing an application that has already been flagged as unworkable. Another benefit of running these tests as part of the CI process is that it does not tie up development resources while the tests are running. CI servers can execute long-running tests as part of the build process and report on which tests, if any, fail. In the meantime the development staff can continue working on other features or user stories. This is an attractive feature for teams who are working on applications where the integration and end-to-end tests can take a long time to run. Needless to say, any tests that fail as part of the CI process should become the top priority of the application development team. All other activities should be suspended until the build is in an "all green" state again.

SUMMARY

Integration tests are important to the quality of your application. Unit tests ensure that the individual components meet the business requirements as documented by the features and user stories. Integration tests ensure that these individual components work together correctly to create a functioning application.

When writing integration tests, you want to concentrate on the seams between the individual components in your application. In addition to the seams between the various internal components, you want to target the seams between your application and external resources such as databases, web services, file systems, and anything else that is not specifically a part of your application.

Like unit tests, integration tests expect to execute in an environment that is in a predictable state. Unlike unit tests, which rely on injected dependency objects and mocking to provide a stubbed environment, integration tests must use test versions of the actual external resources objects. As part of your integration test suite, you need to ensure that you are returning the test execution environment to a consistent state before the integration tests run.

Unit tests test the internal functioning of your application's individual components, and integration tests test the seams between the individual components of your application. End-to-end tests are a specialized type of integration test that verifies that the application code can execute entire business workflows based on the application's user stories. Your application test suite will contain many unit and integration tests, each of which will focus on a relatively small piece of functionality. By contrast, your application test suite will contain comparatively few end-to-end tests, each of which will cover a broader scope of functionality.

Integration and end-to-end tests take longer to execute than unit tests because of how they use non-mocked components and external resources. Due to this longer runtime, it's advisable for developers not to run integration and end-to-end tests as often as they run unit tests. Integration tests should be run periodically throughout the course of developing a feature or user story. End-to-end tests should be run before the developer commits the code to the main source repository branch. Integration tests, as well as end-to-end and unit tests, should be run as part of the development team's CI process. Any build with a failing test should be considered a failed build, and the development team's priority should shift to getting the tests and the build working again. The overarching goal is always to put quality software in front of the users. This can be done only with a successful CI process.

PART III
TDD Scenarios

TDD on the Web

by Jeff McWherter

WHAT'S IN THIS CHAPTER?

➤ TDD with Web Forms

➤ TDD with MVC

➤ TDD with JavaScript

Previous chapters have discussed tools and theory to describe exactly what test-driven development is. It's now time to apply this knowledge to practical examples and bring test-driven development to the world that many software developers live in: the web.

You might be thinking that web frameworks (primarily ASP.NET Web Forms) do not separate concerns very well. The single reasonability principal is something we have been very strict about not breaking while performing TDD. From C# or Visual Basic code mixed into the ASPX files, to common JavaScript functions being copied from page to page, many web frameworks don't follow many of the rules outlined in previous chapters. This chapter discusses patterns that will make it easier to test web applications, including frameworks that don't separate concerns very well. This chapter will start with ASP.NET Web Forms and move onto a fairly new Microsoft framework called ASP.NET MVC, you will learn the techniques required to not only make your web applications more testable, create them using TDD.

Entire books have been written about testing for the web, such as *Testing ASP.NET Web Applications* by Jeff McWherter and Ben Hall (Wrox, 2009, ISBN: 978-0-470-49664-0). This chapter summarizes the important points about this topic. By the end of this chapter, you will understand how to develop your web applications using TDD.

ASP.NET WEB FORMS

In January 2002, ASP.NET was released with version 1.0 of the .NET Framework. This release marked a major milestone for web developers using Microsoft technologies, allowing them to produce powerful web applications using languages such as Visual Basic.NET and C#. ASP .NET includes tools you can use to develop web applications quickly by taking advantage of built-in controls that take care of the basic create, read, update, and delete (CRUD) operations for you. Components that shipped with the ASP.NET framework enabled you to drag and drop controls into your applications. This functionality allowed for a quick development process. But during that process the architecture and testability of many applications were never considered. Because these web applications stayed in the field as developers moved on to different companies or projects, patch after patch was applied to applications developed in this way, and the cost to maintain them increased.

Although these issues still exist to this day, you can use some techniques and patterns to unit-test ASP.NET Web Form applications.

Web Form Organization

A Web Form is made up of two parts. The ASPX file contains HTML, CSS, JavaScript, and ASP.NET markup. The second part is the code-behind file, either a CS or VB file that contains the executable code. Let's take a moment to discuss what should be contained in these files.

ASPX Files

ASPX files are the view of your web application pages that the user sees. As such, no business logic should be contained within them. ASPX files should be clean and easy for web and graphic designers to read. Not everyone has the luxury of sending ASPX files to a designer, but when you do, you want the designer to be able to understand the files. Logic that accesses the database inside ASPX files not only violates the rules about separation of concern but also makes your code difficult for other people to read. Your ASPX files should not be littered with <% tags.

Code-Behind Files

You should think of code-behind files as the controller for what the view renders. Code-behind files hook into the ASP.NET page life cycle and have a tight dependency to the ASP.NET runtime, which can make testing these files difficult. Therefore, you should keep code-behind files as thin as possible so that they contain only "glue code." The default way that Visual Studio and ASP.NET Web Forms currently act encourages developers to store a large amount of logic in these files, which is actually in opposition to the patterns required for TDD.

 Glue code is code that does not contribute functionality to the application. The purpose of glue code is only to "glue" together parts of code that normally would be incompatible. Most of the time, due to its simplistic nature, glue code does not need to be tested.

One of the best ways within ASP.NET Web Forms to keep clean code-behind files and have a good separation of concern is to follow the model-view-presenter (MVP) design pattern, shown in Figure 9-1.

At its core the presenter acts as the middle layer, similar to the controller object within the model-view-controller (MVC) pattern, which is covered later in this chapter. The presenter retrieves the data, persists it, and then formats it for display in the view. The view is the interface that displays the data, and the model represents the data or the domain model. The MVP pattern has been around since the early '90s and is a popular method for following the SOLID design principles.

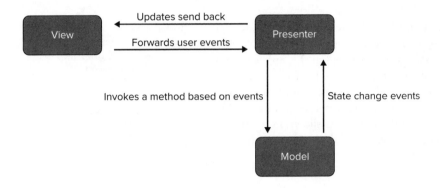

FIGURE 9-1

Implementing Test-Driven Development with MVP and Web Forms

This example creates an application that lists recently read books. You will be concerned with displaying the data to the user. Figure 9-2 shows what you will be building.

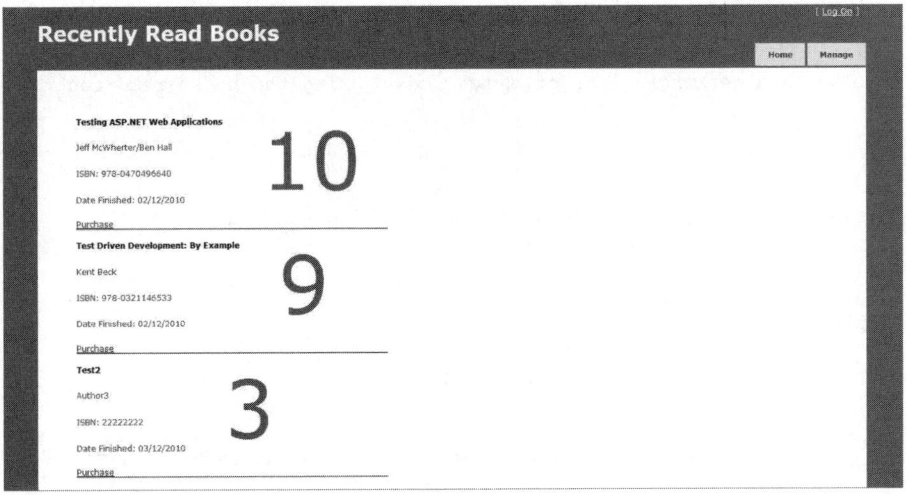

FIGURE 9-2

Project Layout

Before you begin creating your first test, you should start with the organization of the project. You create an ASP.NET web application and name it **Wrox.BooksRead.Web**. This name is created from a standard `Company.ProjectName.Component` naming schema. Keeping a project organized and clean will help with maintenance down the road. The key is to be consistent when naming your projects. Nothing fancy has been added to the `Wrox.BooksRead.Web` project; currently it is just a default ASP.NET web application.

Another Windows Class Library project, `Wrox.BooksRead.Tests`, also needs to be added. This project will hold your tests for the web application. Included in this application is a `Lib` folder that will hold the external binaries required for testing the `Wrox.BooksRead.Web` application. NUnit and Rhino Mocks (a popular mocking framework) also need to be added. At this point all the projects shown in Figure 9-3 should be compiled, and you are ready to create your first test.

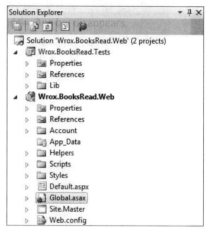

FIGURE 9-3

The First Test

Often it's difficult to choose where to start when using a pattern such as MVP or MVC. The controller or presenter usually is the best place to start because of the amount of application logic that each object contains. You could start with tests around the model, but working with the controller/presenter helps you define exactly what the model will look like. Here is the first test:

```
public class when_using_the_books_read_controller : Specification
{
}

public class and_getting_a_list_of_books : when_using_the_books_read_controller
{

}

public class and_when_calling_getdata_bind_should_be_called :
    and_getting_a_list_of_books
{
    IDisplayBooksReadView _view;
    DisplayBooksReadController _controller;

    protected override void Establish_context()
    {
        base.Establish_context();
        _view = MockRepository.GenerateMock<IDisplayBooksReadView>();
```

```
        _view.Expect(v => v.Bind());
        _controller = new DisplayBooksReadController(_view);

    }

    protected override void Because_of()
    {
        _controller.GetData(this, EventArgs.Empty);
    }

    [Test]
    public void then_getdata_should_call_bind()
    {
        _view.VerifyAllExpectations();
    }
}
```

DisplayBookReadControllerTests.cs

As you examine this test, you should be able to pick out a few recognizable parts. At first glance you may wonder what, if anything, this code has to do with a Web Form application. In this example you try to create a fake view and a real controller. Then you try to load the data using the methods in the controller and check to make sure that the fake view has the data from the controller. Remember, at this point you are testing the interaction of the controller, not the view. This is why you can use a fake view. As expected, the class won't compile, because so many things are missing.

When it's time to implement the code, it may be easier to do so within one file, use a refactoring tool such as Resharper or Refactor, and then select the Move Type To File menu option, as shown in Figure 9-4.

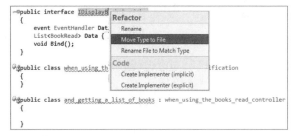

Just to get the test to compile, you need to add the following components:

FIGURE 9-4

➤ IDisplayBooksReadView

➤ The BookRead object

➤ DisplayBooksReadController

IDisplayBooksReadView is the contract that your views need to adhere to. The view needs to be aware of the data that will be displayed, and this is handled in the Data field that you added to the view. In this case it happens to be a List of BookRead objects, and right now you really don't care what it looks like. The Bind method binds the data to the controls on the view, and the view uses the `DataRequested` event to ask the controller for the data. `IDisplayBooksReadView` should look like this:

```
public interface IDisplayBooksReadView
{
    event EventHandler DataRequested;
    List<BookRead> Data { get; set; }
    void Bind();
}
```

IDisplayBooksReadView.cs

The `BookRead` object, as shown here, is the model. At this point you don't need to define that it is contained in this object; you just need to create it so that your tests will compile:

```
public class BookRead
{
}
```

BookRead.cs

`DisplayBooksReadController` is the presenter for part of the application. The presenter is responsible for the communication between the view and the model. As such, the presenter has a field that contains the view you are working with which eventually will get passed into the constructor of the presenter object, and a function that will get the data from whatever type of data source you determine is necessary. Here is the code for `DisplayBooksReadController`:

```
public class DisplayBooksReadController
{
    public IDisplayBooksReadView View { get; set; }

    public DisplayBooksReadController(IDisplayBooksReadView view)
    {
    }

    public void GetData(object sender, EventArgs e)
    {
    }
}
```

DisplayBooksReadController.cs

As shown in Figure 9-5, the test is still failing, but at least it is compiling. You are getting a null reference exception when trying to count the number of data items that the controller passed into the view. There are two ways to fix this. You can use a mocking framework and mock the data, or you can just hard-code some objects and call it good (also known as stubbing). This example shows how to stub the `ReadBook` data. Later in this chapter, you will work with the relationship between tests, databases, and mock objects.

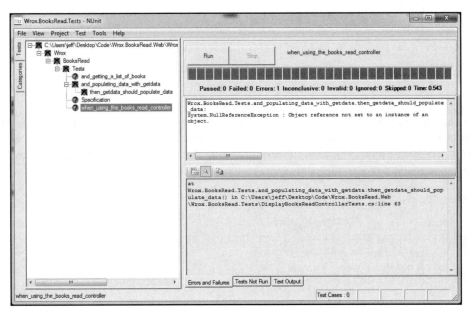

FIGURE 9-5

To complete this task, you need to implement the controller:

Available for
download on
Wrox.com

```
public class DisplayBooksReadController
{
    public IDisplayBooksReadView View { get; set; }

    public DisplayBooksReadController(IDisplayBooksReadView view)
    {
        View = view;
        View.DataRequested += GetData;
    }

    public void GetData(object sender, EventArgs e)
    {
        View.Data = new List<BookRead> {
                new BookRead{ReadBookId = 1, Name = @"Testing ASP.NET Web
                Applications", Author = "Jeff McWherter/Ben Hall", ISBN =
                "978-0470496640", StartDate = new DateTime(2010, 2, 1),
                EndDate = new DateTime(2010, 2, 12), Rating = 10,
                PurchaseLink = "http://www.amazon.com" },
                new BookRead{ReadBookId = 2, Name = @"Test Driven Development:
                By Example", Author = "Kent Beck", ISBN = "978-0321146533",
                StartDate = new DateTime(2010, 2, 1), EndDate =
                new DateTime(2010, 2, 12), Rating = 9, PurchaseLink =
                "http://www.amazon.com" },
                new BookRead{ReadBookId = 3, Name = "Test2", Author =
                "Author3", ISBN = "22222222", StartDate = new DateTime(2010, 3,
                1), EndDate = new DateTime(2010, 3, 12), Rating = 3,
                PurchaseLink = "http://www.msu.edu" }
```

```
        };
        View.Bind();
    }
}
```

DisplayBooksReadController.cs

Starting with the constructor of the `DisplayBooksReadController` class, you set the view property to the view that was passed into the controller and then wire up the `DataRequested` event to the `GetData` method. `GetData` returns three stubbed-out `ReadBook` objects. Implementing the controller means that it's time to define the model as follows:

Available for download on Wrox.com

```
public class BookRead
{
    public int ReadBookId { get; set; }
    public string Name { get; set; }
    public string Author { get; set; }
    public string ISBN { get; set; }
    public DateTime StartDate { get; set; }
    public DateTime EndDate { get; set; }
    public int Rating { get; set; }
    public string PurchaseLink { get; set; }
}
```

BookRead.cs

The first test of the Web Forms MVP project should pass. Because of the MVP pattern, you can isolate the class from the ASP.NET life cycle and create tests to ensure that the functionality of this class works correctly.

Creating More Tests

Now the controller is fully implemented. Because the example started with the controller, you don't have any tests regarding the view. You need to test to ensure that the constructor on the view is wiring up all the events you expect, which is only one at this point — the `DataRequested` event. You can create a `Mock` object for the view, inject it into the controller, and then verify that the `DataRequested` event was wired up. Remember that the `DataRequested` event is wired up in the controller to the `GetData` function. Because you already implemented the functionality, this test should pass without your having to add any more code.

Available for download on Wrox.com

```
public class and_wireing_the_events_by_the_constructor :
    and_getting_a_list_of_books
{
    IDisplayBooksReadView _view;

    protected override void Establish_context()
    {
        base.Establish_context();
        _view = MockRepository.GenerateMock<IDisplayBooksReadView>();
        _view.Expect(v => v.DataRequested += null).IgnoreArguments();
```

```
        }

        protected override void Because_of()
        {
            new DisplayBooksReadController(_view);
        }

        [Test]
        public void then_the_constructor_should_wire_up_events()
        {
            _view.VerifyAllExpectations();
        }
    }
```

After the GetData function and the DataRequested event fire, the controller calls the Bind method on the view. The bind method within the view is where the data is bound to the controls in the ASPX file. Code that looks like ListBox1.DataSouce = data would be found in this method, but I'm getting a bit ahead of myself. First you need to ensure that the bind method is called, from the GetData function within the controller. To do this you create another mock of the view and then verify that the Bind method was called. Again, after you implement all this logic, this should pass.

Available for
download on
Wrox.com

```
public class and_when_calling_getdata_bind_should_be_called :
    and_getting_a_list_of_books
{

    IDisplayBooksReadView _view;
    DisplayBooksReadController _controller;

    protected override void Establish_context()
    {
        base.Establish_context();
        _view = MockRepository.GenerateMock<IDisplayBooksReadView>();
        _view.Expect(v => v.Bind());
        _controller = new DisplayBooksReadController(_view);
    }

    protected override void Because_of()
    {
        _controller.GetData(this, EventArgs.Empty);
    }

    [Test]
    public void then_getdata_should_call_bind()
    {
        _view.VerifyAllExpectations();
    }
}
```

All the "plumbing" code needed to display the recently read books in an ASP.NET Web Form is now implemented. Before I show you the glue code for wiring all this together, I want to briefly cover the concept of helpers.

Helpers

Helper methods help other methods perform tasks. Usually they are common tasks shared between other methods in your application. For example, on the web it's common to truncate text to a set number of characters and then append ellipses to the end to indicate that the text has been truncated. This type of method is not specific to the Read Book view; it can be used with any other view in this application, so you would create an `HTMLHelper` class that contains a truncate method to help you display text in this manner. If I haven't said it before, I'll say it now: TDD is about repetition. You start by creating a test for the `Truncate` method:

```
public class when_using_the_html_helper_to_truncate_text : Specification
{
    protected string _textToTruncate;
    protected string _expected;
    protected string _actual;
    protected int _numberToTruncate;

    protected override void Because_of()
    {
        _actual = HTMLHelper.Truncate(_textToTruncate, _numberToTruncate);
    }
}

public class and_passing_a_string_that_needs_to_be_truncated :
        when_using_the_html_helper_to_truncate_text
{
    protected override void Establish_context()
    {
        _textToTruncate = "This is my text";
        _expected = "This ...";
        _numberToTruncate = 5;
    }

    [Test]
    public void then_the_text_should_be_truncated_with_ellipses()
    {
        _expected.ShouldEqual(_actual);
    }
}
```

HTMLHelpersTests.cs

Next, you implement enough code to get the test to pass:

```
public static string Truncate(string input, int length)
{
    if (input.Length <= length)
        return input;
```

```
        else
            return input.Substring(0, length) + "...";

    }
```

HTMLHelper.cs

Now go back and create more tests:

```
public class and_passing_a_string_that_does_not_need_to_be_truncated :
    when_using_the_html_helper_to_truncate_text
{
    protected override void Establish_context()
    {
        _textToTruncate = "This is my text";
        _expected = "This is my text";
        _numberToTruncate = 0;
    }

    [Test]
    public void then_the_text_should_not_be_truncated()
    {
        _expected.ShouldEqual(_actual);
    }
}

public class and_passing_a_string_that_is_less_that_what_needs_to_be_truncated :
    when_using_the_html_helper_to_truncate_text
{
    protected override void Establish_context()
    {
        _textToTruncate = "This is my text";
        _expected = "This is my text";
        _numberToTruncate = 50;
    }

    [Test]
    public void then_the_text_should_not_contain_ellipses()
    {
        _expected.ShouldEqual(_actual);
    }
}

public class and_pass_a_null_value : when_using_the_html_helper_to_truncate_text
{
    protected override void Establish_context()
    {
        _textToTruncate = null;
        _expected = string.Empty;
        _numberToTruncate = 50;
    }

    [Test]
```

```
    public void then_the_text_should_return_empty_string()
    {
        _expected.ShouldEqual(_actual);
    }
}
```

HTMLHelpersTests.cs

Then refactor the implementation to make the tests pass:

```
public static string Truncate(string input, int length)
{
    if (length == 0)
        return input;

    if (String.IsNullOrEmpty(input))
        return string.Empty;

    if (input.Length <= length)
        return input;
    else
        return input.Substring(0, length) + "...";

}
```

HTMLHelper.cs

Gluing Everything Together

At this point all the logic needed to display Read Books has been created. All that's left is gluing this logic to the Web Form. The following code is the default page of the Read Books Web Form application. The first thing to notice is that the Default page needs to implement `IDisplayBooksReadView`. Adding module-level variables enables you to persist the controller and the data. You should also define an event for `DataRequested`. In the `Page_Load` function, you simply create a new controller and then fire the `DataRequested` event.

As a result of the `DataRequested` event's being fired, the `Bind` function is called, and the data is bound to the screen. This is clean and easy to read once you understand the concept:

```
public partial class _Default : System.Web.UI.Page, IDisplayBooksReadView
{
    private DisplayBooksReadController Controller;
    public event EventHandler DataRequested;
    public List<BookRead> Data { get; set; }

    protected void Page_Load(object sender, EventArgs e)
    {
        Controller = new DisplayBooksReadController(this);
        DataRequested(sender, e);
    }
```

```
    public void Bind()
    {
        rptBooksRead.DataSource = Data;
        rptBooksRead.DataBind();
    }
}
```

As a developer, you may not think about what designers have to go through when they receive your code. Just like everything in the code-behind, your goal should be to keep your markup as clean as possible. The following example uses a repeater. You want to try to avoid datagrids because they add ugly code that is not easy to test and that is difficult for designers to work with. Keep <% tags to a minimum; implement them only when you need to show a field. These strategies allow you to create markup that most designers or developers can go into and understand easily.

```
<asp:Repeater ID="rptBooksRead" runat="server">
    <ItemTemplate>
        <div class="readBook">
            <div class="bookInfo">
                <h2><%#Wrox.BooksRead.Web.Helpers.HTMLHelper.Truncate(((
                    Wrox.BooksRead.Web.BookRead)Container.DataItem).Name, 25) %>
                </h2>
                <p><%# ((Wrox.BooksRead.Web.BookRead)Container.DataItem)
                    .Author %></p>
                <p>ISBN: <%# ((Wrox.BooksRead.Web.BookRead)Container.DataItem).ISBN
%>></p>
                <p>Date Finished: <%# ((Wrox.BooksRead.Web.BookRead)Container
                    .DataItem)
                    .EndDate.ToString("MM/dd/yyyy")%>
                </p>
                <a href='<%#
((Wrox.BooksRead.Web.BookRead)Container.DataItem).PurchaseLink %>'
                    target="_blank">Purchase</a>
            </div>

            <div class="ratingContainer">
                <span class="rating"><%#
((Wrox.BooksRead.Web.BookRead)Container.DataItem)
                    .Rating %>
                </span>
            </div>

            <div style="clear:both;" />
            <hr />
        </div>
    </ItemTemplate>
</asp:Repeater>
```

As you can see in Figure 9-6, three read books are displayed.

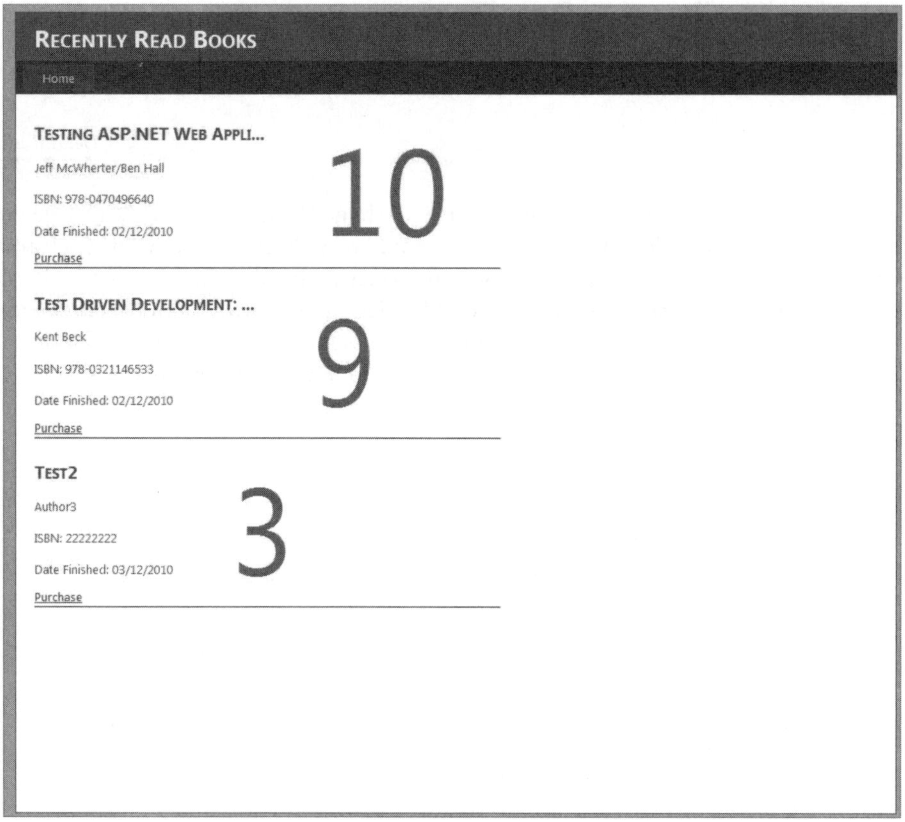

RECENTLY READ BOOKS

Home

TESTING ASP.NET WEB APPLI...

Jeff McWherter/Ben Hall

ISBN: 978-0470496640

Date Finished: 02/12/2010

Purchase

10

TEST DRIVEN DEVELOPMENT: ...

Kent Beck

ISBN: 978-0321146533

Date Finished: 02/12/2010

Purchase

9

TEST2

Author3

ISBN: 22222222

Date Finished: 03/12/2010

Purchase

3

FIGURE 9-6

In the MVP example, I showed you how to isolate objects and create Web Forms that are testable. The MVP pattern was never adopted as a mainstream approach to developing ASP.NET Web Forms, but it's a good place to start when you are forced to continue development with ASP.NET Web Forms and don't have the option of using new frameworks such as ASP.NET MVC.

This was a simple example, but testing the MVP pattern breaks down when you are working at the lower levels of the ASP.NET Framework and need to start mocking objects, such as the HTTPResponse object. With the recent demand from Microsoft developers to deliver a framework that is highly testable, the ASP.NET MVC framework was born.

WORKING WITH THE ASP.NET MVC

In 1979, while working at Xerox PARC, Trygve Reenskaug, a Norwegian computer scientist, published a paper titled "Applications Programming in Smalltalk-80: How to Use Model-View

Controllers." It was in this paper that Reenskaug formally documented this software design pattern. Even though the MVC design pattern has been around for over 30 years, it has gained popularity recently mostly because of the success of Ruby on Rails. Ruby on Rails helped show developers that highly testable web applications can be created. Developers who use Ruby on Rails are always bragging about how testable their code is. It was only a matter of time before other web platforms implemented MVC frameworks. In 2011, just about every programming language, from Cold Fusion to PHP, has a framework for MVC. The code may look different, but each framework is based on Reenskaug's work. MVC is not just for the web. Many GUI frameworks, including Cocoa (the programming environment for Mac OS X), took inspiration from Reenskaug's Small Talk framework. In Cocoa, developers are encouraged to use this pattern.

In March 2009, Microsoft released the ASP.NET MVC Framework 1.0 to the public. The code was released as open source under the Microsoft Public License, so if you want to see what the framework is doing under the covers, you can have a look. The ASP.NET MVC Framework team is agile, releasing early and often to get feedback from the community. It has been great to see the feedback given to this team implemented! Microsoft has made it clear that the ASP.NET MVC framework is not intended to replace ASP.NET Web Forms. It was created to give developers a choice.

When this book was being written, we counted 16 ASP.NET MVC books on the market, and numerous others mentioned ASP.NET MVC in some way. It is not our intention to make you an MVC expert, but we do hope to give you a good idea of how MVC web applications can be created using the TDD techniques you have learned thus far.

MVC 101

Reenskaug states that he "created the model-view-controller pattern as an obvious solution to the general problem of giving users control over their information as seen from multiple perspectives." Figure 9-7 shows the MVC design pattern.

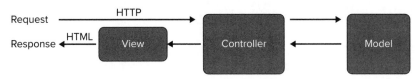

FIGURE 9-7

For this chapter, we define MVC as follows:

> ➤ **Model** — The model manages the data in the application. Classes that store and manipulate the database are combined with business logic.

> ➤ **View** — The view renders the model into an interface that the users can interact with. HTML, JSON, and XML are common forms of views.

> ➤ **Controller** — The controller orchestrates the communication between the model and the view. The controller receives input from the view and initiates a response from the model. The controller decides which view to render — HTML, XML, or JSON — depending on which view was requested. Validation logic also lives within the controller.

Microsoft ASP.NET MVC 3.0

Previous chapters implemented the OSIM example using various technologies such as WCF. Visual Studio 2010 ships with ASP.NET MVC 2.0, but this example uses ASP.NET MVC 3.0, which is available for download at http://www.asp.net/mvc/mvc3.

MVC frameworks rely on convention over configuration, so as long as you follow the convention, things tend to "just work." Routes are an important tenet of the ASP.NET MVC. Simply put, routes in the MVC framework specify how an HTTP request should be handled. In the past, with ASP .NET Web Forms, you had little control over how requests worked. Requests were tightly coupled to the page handling the request. The following code is default code that is added to the Global.asax file when you create an ASP.NET MVC application:

```
routes.MapRoute("Default", // Route name
    "{controller}/{action}/{id}", // URL with parameters
    new { controller = "Home", action = "Index", id =
    UrlParameter.Optional });
```

Global.asax.cs

It's important to note this, because many newcomers to ASP.NET MVC overlook this fact. Basically the code states that the URL will look like this: http://*url*/*controller*/*action*/*id* or http://*localhost* /*home*/*index*, assuming that you have an index method within a controller class named home.

Creating an ASP.NET MVC Project

Creating an ASP.NET MVC project is as simple as selecting MVC 3 Web Application, found under the Web project types when you create a new project, as shown in Figure 9-8.

FIGURE 9-8

After you select the MVC 3.0 project type, you can choose from two default templates — Empty or Internet Application. When you select the Internet Application template, a new project that contains default HTML/CSS styling is created. Also included in this project are default views and controllers for a home page, as well as the basics for authentication. To follow along with this example, select the Empty template, as shown in Figure 9-9.

Figure 9-10 shows the default structure that the framework creates. It includes the following folders:

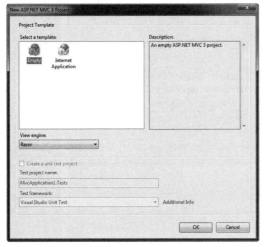

FIGURE 9-9

FIGURE 9-10

➤ `Content` contains HTML, CSS, and image files.

➤ `Controllers` contains your controller classes.

➤ `Models` contains model classes.

➤ `Scripts` contains JavaScript needed for your application.

➤ `Views` contains your views. Each controller has a subdirectory under this directory that contains views for the CRUD operations.

Creating Your First Test

Based on previous examples, this example implements the same functionality used in the OSIM project, revolving around the item type concept. You list, create, and edit the item types.

In many situations developers start a project with the data model already in place. This is one of those projects, because we discussed testing the data layer in depth in previous chapters. You know that the developer who created the `OSIM.Core` module, which contains the data layer, has a full test suite surrounding it, so there is no need to create tests for this assembly. Because you will be working with item types, let's start by creating a test for the controller that ensures that the controller will get the item type data to display.

You begin with the setup of our test. The first thing you need to do is set up the item type repository object. You also set up a mock to return a list of three item types when the `GetAll` method is called from this repository:

```
public class when_working_with_the_item_type_controller : Specification
{
    protected Mock<IItemTypeRepository> _itemRepository
        = new Mock<IItemTypeRepository>();
    protected ItemType _itemOne;
    protected ItemType _itemTwo;
    protected ItemType _itemThree;

    protected override void Establish_context()
    {
        _itemOne = new ItemType { Id = 1, Name = "USB drives" };
        _itemTwo = new ItemType { Id = 2, Name = "Nerf darts" };
        _itemThree = new ItemType { Id = 3, Name = "Flying Monkeys" };
        var itemTypeList = new List<ItemType>
        {
            _itemOne,
            _itemTwo,
            _itemThree
        };

        _itemRepository.Setup(x => x.GetAll)
        .Returns(itemTypeList);
    }
}
```

ItemTypeControllerTests.cs

With our setup logic in place for the item type repository, you can create your first test. The first page you will create lists the item types. You want to test to ensure that the controller is working with the repository correctly. The following test ensures that when a controller is created, the model is set correctly from the repository:

```
public class and_trying_to_load_the_index_page :
    when_working_with_the_item_type_controller
{
    Object _model;
    int _expectedNumberOfItemsInModel;

    protected override void Establish_context()
    {
        base.Establish_context();
        _expectedNumberOfItemsInModel = _itemRepository.Object.GetAll.Count;
    }

    protected override void Because_of()
    {
        _model = ((ViewResult)new
```

```
                    ItemTypeController(_itemRepository.Object).Index()).ViewData.Model;
    }

    [Test]
    public void then_a_valid_list_of_items_should_be_retunred_in_the_model()
    {
        _expectedNumberOfItemsInModel.ShouldEqual(((List<ItemType>)_model).Count);
        _itemOne.ShouldEqual(((List<ItemType>)_model)[0]);
    }
}
```

ItemTypeControllerTests.cs

Making Your First Test Pass

Now that you have a test, you can create your controller, named `ItemTypeController`. Right-click the `Controllers` folder and select Add ⇨ Controller to access a dialog box that allows you to create the controller, as shown in Figure 9-11.

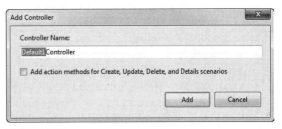

You have the option of letting Visual Studio create all the action methods for create, edit, and so on, but because you do not have tests

FIGURE 9-11

for them, you will want to handle these yourself in the future. For now, implement only the `Index` method. After the `Controller` class is created, you fill in the blanks with the following code:

Available for download on Wrox.com

```
public class ItemTypeController : Controller
{

    IItemTypeRepository _itemTypeRepository;

    public ItemTypeController(IItemTypeRepository itemRepository)
    {

        _itemTypeRepository = itemRepository;
    }

    public ActionResult Index()
    {
        ViewData.Model = _itemTypeRepository.GetAll;
        return View();
    }
}
```

ItemTypeController.cs

Most notable in the `ItemTypeController` code is the addition of a constructor that takes in an `Item` repository. This is how you get the instance of the repository. With this logic in place, your test will pass, but the website will not function as you would expect.

Creating Your First View

You need to create a view that displays the item Types. You will want to create a subdirectory called ItemType under the Views directory to keep things organized. After the subdirectory is created, right-click the newly created ItemType directory and select Add ⇨ View. You see a dialog box similar to the one shown in Figure 9-12.

When creating a view with ASP.NET MVC 3.0, you have two default options for the view engine. It's outside the scope of this book to discuss the view engines in depth, but view engines render the markup for the page. Each view engine renders the markup a bit differently, and some have advantages over others. By default Microsoft ASP.NET MVC 3.0 ships with the Razor and ASPX view engines. Other open source view engines such as Spark and NHaml can be used as well. This example uses the Razor view engine.

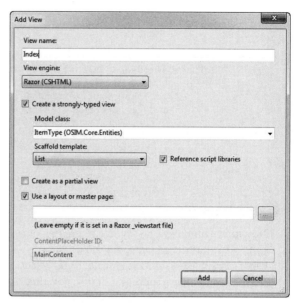

FIGURE 9-12

Checking the "Create a strongly-typed view" check box and selecting your ItemType class from the OSIM.Core.Entities namespace causes the ASP.NET Framework to generate a scaffold for this view. Scaffolding is simply a template containing markup to render your model in a view. Scaffolding gets you from point A to point C quickly. You have different options to select for the scaffold template. In this case you are listing the item types on the screen, so you should choose the List template. The following code is rendered for the Index view:

Available for download on Wrox.com

```
@model IEnumerable<OSIM.Core.Entities.ItemType>

@{
    ViewBag.Title = "ItemType";
}

<h2>ItemType</h2>

<p>@Html.ActionLink("Create New", "Create")</p>
<table>
    <tr>
        <th></th>
        <th>Name</th>
    </tr>
    @foreach (var item in Model) {
        <tr>
            <td>@Html.ActionLink("Edit", "Edit", new { id=item.Id }) |</td>
            <td>@item.Name</td>
        </tr>
    }
</table>
```

Index.cshtml

It's important to name your view in the `ItemType` directory index. This is because MVC is based on convention, and with the defaults you set up in the controller (the `Index` method), the MVC framework will look for a file with this name. Figure 9-13 shows what happens when the framework cannot find the correct file.

Server Error in '/' Application.

The view 'Index' or its master was not found or no view engine supports the searched locations. The following locations were searched:
~/Views/ItemType/Index.aspx
~/Views/ItemType/Index.ascx
~/Views/Shared/Index.aspx
~/Views/Shared/Index.ascx
~/Views/ItemType/Index.cshtml
~/Views/ItemType/Index.vbhtml
~/Views/Shared/Index.cshtml
~/Views/Shared/Index.vbhtml

Description: An unhandled exception occurred during the execution of the current web request. Please review the stack trace for more information about the error and where it originated in the code.

Exception Details: System.InvalidOperationException: The view 'Index' or its master was not found or no view engine supports the searched locations. The following locations were searched:
~/Views/ItemType/Index.aspx
~/Views/ItemType/Index.ascx
~/Views/Shared/Index.aspx
~/Views/Shared/Index.ascx
~/Views/ItemType/Index.cshtml
~/Views/ItemType/Index.vbhtml
~/Views/Shared/Index.cshtml
~/Views/Shared/Index.vbhtml

Source Error:

An unhandled exception was generated during the execution of the current web request. Information regarding the origin and location of the exception can be identified using the exception stack trace below.

Stack Trace:

```
[InvalidOperationException: The view 'Index' or its master was not found or no view engine supports the searched locations. The following locations were searched:
~/Views/ItemType/Index.aspx
~/Views/ItemType/Index.ascx
~/Views/Shared/Index.aspx
~/Views/Shared/Index.ascx
~/Views/ItemType/Index.cshtml
~/Views/ItemType/Index.vbhtml
~/Views/Shared/Index.cshtml
~/Views/Shared/Index.vbhtml]
   System.Web.Mvc.ViewResult.FindView(ControllerContext context) +497
   System.Web.Mvc.ViewResultBase.ExecuteResult(ControllerContext context) +209
   System.Web.Mvc.ControllerActionInvoker.InvokeActionResult(ControllerContext controllerContext, ActionResult actionResult) +39
   System.Web.Mvc.<>c__DisplayClass1e.<InvokeActionResultWithFilters>b__19() +60
   System.Web.Mvc.ControllerActionInvoker.InvokeActionResultFilter(IResultFilter filter, ResultExecutingContext preContext, Func`1 continuation) +391
   System.Web.Mvc.<>c__DisplayClass1e.<InvokeActionResultWithFilters>b__1b() +61
   System.Web.Mvc.ControllerActionInvoker.InvokeActionResultWithFilters(ControllerContext controllerContext, IList`1 filters, ActionResult actionResult) +285
```

FIGURE 9-13

This is not to say that you could not create custom routes. Although you could name the view whatever you wanted, generally this approach is frowned on.

Gluing Everything Together

With the Index view in place, you are one step closer to getting the website application up and running. A bit of glue code needs to be added to handle your dependency injection. As with the examples in previous chapters, this example shows you how to use Ninject to inject dependencies into your controller. Remember the constructor you added to the item type controller that took in the item type repository? This logic injects this dependency of the repository into your controller for you. This code is found in the `Global.asax.cs` file.

Available for
download on
Wrox.com

```csharp
public class MvcApplication : NinjectHttpApplication
{
    protected override void OnApplicationStarted()
    {
        base.OnApplicationStarted();

        AreaRegistration.RegisterAllAreas();
        RegisterGlobalFilters(GlobalFilters.Filters);
        RegisterRoutes(RouteTable.Routes);
    }

    public static void RegisterGlobalFilters(GlobalFilterCollection filters)
    {
```

```
        filters.Add(new HandleErrorAttribute());
    }

    public static void RegisterRoutes(RouteCollection routes)
    {
        routes.IgnoreRoute("{resource}.axd/{*pathInfo}");

        routes.MapRoute(
            "Default", // Route name
            "{controller}/{action}/{id}", // URL with parameters
        new { controller = "ItemType", action = "Index", id =
        UrlParameter.Optional });
    }

    protected override IKernel CreateKernel()
    {
        return new StandardKernel(new PersistenceModule(), new
        CoreServicesModule());
    }
    }
}
```

Global.asax.cs

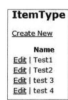

FIGURE 9-14

Most notable in this example is that instead of Global.asax inheriting from System.Web.HttpApplication, it inherits from NinjectHttpApplication, which requires a reference to the Ninject.Web.MVC assembly. Inheriting from NinjectHTTPApplication as well as implementing the CreateKernel method to map your dependencies is all the glue code you need to get your web application up and running. You may also note, in the RegisterRoutes method, in this example you change the default controller name from Home to ItemType so that it defaults to the only controller you created. If you do not do this, your web application looks for a home controller that doesn't exist. Running the web application renders a website similar to the one shown in Figure 9-14.

Now that you have implemented your first feature, you can go back and create tests that involve creating and editing item types. I'll forgo creating the controllers and views for these features and just show the tests:

```
public class and_trying_to_create_a_new_valid_item_type :
    when_working_with_the_item_type_controller
{
    ItemType _newItemType;
    ItemTypeController _controller;
    RedirectToRouteResult _result;
    string _expectedRouteName;

    protected override void Establish_context()
    {
        base.Establish_context();
        _expectedRouteName = "Index";
        _newItemType = new ItemType() { Id = 99, Name = "New Item" };
```

```csharp
            _controller = new ItemTypeController(_itemRepository.Object);
        }

        protected override void Because_of()
        {
            _result = _controller.Create(_newItemType) as RedirectToRouteResult;
        }

        [Test]
        public void then_a_new_item_type_should_be_created_and_
            the_redirected_to_the_correct_view()
        {
            _result.ShouldNotBeNull();
            _result.RouteValues.Values.ShouldContain(_expectedRouteName);
        }
    }

    public class and_trying_to_create_a_new_invalid_item_type :
        when_working_with_the_item_type_controller
    {
        ItemType _newItemType;
        ItemTypeController _controller;
        ViewResult _result;
        string _expectedRouteName;

        protected override void Establish_context()
        {
            base.Establish_context();
            _expectedRouteName = "create";
            _newItemType = new ItemType() { Id = 99, Name = "New Item" };
            _controller = new ItemTypeController(_itemRepository.Object);
            _controller.ModelState.AddModelError("key", "model is invalid");
        }

        protected override void Because_of()
        {
            _result = _controller.Create(_newItemType) as ViewResult;
        }

        [Test]
        public void then_a_new_item_type_should_not_be_created()
        {
            _result.ShouldNotBeNull();
            _result.ViewName.ShouldEqual(_expectedRouteName);
        }
    }

    public class and_trying_to_edit_an_existing_item :
        when_working_with_the_item_type_controller
    {
        string _expectedRouteName;
        ItemTypeController _controller;
        ViewResult _result;
```

```
protected override void Establish_context()
{
    base.Establish_context();
    _expectedRouteName = "edit";
    _controller = new ItemTypeController(_itemRepository.Object);
    _result = _controller.Edit(_itemOne.Id) as ViewResult;
}

protected override void Because_of()
{
}

[Test]
public void then_a_valid_edit_view_should_be_returned()
{
    _expectedRouteName.ShouldEqual(_result.ViewName);
}
}
```

ItemTypeControllerTests.cs

Using the MVC Contrib Project

The open source MVC Contrib project can be found at http://mvccontrib.codeplex.com/. This project adds a great deal of functionality to the ASP.NET MVC framework and is useful for MVC developers. The MVC Contrib project includes features to help with unit testing and much more. The MVC Contrib project fills in gaps in the ASP.NET MVC framework. The MVC Contrib project is a must for anyone who is looking to develop ASP.NET MVC applications.

ASP.NET MVC Summarized

ASP.NET MVC requires a different way of thinking when you are developing web applications on the Microsoft stack. At first it can be a bit overwhelming due to the number of new tools and concepts you need to understand to build even the simplest web application. After you learn the basics, however, you will realize that using the ASP.NET MVC framework forces you and your coworkers to create clean code that is easy to read, test, and maintain.

WORKING WITH JAVASCRIPT

Many web developers have a love-hate relationship with JavaScript. In most situations, web developers don't hate JavaScript per se; they hate the Document Object Model (DOM) in most web browsers. In recent years JavaScript frameworks such as jQuery and Prototype have relieved the pain that the DOM has caused web developers. These frameworks make it easier for you to work with the DOM and reduce the number of tests you need to create to test your JavaScript. Remember, you don't need to test the framework.

One of the most common mistakes web developers make when it comes to JavaScript is not abstracting their logic into different files. Many developers chuck everything into one script file or duplicate functionality over many different web pages. They don't realize that testing frameworks exist for JavaScript, or that you can create JavaScript using TDD methods.

JavaScript is a real language, and code should be treated as such. Rules that you have learned about SOLID apply to JavaScript. When JavaScript code is created in this manner, it is easy to test and maintain. Some web developers complain that an HTML page that is required to download multiple JavaScript files loads slowly, and they are correct. Using techniques such as combining and minifying during the build process resolves these slow page load issues. Testing performance is a different topic; for now I will focus on creating testable code.

JavaScript Testing Frameworks

As with most languages, multiple frameworks allow you to test your JavaScript code. Frameworks such as qUnit, Screw Unit, and jsUnit are all open source testing frameworks that act similarly to NUnit but are designed for testing JavaScript. The examples here use qUnit — the testing framework that the jQuery team has selected to test its popular JavaScript framework. qUnit has been around for quite some time, and because of the success with the jQuery project, it has a large following. When open source projects have large followings, it means you can find documentation and file bugs and get frequent software updates.

In these examples of using TDD with JavaScript, you will look at something a bit more complicated than any JavaScript you would be testing in any of the previous applications covered in this chapter. Most of the JavaScript you would add in these applications would be considered glue code, and testing would occur during the integration or functionality testing phase.

The following example shows how you create JavaScript that represents a bank account. This object holds the current balance, and a function transfers funds between two accounts. The first step is to set up the qUnit framework. Doing so is fairly simple. Figure 9-15 shows the directory set up for this application. You see it includes jQuery, qUnit JavaScript, and the qUnit style sheet. You create your tests in the js folder.

FIGURE 9-15

When the framework is ready, you can write your first test. qUnit tests are written in JavaScript, and the runner is contained within the HTML. Just like testing within C# or Visual Basic, you should keep separate files for each object you are testing. In this case, you are testing the account object, so you create AccountTests.htm, which will contain all the tests for the account object that you will create.

As with other testing frameworks, you want to write your test so that it describes what the test is trying to accomplish. In this example, you just want to create an account object that has an account number as well as a balance:

```
<script type="text/javascript">
test('Should_Create_An_Account_Object_With_Balance', function() {
    var checkingAccount = new Account(564858510, 600);
        equals(checkingAccount.Balance, 600);
});
</script>
```

To finish the implementation of this test, you need to finish adding the test runner implementation code. The following code shows the full implementation of the test you will run.

```html
<html xmlns="http://www.w3.org/1999/xhtml" >
    <head>
        <title>Account Tests</title>
        <link rel="stylesheet" href="QUnit.css" type="text/css"   media="screen" />
        <script type="text/javascript" src="../jquery-1.4.4.js"></script>
        <script type="text/javascript" src="../qunit.js"></script>
        <script type="text/javascript" src="../Account.js"></script>

        <script type="text/javascript">
            test('Should_Create_An_Account_Object_With_Balance', function() {

                var checkingAccount = new Account(564858510, 600);
                equals(checkingAccount.Balance, 600);

            });

        </script>
    </head>
    <body>
        <h1 id="qunit-header">Account Unit Tests</h1>
        <h2 id="qunit-banner"></h2>
        <div id="qunit-testrunner-toolbar"></div>
        <h2 id="qunit-userAgent"></h2>
        <ol id="qunit-tests"></ol>
        <div id="qunit-fixture">test markup</div>
    </body>
</html>
```

AccountTests.htm

After your test and running logic are in place, you are ready to run the test. You should expect this test to fail, because you have not implemented the account object yet. Figure 9-16 represents this.

FIGURE 9-16

With your test failing, you are ready to implement the account JavaScript:

```javascript
function Account(accountNumber, balance)
{
    this.AccountNumber = accountNumber;
    this.Balance = balance;
}
```

Account.js

As shown in Figure 9-17, the test now passes.

FIGURE 9-17

Let's now fulfill the requirement for the account object to transfer funds between objects. In a test named `Should_Transfer_From_Checking_To_Savings_Successfully`, create two accounts with balances, and then transfer funds from one of them to the other. When you run the test, you expect failure, as shown in Figure 9-18.

```
test('Should_Transfer_From_Checking_To_Savings_Successfully',
function() {
        var checkingAccount = new Account(564858510, 600);
        var savingsAccount = new Account(564858507, 100);

        checkingAccount.Transfer(savingsAccount, 100);
        equals(savingsAccount.Balance, 200);
        equals(checkingAccount.Balance, 500);
});
```

AccountTests.htm

FIGURE 9-18

After the test fails, you can implement the code required to transfer funds. All the tests pass, as shown in Figure 9-19.

```
function Account(accountNumber, balance)
{
    this.AccountNumber = accountNumber;
    this.Balance = balance;
}

Account.prototype. Transfer = function(toAccount, amount)
{
    toAccount.Balance += amount;
    this.Balance = this.Balance - amount;
}
```

Account.js

FIGURE 9-19

You have implemented only the bare minimum for the JavaScript account object tests to pass, but you are not done yet. Business rules and boundary conditions need to be tested as well. The first one would be to test what happens if an account tries to transfer more than it has. Let's write a test to see:

Available for download on Wrox.com

```
test('Should_Not_Transfer_From_When_The_From_Account_Has_Insufficent_Funds',
function () {
        var checkingAccount = new Account(564858510, 600);
        var savingsAccount = new Account(564858507, 100);

        checkingAccount.Transfer(savingsAccount, 700);
        equals(savingsAccount.Balance, 100);
        equals(checkingAccount.Balance, 600);
    });
```

Account.js

As shown in Figure 9-20, this test fails.

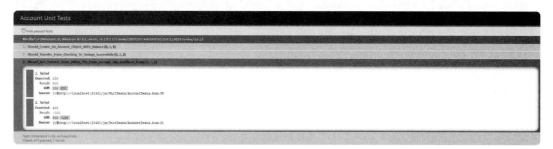

FIGURE 9-20

The test you wrote expects that when you try to transfer $700 from an account that has only $600, the accounts will still have the same balance, meaning that the transfer did not occur. If you look closely at the error shown in Figure 9-20, you see that the transfer did occur. The application has a bug, and you should fix it before someone notices. This problem can be resolved quickly by simply placing a guard statement that checks to see if the amount being transferred is more than the current balance. If it is, don't perform the transfer; just return:

```javascript
Account.prototype.Transfer = function (toAccount, amount) {
    if (this.Balance < amount) {
        return;
    }

    toAccount.Balance += amount;
    this.Balance = this.Balance - amount;
}
```

Account.js

Figure 9-21 shows that all the tests now pass.

FIGURE 9-21

By now you should start feeling the repetition of TDD, which is important. In a real-world situation, you would have tests that cover all scenarios. Previous chapters discussed what exactly to test, but for our purposes, this example is sufficient.

After you have created tests for the entire object, you can implement your newly developed object in production code. The following code is the implementation of the JavaScript account object. I have written a suite of tests around the account object, and the code shown is considered glue code or jQuery framework code that does not need to be tested at this level:

```html
<html xmlns="http://www.w3.org/1999/xhtml" >
<head>
    <title>Simple qUnit Test</title>
    <script type="text/javascript" src="js/account.js"></script>
    <script type="text/javascript" src="js/jQuery-1.4.4.js"></script>
</head>
    <body>
        <div>
            Savings Balance:<span id="SavingsBalance"></span>
        </div>
        <div>
            Checking Balance:<span id="CheckingBalance"></span>
        </div>
    </body>

    <script type="text/javascript">
        var checkingAccount = new Account(564858510, 600);
        var savingsAccount = new Account(564858507, 100);

        savingsAccount.Transfer(checkingAccount, 100);

        jQuery("document").ready(function () {
            jQuery("#SavingsBalance").text(savingsAccount.Balance);
```

```
            jQuery("#CheckingBalance").text(checkingAccount.Balance);
        });
    </script>
</html>
```

Default.aspx

Figure 9-22 shows the project's final organization.

SUMMARY

Test-driven development on the web can sometimes be
cumbersome. This chapter introduced frameworks and concepts
that allow you to start creating highly testable web applications.
You have probably worked in environments where teams do not
want to try new concepts, but many of the concepts in this chapter
can be introduced slowly to teams using existing tools they have
access to.

ASP.NET MVC is a new way of thinking for many Microsoft web
developers. Microsoft has stated that ASP.NET Web Forms is not
going away anytime soon. The MVC framework is an additional
tool that you can choose to use.

FIGURE 9-22

Like all the TDD practices discussed previously, the best way to learn these practices is to get out
and meet other developers who practice them every day. Free conferences such as Day of .NET and
Code Camps are a great way to meet people and hone your newly developed skills.

10

Testing Windows Communication Foundation Services

WHAT'S IN THIS CHAPTER?

➤ Understanding why Windows Communication Foundation (WCF) services are an important part of your application

➤ Recognizing WCF services as interface code, similar to a Windows form or web page

➤ Refactoring your WCF services to employ dependency injection

➤ Understanding the role that transports play in testing WCF services

Like web pages or desktop windows, services are an interface to your application. As with the other interfaces to your application, your application's services need to be tested to ensure that they meet all the requirements that have been specified for them as an interface to your application. Testing services is especially necessary, because unlike Windows forms or web pages, errors and defects can be easily obfuscated or swallowed by a services layer in ways that make diagnosing defects extremely difficult.

WCF is the standard framework for creating services in .NET. However, many developers are intimidated by even the basics of WCF. As a result, even developers who are willing to learn WCF find testing services to be a daunting proposition. The skills to properly test WCF services are not difficult to learn. This chapter provides you with the tools and knowledge you need to test your WCF services.

This chapter assumes a basic level of knowledge and skill with WCF. If you are unfamiliar with WCF, many books are available on the subject. My blog at www.jamescbender.com hosts an ongoing WCF instructional series that is perfect for developers who have not used WCF.

WCF SERVICES IN YOUR APPLICATION

Services are important to your application. As an architectural tool, services allow you to develop broad, adaptive systems that would not be possible using only static binding or an application confined to a single physical machine. Services enhance scalability and increase flexibility. Some would argue that services are the last word in the quest for the loosely coupled system. The rising popularity of mobile devices, the desire for more responsive web applications via JavaScript and AJAX calls, frameworks such as Silverlight, and the resurgence of REST are all breathing new life into an architectural concept that until a few years ago was seen as the sole domain of ivory-tower architects and service-oriented architecture (SOA) geeks. For these reasons, more and more applications will begin to include a service interface requirement of some kind.

Services Are Code Too

The actual code in your service should be very simple. In other words, the code should do almost nothing. The most complicated action a service should perform on its own is translate data between data transfer objects (DTOs) and domain entity objects. The service may also perform some simple data validation, similar to what would be done on a web page or a Windows form. Aside from that, your service should call methods only on domain services or a business model object of some sort.

In spite of how simple the code for your service should be, your service is still code. As such, it is still prone to defects and sensitive to changes made in other areas of the application. You need to ensure that your service is using the correct domain service or model. Validation rules must be verified. Data translations must be rechecked periodically to ensure that changes to an entity domain class have not disrupted the service's operation. Services are external entry points to an application, meaning that they enable the automated input of data; much like a web page or web form would for a user. This means that the validation and verification of services must be verified as well to ensure proper security for the application. For these reasons, it's important to test services as much as you would test any other interface to an application.

TESTING WCF SERVICES

Unlike domain services or entities, you do not have direct control over the instantiation of your WCF services. This has led to the belief that WCF services cannot take advantage of dependency injection and therefore cannot be unit-tested. This is a fallacy. Most of the popular dependency injection frameworks available today provide some facility for injecting dependencies into WCF services. All you need are some changes to how the service implementation is constructed, and a couple of minor tweaks to how the WCF projects are configured.

Refactoring for Testability

Like domain services and entities, in an ideal world you write the tests for your WCF services before you write the code. Test first is a major tenet of TDD (remember, the second D stands for driven). This chapter starts with an existing WCF service and refactors it to make it testable. There are a couple reasons for this demonstration. You are far more likely to encounter codebases where the domain-specific code, and even the ASP.NET MVC or WPF interfaces, have been designed for testability — specifically, the ability to accept dependencies. WCF services are in the unique position of being relatively easy to refactor to accept dependencies. The service is an interface. As such, it is at the edge of the application, which means that it should have no references that would break from the creation of a new constructor to accept dependencies. Additionally, because access to services is done via proxy, and the caller has no role in the instantiation of the service class, the instantiation provider can be changed at will with almost no risk of introducing a breaking change.

Finally, I recognize the learning curve that some developers experience with WCF. I hope that, by starting with a working service, you will have more confidence in attempting to introduce dependency injection into a working WCF service than you would by trying to build a working service and introduce dependency injection at the same time. You should apply all the techniques in this chapter to future development of WCF services, and you should adopt a test-first paradigm when you feel comfortable with the frameworks.

I've added a simple WCF service to the OSIM application that returns a list of `ItemTypes` as a string array. (This demo, as well as all the demos for this book, are available on `wrox.com`.) I've called this `InventoryService` and created it in the `OSIM.ExternalServices` project, as shown in Figure 10-1.

FIGURE 10-1

The implementation of the `InventoryService` service simply creates an instance of the `ItemTypeService` domain service class (which I created to support this service). It also returns the result of a call to the `GetItemTypes` method of the `ItemTypeService` after that result has been flattened to a string array:

Available for download on Wrox.com

```
using System.Linq;
using Ninject;
using OSIM.Core.Services;
using OSIM.Persistence;

namespace OSIM.ExternalServices
{
    public class InventoryService : IInventoryService
    {

        public string[] GetItemTypes()
        {
            var kernel =
                new StandardKernel(new PersistenceModule(), new
    CoreServicesModule());
            var itemTypeService = kernel.Get<IItemTypeService>();

            var itemTypeList = itemTypeService.GetItemTypes()
                .Select(x => x.Name)
```

```
            .ToArray();

        return itemTypeList;
    }
  }
}
```

InventoryService.svc.cs

To follow along in the implementation of the `GetItemTypes` method of `InventoryService`, you create an instance of a Ninject `StandardKernel` class and provide it with implementations of the `PersistenceModule` (which contains the rules and logic to create `ItemTypeRepository` and connect it to the database) and `CoreServicesModule` (which contains the rules for instantiation of a class that implements the `IItemTypeService` interface). The code in these modules is simple and is irrelevant to the rest of this example, so I will not provide a detailed explanation of it here. Feel free to examine the code in the downloadable sample available at www.wrox.com.

First the instance of the `StandardKernel` is used to get an instance of an object that implements the `IItemTypeService` interface. Then call the `GetItemTypes` method on that implementation of the `IItemTypeService` interface is called, which returns an instance of an object that implements the `IList<ItemType>` interface (a list of `ItemType` objects).

The `ItemType` class has two properties: `Id` and `Name`. The `GetItemTypes` method returns `ItemTypes` used in the system (presumably retrieved from a data store). Because you need only the names, you can use the `Select` LINQ command to select only the names from each item in the list of `ItemTypes` returned from the `GetItemTypes` method call. Then employ the `ToArray` extension method to convert the result of the `Select` command to a string array, which the service returns, as shown in Figure 10-2.

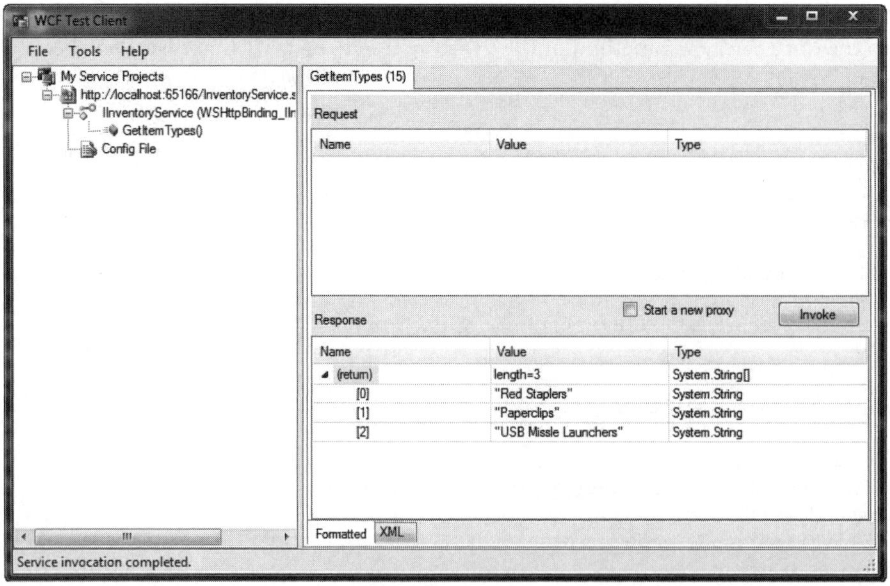

FIGURE 10-2

Introducing Dependency Injection to Your Service

Even though the code in the `InventoryService` is very simple, it still needs to be tested. A fundamental barrier to testing the `InventoryService` is that it's dependent on an implementation of the `IItemTypeService` interface, but currently there is no way to inject an instance of an object that implements the `IItemTypeService` interface. This means that the test is dependent on whatever implementation of the `IItemTypeService` interface is provided by the statically bound Ninject modules.

WCF service applications share a similar trait with ASP.NET applications and Windows Forms/WPF applications in that the instantiation of WCF services, ASP.NET pages, and Windows forms is performed by the .NET runtime. This limits what can be done in terms of instantiation of these objects without delving deep into the .NET runtime. In response to the desire of more and more developers to use dependency injection with these objects, Microsoft has built some hooks into the .NET runtime that enable you to use dependency injection with these types of objects.

Ninject has a large library of extensions that are designed to enable dependency injection via Ninject in a variety of situations. Among them are the `Ninject.Extensions.Wcf` extensions, which provide a set of classes that enable dependency injection via Ninject for WCF services. Adding these extensions takes only a few steps, and it allows your WCF services to use dependency injection seamlessly.

The Ninject WCF extension contains two assemblies used in this example: `Ninject.Extensions.Wcf` and `Ninject.Extensions.Wcf.CommonServiceLocator`. You add these as references to the `OSIM.ExternalServices` projects, as shown in Figure 10-3.

FIGURE 10-3

These two assemblies contain the Ninject classes needed to retrofit the WCF service application (`OSIM.ExternalServices`) to be a Ninject application.

The first change you need to implement is to make the `OSIM.ExternalServices` application an instance of a Ninject WCF application. You do so by changing the class that the `OSIM.ExternalServices` application inherits from. This information is located in the `Global.asax.cs` file. By default, this file is not added to the WCF Services project at creation time. The convention is that you create this file only if you need to modify some behavior it provides, such as application start activities. If this file is not included, the .NET runtime uses a standard definition of this class to create your application.

In this case you need to change the base class for the `Global` class, so add this file to the `OSIM.ExternalServices` project. To do this, right-click the `OSIM.ExternalServices` project and select Add --> New Item. The Add New Item dialog, shown in Figure 10-4, is displayed.

FIGURE 10-4

As shown in Figure 10-4, you select the Global Application Class file type. Leave the default name of Global.asax, and click the Add button. The Global.asax file is added to the OSIM.ExternalServices project, as shown in Figure 10-5.

FIGURE 10-5

Viewing the contents of the Global.asax file reveals that the Global class currently inherits from System.Web.HttpApplication:

Available for
download on
Wrox.com

```
namespace OSIM.ExternalServices
{
    public class Global : System.Web.HttpApplication
    {
    ...

    }
}
```

Global.asax.cs

To use the Ninject WCF extensions in the OSIM.ExternalServices project, you need to change the declaration of the Global class to inherit from the NinjectWcfApplication base class. The NinjectWcfApplication class is located in the Ninject.Extensions.Wcf namespace. Because you also need access to a class in the Ninject root namespace, you add `using` statements to include these namespaces in the `Global.asax.cs` file:

```
using Ninject;
using Ninject.Extensions.Wcf;
```

Next you change the declaration of the `Global` class so that it inherits from `NinjectWcfApplication` instead of `System.Web.HttpApplication`:

```
namespace OSIM.ExternalServices
{
    public class Global : NinjectWcfApplication
    {

        . . .

    }
}
```

Global.asax.cs

The `NinjectWcfApplication` base class defines an abstract method called `CreateKernel` that must be implemented by the `Global` class:

```
protected override IKernel CreateKernel()
{
    throw new NotImplementedException();
}
```

Global.asax.cs

The purpose of the `CreateKernel` method is to provide the developer with a place to reference the Ninject modules that contain the rules for creating the various classes that will be used by the WCF services in the current application. You return to this method after you finish retrofitting the `OSIM .ExternalServices` application and create a Ninject module for the `InventoryService` WCF service.

In the `OSIM.ExternalServices` project is a file called `InventoryService.svc`. This file is similar to `.aspx` files in that it provides some runtime metadata about the `InventoryService` service endpoint and a link to the actual implementation of `InventoryService` in the `InventoryService .svc.cs` code-behind file:

```
<%@ ServiceHost Language="C#" Debug="true"
    Service="OSIM.ExternalServices.InventoryService"
CodeBehind="InventoryService.svc.cs" %>
```

InventoryService.cs

One of the attributes of the `ServiceHost` directive is `Factory`. The `Factory` attribute specifies what class should be used to instantiate the WCF service. When the attribute is not supplied, the .NET runtime uses the standard WCF service factory to create the instance of the service implementation. As part of the retrofit to enable dependency injection in the `OSIM.ExternalServices` project, you change the factory used to instantiate `InventoryService` to `NinjectServiceHostFactory`:

```
<%@ ServiceHost Language="C#" Debug="true"
Service="OSIM.ExternalServices.InventoryService"
CodeBehind="InventoryService.svc.cs"
Factory="Ninject.Extensions.Wcf.NinjectServiceHostFactory"%>
```

InventoryService.cs

That is the last step needed to convert the internal mechanics of `OSIM` `.InventoryService` and the `InventoryService.svc` file to use Ninject. The next steps are the standard steps to employ dependency injection in a class with Ninject.

First, you need to create a Ninject module to store the rules for how the service implementation classes are created. Call this module **ExternalServicesModule**, and place it in a new folder in the `OSIM` `.ExternalServices` project called **Modules**, as shown in Figure 10-6.

FIGURE 10-6

In the `ExternalServicesModule.cs` file, create the `ExternalServicesModule` class in the same manner you created the other Ninject modules in the previous chapters:

```
using Ninject.Modules;

namespace OSIM.ExternalServices.Modules
{
    public class ExternalServicesModule : NinjectModule
    {
        public override void Load()
        {
            Bind<IInventoryService>().To<InventoryService>();
        }
    }
}
```

ExternalServicesModule.cs

The `OSIM.ExternalServices` project has only one service, `InventoryService`, so that's the only interface/class pair you need to provide binding information for. You use the other modules from the appropriate projects to provide the rules for the `ItemTypeService` and all its needed dependencies.

It's time to return your attention to the `CreateKernel` method of the `Global` class in the `Global` `.asax.cs` file. Now that you have a module for the `OSIM.ExternalServices` classes, you can provide the implementation of this method that will create a kernel for the `OSIM.ExternalServices` WCF Services application to use. First, you need to add `using` statements for the various Ninject modules you will need in the `OSIM.ExternalServices` project:

```
using OSIM.Core.Services;
using OSIM.ExternalServices.Modules;
using OSIM.Persistence;
```

ExternalServicesModule.cs

Now add the implementation of the `CreateKernel` method that provides an instance of the Ninject `StandardKernel` that is based on the `PersistenceModule`, `CoreServicesModule`, and `ExternalServicesModule`:

```
protected override IKernel CreateKernel()
{
    return new StandardKernel(new PersistenceModule(),
        new CoreServicesModule(),
        new ExternalServicesModule());
}
```

ExternalServicesModule.cs

Now we'll return to the actual `InventoryService` implementation. Currently, it looks like this:

```
public class InventoryService : IInventoryService
{
    public string[] GetItemTypes()
    {
        var kernel =
                new StandardKernel(new PersistenceModule(), new
CoreServicesModule());
        var itemTypeService = kernel.Get<IItemTypeService>();

        var itemTypeList = itemTypeService.GetItemTypes()
            .Select(x => x.Name)
            .ToArray();

        return itemTypeList;
    }
}
```

InventoryService.svc.cs

To complete the conversion of `InventoryService` from relying on statically bound services to injected services, you need to add a constructor to the `InventoryService` class that accepts an instance of an object that implements the `IItemTypeService` interface and stores it in a member variable:

```
private IItemTypeService _itemTypeService;

public InventoryService(IItemTypeService itemTypeService)
{
    _itemTypeService = itemTypeService;
}
```

ItemTypeService.svc.cs

The final step is to remove the code from the `GetItemTypes` method that creates the Ninject kernel and uses the kernel to get an instance of a class that implements `IItemTypeService`. You also need to change any code that calls the local instance of `IItemTypeService` to use the member variable `_itemTypeService` instead:

```
public string[] GetItemTypes()
{
    var itemTypeList = _itemTypeService.GetItemTypes()
        .Select(x => x.Name)
        .ToArray();

    return itemTypeList;
}
```

ItemTypeService.svc.cs

Immediately you should notice that the code in the `GetItemTypes` method is much cleaner and easier to understand. You compile that application and call the `GetItemTypes` method from the WCF Test client again to verify that the service is still working correctly, as shown in Figure 10-7.

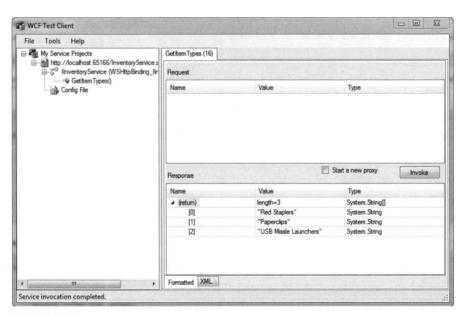

FIGURE 10-7

Writing the Test

Now that you can inject a mocked instance of a class that implements the `IItemType` interface, you can write a unit test for the `InventoryService` WCF service. You start by creating a `cs` file to hold your unit tests. I've placed this file in the `OSIM.ExternalServices` folder of the `OSIM.UnitTests` project and called it `InventoryServiceTests.cs`, as shown in Figure 10-8.

To test the `InventoryService`, you need to add a reference to the `OSIM.ExternalServices` project to the `OSIM.UnitTests` project, as shown in Figure 10-9.

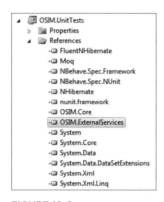

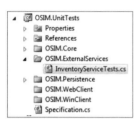

FIGURE 10-8   **FIGURE 10-9**

Next you create your test class, and its base class, using the same BDD naming style used previously:

Available for
download on
Wrox.com

```
namespace OSIM.UnitTests.OSIM.ExternalServices
{
    public class when_using_the_external_inventory_service : Specification
    {

    }

    public class and_getting_a_list_of_item_types :
    when_using_the_external_inventory_service
    {

    }
}
```

InventoryServiceTests.cs

To use the attributes in the NUnit framework, you need to add a `using` statement to bring in the `NUnit.Framework` namespace. You also need to create an instance of the `InventoryService` class, so you need the `OSIM.ExternalServices` namespace as well. Because you will be creating a mocked instance of the `IItemTypeService` core domain service, you need to add `using` statements for the Moq namespace as well as the `OSIM.Core.Services` namespace. Finally, as with the previous unit tests, you use the extension methods provided by NBehave to evaluate the results, so you need to include the NBehave.Spec.NUnit namespace:

```
using Moq;
using NBehave.Spec.NUnit;
using NUnit.Framework;
using OSIM.Core.Services;
using OSIM.ExternalServices;
```

InventoryServiceTests.cs

The Because_of method for the test exercises the GetItemTypes method of InventoryService and stores the resulting string array in the member variable results:

```
protected override void Because_of()
{
    _result = _inventoryService.GetItemTypes();
}
```

InventoryServiceTests.cs

Of course, this requires that you declare the _result and _inventoryService member variables:

```
private IInventoryService _inventoryService;
private string[] _result;
```

InventoryServiceTests.cs

Next you create the actual test method for this test class. To ensure that the InventoryService is performing correctly, you need to verify that the correct number of elements exists in the _result array and that the three items that you have the mock of IItemTypeService return are each represented in the _results array. I'll call this method then_a_list_of_item_types_should_be_returned:

```
[Test]
public void then_a_list_of_item_types_should_be_returned()
{
    _result.Count().ShouldEqual(_expectedNumberOfItems);
    _result.OfType<string>().Select(x => x == _itemOneName)
        .FirstOrDefault()
        .ShouldNotBeNull();
    _result.OfType<string>().Select(x => x == _itemTwoName)
        .FirstOrDefault()
        .ShouldNotBeNull();
    _result.OfType<string>().Select(x => x == _itemThreeName)
        .FirstOrDefault()
        .ShouldNotBeNull();
}
```

InventoryServiceTests.cs

This example uses the `Select` LINQ statement to verify that the items that were given names in the test setup exist in the `_results` string array. You need to add a `using` statement to bring the LINQ namespace into this class:

```
using System.Linq;
```

InventoryServiceTests.cs

Several member variables are used in the `then_a_list_of_item_types_should_be_returned` test method to represent the expected values for this test. You need to declare them in the test class:

```
private int _expectedNumberOfItems;
private string _itemOneName;
private string _itemTwoName;
private string _itemThreeName;
```

InventoryServiceTests.cs

The test compiles, so it's time to run it and observe the results. At this point I expect the test to fail, as it does (see Figure 10-10).

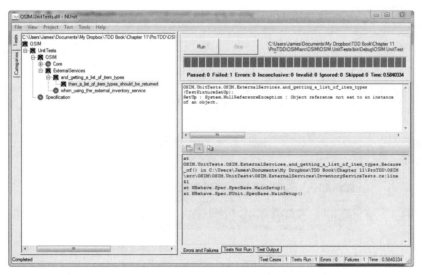

FIGURE 10-10

Stubbing the Dependencies

Line 41 of the `InventoryServiceTests.cs` file is the call to the `GetItemTypes` method of the `_inventoryService` member variable. In previous chapters I stressed that you should not write any code unless you have a failing test that requires that the code be written. When you are writing tests, the same rule applies. Because `InventoryService` has existing application code, you may not need to write any additional code for it. But you want to make sure that you're not creating an overly complicated test to verify the existing logic. From the failing test, you can see that you need to supply an instance of a class that implements the `IInventoryService` interface in the `_inventoryService` member variable. You add an `Establish_context` method to the `and_getting_a_list_of_item_types` test class so that you can provide an instance of a class that implements the `IInventoryService` interface:

```
protected override void Establish_context()
{
    base.Establish_context();

    _itemTypeService = new Mock<IItemTypeService>();
    _inventoryService = new InventoryService(_itemTypeService.Object);
}
```

InventoryServiceTests.cs

`InventoryService` requires an instance of a class that implements the `IItemTypeService` interface. Because this is a unit test, you want to supply a mocked object based on the `IItemTypeService` interface to stand in for that dependency. This means you need to add a declaration of the `_itemTypeService` member variable to the class definition:

```
private Mock<IItemTypeService> _itemTypeService;
```

InventoryServiceTests.cs

At this point you've satisfied the defect that caused the test to fail. It's time to run it again and see if you have done enough to make the test pass, as shown in Figure 10-11.

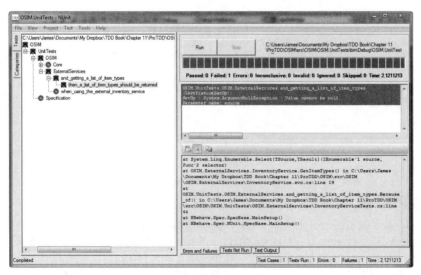

FIGURE 10-11

This new error points out something interesting: Line 19 of the `InventoryService.svc.cs` file raised `ArgumentNullException`:

```
var itemTypeList = _itemTypeService.GetItemTypes()
    .Select(x => x.Name)
    .ToArray();
```

InventoryServiceTests.cs

This line of code works fine, provided that the result of the `GetItemTypes` method of the `ItemTypeService` does not return null. What has happened is that as I was attempting to write a test that I could use to verify functionality that seemed to be working, I uncovered a potential defect. Without this effort, the defect would have gone undiscovered. By thoroughly unit testing, even something as seemingly simple as the `GetItemTypes` method of the `InventoryService` class, I uncovered a potential bug in the system. This bug easily could have made its way through the QA process and not been discovered until production. This should be a lesson: Don't underestimate the power of tests. It doesn't matter how simple code seems; defects can lurk anywhere.

Chapter 12 covers testing and correcting this defect. For the time being, the solution for this test is to provide a stub for the mock of `IItemTypeService` that returns a populated `ItemType` array to `InventoryService`:

```
_itemOneName = "USB drives";
_itemTwoName = "Nerf darts";
_itemThreeName = "Flying Monkeys";
var itemTypeOne = new ItemType {Id = 1, Name = _itemOneName};
var itemTypeTwo = new ItemType {Id = 2, Name = _itemTwoName};
var itemTypeThree = new ItemType {Id = 3, Name = _itemThreeName};
var itemTypeList = new List<ItemType>
    {
        itemTypeOne,
        itemTypeTwo,
        itemTypeThree
    };
_expectedNumberOfItems = itemTypeList.Count;
_itemTypeService.Setup(x => x.GetItemTypes())
    .Returns(itemTypeList);
```

InventoryServiceTests.cs

`ItemType` resides in the `OSIM.Core.Entities` namespace, so you need to add a `using` statement to bring that namespace into this test class. Likewise, you use the `List` class from the `System .Collections.Generic` namespace, which requires a `using` statement as well:

```
using System.Collections.Generic;
using OSIM.Core.Entities;
```

InventoryServiceTests.cs

The complete implementation of the test in the `InventoryServiceTests.cs` file should now look like this:

```csharp
using System.Collections.Generic;
using OSIM.Core.Entities;
using System.Linq;
using Moq;
using NBehave.Spec.NUnit;
using NUnit.Framework;
using OSIM.Core.Services;
using OSIM.ExternalServices;

namespace OSIM.UnitTests.OSIM.ExternalServices
{
    public class when_using_the_external_inventory_service : Specification
    {

    }

    public class and_getting_a_list_of_item_types :
  when_using_the_external_inventory_service
    {
        private IInventoryService _inventoryService;
        private string[] _result;
        private Mock<IItemTypeService> _itemTypeService;
        private int _expectedNumberOfItems;
        private string _itemOneName;
        private string _itemTwoName;
        private string _itemThreeName;

        protected override void Establish_context()
        {
            base.Establish_context();

            _itemTypeService = new Mock<IItemTypeService>();
            _inventoryService = new InventoryService(_itemTypeService.Object);

            _itemOneName = "USB drives";
            _itemTwoName = "Nerf darts";
            _itemThreeName = "Flying Monkeys";
            var itemTypeOne = new ItemType {Id = 1, Name = _itemOneName};
            var itemTypeTwo = new ItemType {Id = 2, Name = _itemTwoName};
            var itemTypeThree = new ItemType {Id = 3, Name = _itemThreeName};
            var itemTypeList = new List<ItemType>
                                {
                                    itemTypeOne,
                                    itemTypeTwo,
                                    itemTypeThree
                                };
            _expectedNumberOfItems = itemTypeList.Count;
            _itemTypeService.Setup(x => x.GetItemTypes())
                .Returns(itemTypeList);
        }
```

```
    protected override void Because_of()
    {
        _result = _inventoryService.GetItemTypes();
    }

    [Test]
    public void then_a_list_of_item_types_should_be_returned()
    {
        _result.Count().ShouldEqual(_expectedNumberOfItems);
        _result.OfType<string>().Select(x => x == _itemOneName)
            .FirstOrDefault()
            .ShouldNotBeNull();
        _result.OfType<string>().Select(x => x == _itemTwoName)
            .FirstOrDefault()
            .ShouldNotBeNull();
        _result.OfType<string>().Select(x => x == _itemThreeName)
            .FirstOrDefault()
            .ShouldNotBeNull();
    }
  }
}
```

InventoryServiceTests.cs

Verifying the Results

The next step is to rerun the test, as shown in Figure 10-12.

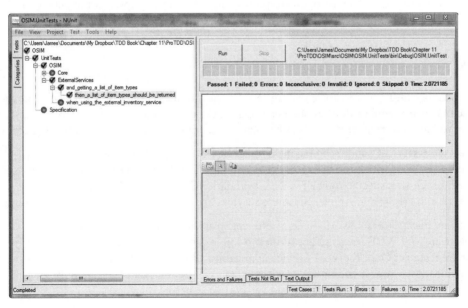

FIGURE 10-12

The passing test indicates that you have verified the functionality of `InventoryService`. As development goes forward, you have this and other tests to verify that functionality of `InventoryService` is not damaged.

Trouble Spots to Watch

WCF services are unlike other classes that you work with in your application. By design, they communicate with other applications and processes via a communications channel. This communications channel employs some sort of transport to deliver messages to and from your WCF service.

The most commonly used transports are HTTP and TCP. WCF also offers inter-machine communication via named pipes and queued delivery via Microsoft Message Queuing (MSMQ). In addition to these primary transport methods, WCF provides an open architecture that enables you to create custom channels to use any transport available.

Most of the time, the choice of transport employed by a service does not pose an issue for testing. In some cases a WCF service may be designed to take advantage of a particular attribute of a specific transport type. Testing WCF services can also be complicated by the ability of WCF services to be called asynchronously.

You need to put a bit more thought into these cases. You should think about how the method under test of the service implementation can be called in a way that closely replicates the attributes of the transport that you are attempting to exploit. These situations represent edge cases in the development of services, but it's important to know they exist. As these situations arise, I find myself turning to the Internet. Websites such as Stack Overflow (`stackoverflow.com`) and the MSDN developer forums (`social.msdn.microsoft.com/Forums/en-US/categories`) are visited daily by developers who are dealing with challenges similar to yours. When in doubt, ask the people on these sites for advice. It can save you a lot of frustration and help keep your WCF services testable.

SUMMARY

WCF services are becoming more widespread in .NET applications. As the users' needs change and new form factors such as mobile devices become popular, the need for services will only increase. It's important to have a testing strategy for WCF services in your application development practice.

Well-designed WCF services contain no business logic. Instead, they rely on the business logic in the application domain layer, which the WCF service consumes. The WCF service itself should concern itself only with processing specific to itself, such as validation and type translation. This results in WCF services that are short and simple. But these services are still code and still need to be tested.

With dependency injection frameworks such as Ninject, you can eliminate statically bound dependencies from your WCF services. The ability to inject dependencies opens the door to WCF services that are testable. Once the WCF service application can support dependency injection, it becomes a simple matter to test your WCF services as you would any other class: Supply the test implementation with mocked dependencies, and verify their functionality.

11

Testing WPF and Silverlight Applications

by Michael Eaton

WHAT'S IN THIS CHAPTER?

➤   Why testing WPF and Silverlight applications is hard

➤   The basics of the MVVM pattern

Windows Presentation Foundation (WPF) and Silverlight are both powerful frameworks that allow you to create visually stunning applications. Both frameworks use Extensible Application Markup Language (XAML) as their markup language. WPF is used for creating desktop-based applications, and Silverlight is used to develop mostly browser-based applications and Windows Phone 7 applications. Despite the fact that these technologies are extremely powerful, testing applications developed using these frameworks can be difficult. Following in the footsteps of previous technologies such as ASP.NET and WinForms, WPF and Silverlight both default to using code-behind files. Code-behind files are great for getting an application up and running quickly, but they make it extremely difficult, if not impossible, to write automated tests for your applications. Code-behind-based applications can also be difficult to maintain, especially as more and more functionality is added. In the world of ASP.NET, the MVC pattern has become the standard for creating highly testable applications while avoiding the pain points of the code-behind.

By the end of this chapter, you will have an understanding of why testing the user interface is difficult. You will learn about patterns that help alleviate some, if not most, of the difficulty of testing WPF and Silverlight-based applications and you will see how to create a WPF application using test-driven development.

This chapter assumes a basic level of knowledge and skill with WPF and Silverlight. If you are unfamiliar with these technologies, many books and websites on these subjects are available.

THE PROBLEM WITH TESTING THE USER INTERFACE

Even though XAML enforces a clean separation of the user interface and your logic, using the code-behind file actually tightly couples the two. This coupling means that you can't instantiate the code-behind without the user interface. In a code-behind-based application, all user code that handles user interactions, validation, and even calls to the database or other services can end up in the code-behind. In an automated test, you don't really want to be forced to create the UI just to test the logic behind it. It's possible to create the UI from a unit test, but this makes testing more difficult and error-prone. It becomes even more difficult when the code-behind interacts with other services.

To write automated tests for WPF and Silverlight applications, you need to fully separate the logic from the user interface in such a way that you can instantiate one without the other. There are many ways to do this, but one pattern has recently emerged and become the de facto standard for WPF development and is becoming more popular in Silverlight development, as discussed next.

The MVVM Pattern

Although it's not a silver bullet, the Model-View-ViewModel (MVVM, sometimes pronounced "moovem") pattern facilitates testing by putting screen-level code into a class that's completely separated from XAML. Not only does MVVM help with testability, but it also helps with reusability. If you work with a user experience (UX) designer, you can focus solely on the markup instead of worrying about any programming or the business logic. Microsoft Expression Blend is a great designer-centric tool that works perfectly with the MVVM model. Figure 11-1 is a high-level overview of how MVVM works.

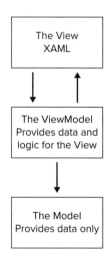

FIGURE 11-1

In a nutshell, the model contains your data, the view presents your data, and the ViewModel ties the two together, sorting and filtering the data as needed. The ViewModel also provides methods and commands for the view. Each view (the XAML) has a corresponding ViewModel. The ViewModel has no knowledge of the view, but the view usually has intimate knowledge of the ViewModel, at least in terms of what it's binding to. It's also possible for multiple views to use the same ViewModel. Each ViewModel pulls in the necessary models based on its needs. The models themselves tend to be plain old code objects that aren't much more than containers for your data, although they may or may not be your domain models.

For the view to use the ViewModel, it must bind to public properties exposed by the ViewModel. This is normally done by setting the view's `DataContext` to be an instance of the ViewModel and then binding each control to individual properties of the ViewModel. Because of this, you can avoid almost any code in the code-behind, at least as it relates to populating controls. If you're coming from a WinForms or possibly a Classic Visual Basic (versions 3 through 6) background, data binding always sounded good, but it tended to fall apart when used outside of basic scenarios. The data binding in Silverlight and WPF is a huge improvement over previous incarnations, and it makes MVVM easy to use. The following code shows basic examples of a model, a ViewModel, and a view:

```csharp
public class MyModel
{
    public string FirstName { get; set; }
    public string LastName { get; set; }
}

public class MyViewModel : INotifyPropertyChanged
{
Private MyModel _instanceOfMyModel;
public MyViewModel(MyModel instanceOfMyModel)
    {
        _instanceOfMyModel = instanceOfMyModel;
    }

    private string _firstName;
    public string FirstName
    {
        get { return _firstName; }
        set
        {
            _firstName = value;
            OnPropertyChanged("FirstName");
        }
    }

    private string _lastName;
    public string LastName
    {
        get { return _lastName; }
        set
        {
            _lastName = value;
            OnPropertyChanged("LastName");
        }
    }

    public event PropertyChangedEventHandler PropertyChanged;
    private void OnPropertyChanged(string propertyName)
    {
        if(PropertyChanged != null)
            PropertyChanged(this, new PropertyChangedEventArgs(propertyName));
    }
}

<Window x:Class="WpfApplication1.MainWindow"
        xmlns="http://schemas.microsoft.com/winfx/2006/xaml/presentation"
        xmlns:x="http://schemas.microsoft.com/winfx/2006/xaml"
        Title="MainWindow" Height="350" Width="525">
    <Grid>
        <TextBox Text="{Binding FirstName}" />
        <TextBox Text="{Binding LastName}" />
    </Grid>
</Window>
```

The code to make it all work together can be as simple as this:

```
var vm = new MyViewModel(new MyModel { FirstName = "John", LastName = "Doe" };
var view = new MainWindow { DataContext = vm };
view.Show();
```

You'll notice that the constructor in the example takes a single argument:

```
public MyViewModel(MyModel instanceOfMyModel)
    {
        _instanceOfMyModel = instanceOfMyModel;
    }
```

The argument in this case is an instance of the model that holds the data we want the view to display. While it may seem strange to pass in our data this way, it sets us up for using a dependency injection framework like Ninject if and when we need it.

The `INotifyPropertyChanged` interface is a key component of data binding. It is used to notify binding clients when a property has changed. For example, if a text box is bound to the property of a `ViewModel` and the `ViewModel` implements `INotifyPropertyChanged`, as long as the property raises the `NotifyPropertyChanged` event whenever that property is changed, the view will be notified and updated.

Although it is possible to use the MVVM pattern without a framework, I strongly suggest that you avoid writing all the MVVM plumbing yourself and find a framework you're comfortable with. Using a framework lets you focus more on the business and less on the pattern's implementation details. Some of the more popular MVVM frameworks include Prism (`http://compositewpf .codeplex.com`), created and maintained by the Microsoft Patterns and Practices team, MVVM Light (`http://mvvmlight.codeplex.com/`), written by Laurent Bugnion; MVVM Foundation (`http:// mvvmfoundation.codeplex.com/`), written by Josh Smith; Cinch (`http://cinch.codeplex.com/`), written by Sacha Barber; and Caliburn.Micro (`http://caliburnmicro.codeplex.com/`), written by Rob Eisenberg.

Each has its own strengths and weaknesses, so you should check them all out and make an informed decision based on your needs. My preferred framework is Caliburn.Micro, so unless otherwise noted, all the examples in this chapter use it. One of the great things it brings to the table is the ability to bind without actually writing any binding statements. It's able to do this based simply on how you name your classes, properties and methods. It may sound confusing, but behind the scenes, Caliburn.Micro is actually creating the necessary binding statements – it's just removing that particular step for us. Caliburn.Micro is extremely flexible and allows you to tweak much of its behavior. Because it is open source, if it doesn't do exactly what you want, you can do what I've done on several occasions and modify the code. I'll barely scratch the surface of what Caliburn. Micro can do, so be sure to check the website and Eisenberg's blog. If your company has an aversion towards open source, Prism is a great framework.

How MVVM Makes WPF/Silverlight Applications Testable

MVVM allows you to completely separate your user interface from the code that manages it. Because of this separation, you can instantiate the management code without having to worry about displaying the user interface. In an automated test suite, the last thing you want to do is worry about a window appearing that needs you to click a button or enter some text.

A typical WPF application that uses the MVVM pattern has, in some form or another, Models, Views, and ViewModels, along with various other folders and classes. I structure my applications so that they look like Figure 11-2.

Many times, the models are in a project that is entirely separate from your Views and ViewModels.

FIGURE 11-2

When it comes to testing an application that uses the MVVM pattern, you focus all your testing efforts on the ViewModel. In fact, a good way to think about it is that interacting directly with the ViewModel should be exactly like working with the view, at least from the end users' perspective.

Let's consider the following user story:

A user should be able to search for item types.

If you break this into smaller pieces, you need the following:

➤ A text box for entering the item to search for

➤ A Search button that initiates the search process

➤ A list box to display the search results

➤ A Clear button in case the user wants to reset the search criteria

➤ A Cancel button to close the Search screen

I'm a strong believer in not allowing the user to perform an action until all the requirements are met. In this case, the following requirements must be dealt with during the sign-in process:

➤ The user cannot click the Search button to initiate the search process until the search criteria has been entered.

➤ The user can click the Clear button only if he or she has entered something to search for.

➤ If the user successfully searches, the results must be displayed in a list box.

➤ The user can click the Cancel button at any time.

If you use the standard code-behind to handle the button click events and data entry validation, you would have a tough time automating the test and would end up manually starting the application and typing whatever came to mind to see if you get the expected results. A much better way is to start writing tests against a yet-to-be-written ViewModel.

 One of the tenets of Caliburn.Micro is the idea of convention over configuration. Because of this, I have adopted a specific naming convention for my ViewModels and the methods and properties they contain. Don't be too concerned if my conventions seem strange or don't match what you currently use, because Caliburn.Micro allows you to customize the conventions used.

Using the BDD naming style, you start by writing the base class for the initial set of tests:

```
public class when_attempting_to_search : Specification
{
}
```

SearchTests.cs

Once you have your base class, you can move on to writing the test to handle the case where the search criteria property is empty. Remember, if the search criteria property is empty, meaning that the user didn't enter anything, the user should not be allowed to search. The Because_of method for this test sets the Criteria property to string.Empty and then puts the Boolean result of the CanSearch property of SearchViewModel in the _result variable:

```
Using System;
Using NBehave.Spec.NUnit;
Using NUnit.Framework;
Namespace OSIM.UnitTests.OSIM.WinClient
{
    Public class and_the_search_criteria_is_blank : when_attempting_to_search
    {
        Protected override void Because_of()
        {
            _searchViewModel.Criteria = string.Empty;
            _result = _searchViewModel.CanSearch;
        }
        . . .
    }
}
```

SearchTests.cs

Immediately after the Because_of method, you declare the variables you need and then create the actual SearchViewModel instance in the Establish_context method:

```
Private bool _result;
Private ISearchViewModel _searchViewModel;
Protected override void Establish_context()
{
    base.Establish_context();
    _searchViewModel = new SearchViewModel();
}
```

SearchTests.cs

The then_cansearch_should_be_false test simply checks the _result variable, which holds the value of the CanSearch property, to ensure that it's false:

```
[Test]
Public void then_cansearch_should_be_false()
{
    _result.ShouldEqual(false);
}
```

SearchTests.cs

Again, because you write your tests first, you can't build successfully, because you are missing `ISearchViewModel`. You start with the basics with this interface and then write just enough code to get the test to pass:

```
public interface ISearchViewModel
{
    string Criteria { get; set; }
    bool CanSearch { get; }
}
```

SearchViewModel.cs

Next is a bare-bones concrete implementation of `ISearchViewModel`:

```
public class SearchViewModel : PropertyChangedBase,ISearchViewModel
{
    public string Criteria { get; set; }
    public bool CanSearch { get { return true; } }
}
```

SearchViewModel.cs

`PropertyChangedBase` is part of the Caliburn.Micro framework. It is an implementation of `INotifyPropertyChanged`, including a convenience method that eliminates the need to scatter magic strings all over the ViewModels. The whole idea behind `INotifyPropertyChanged` is that when a property in a ViewModel is bound to a control in a view, any changes made to that property automatically are reflected in the view. Although implementing `INotifyPropertyChanged` isn't a requirement of these tests, if you know the application will need it, as is the case with this example, you can include it here even though the need at this point isn't quite apparent. `INotifyPropertyChanged` is one of those things that makes binding really awesome, but it does add some friction to the process of writing the ViewModels. Using a framework such as Caliburn .Micro reduces a bit of that friction.

After you add `PropertyChangedBase` to `SearchViewModel`, you need to modify your property set methods to raise the notification. Caliburn.Micro provides two methods to do so. One method takes the name of the property as a string, much as if you had implemented `INotifyPropertyChanged` yourself:

```
NotifyOfPropertyChange("Criteria");
```

The other method takes a lambda expression:

```
NotifyOfPropertyChange(() => Criteria);
```

My preference is the lambda expression, so for this example you need to expand the `Criteria` property in `SearchViewModel` to use the second version:

```
Private string _criteria;
Public string Criteria
{
    Get { return _criteria; }
    set
    {
        _criteria = value;
        NotifyOfPropertyChange(() => Criteria);

    }
}
```

SearchViewModel.cs

Running the test should give you a failure and the familiar red bar. Remember this line of code?

```
Public bool CanSearch { get { return true; }
```

SearchViewModel.cs

In `CanSearch` the value of `true` is hard-coded because you want to ensure a failing test so that you can stick with the red-green-refactor work flow. Because the test is meant to ensure that something must be in the `Criteria` property, and because you want a passing test now, change this property as follows:

```
Public bool CanSearch
{
    Get { return !string.IsNullOrEmpty(Criteria); }
}
```

SearchViewModel.cs

Rerunning the test should give you a pass and a green bar. Now it's time to refactor to make sure the code does something other than return a hard-coded value:

```
Public bool CanSearch
```

When you run the test again, you get a pass and the green bar.

The next test makes sure the user can search if the `Criteria` property has a value:

```
Public class and_the_search_criteria_is_not_blank : when_attempting_to_search
{
    Private bool _result;
    Private ISearchViewModel _searchViewModel;

    Protected override void Establish_context()
    {
        base.Establish_context();
        _searchViewModel = new SearchViewModel();
    }

    Protected override void Because_of()
    {
        _searchViewModel.Criteria = "foo";
        _result = _searchViewModel.CanSearch;
    }

    [Test]
    Public void then_cansearch_should_be_true()
    {
        _result.ShouldEqual(true);
    }
}
```

SearchTests.cs

Because of the code you wrote to get `and_the_search_criteria_is_blank`, this test passed the first time.

To meet the requirements of the user story, you still must write tests to help drive out the rest of the ViewModel. The first tests you wrote simply checked to make sure the user could initiate the search process if the search criteria property was not empty.

What about the case where the user wants to click the Clear button and reset the Search criteria property to a blank? The Clear button should be enabled only if the user has entered something to search for. You write two tests for this requirement. The first tests the case when `Criteria` is empty:

```
Public class and_wanting_to_clear_when_criteria_is_empty :
 when_attempting_to_search
{
    Private bool _result;
    private ISearchViewModel _searchViewModel;
    protected override void Establish_context()
    {
        base.Establish_context();
        _searchViewModel = new SearchViewModel();
    }

    Protected override void Because_of()
    {
        _result = _searchViewModel.CanClear;
    }
```

```
[Test]
Public void then_canclear_should_be_false()
{
    _result.ShouldEqual(true);
}
}
```

SearchTests.cs

Of course, this won't compile, because `SearchViewModel` doesn't have a `CanClear` property. Adding this is pretty simple. First you need to update the `ISearchViewModel` interface:

```
bool CanClear { get; }
```

SearchViewModel.cs

The implementation of the `CanClear` property in `SearchViewModel` is about as simple as it gets:

```
public bool CanClear
{
    get { return false; }
}
```

SearchViewModel.cs

The green bar shows that the test failed, so now it's time to make it pass. This is as simple as changing the `CanClear` property:

```
public bool CanClear
{
    get { return !string.IsNullOrEmpty(Criteria); }
}
```

SearchViewModel.cs

The green bar should appear after that change. Now it's time to write the opposite test:

```
public class and_wanting_to_clear_when_criteria_is_not_empty :
  when_attempting_to_search
{
    private bool _result;
    private ISearchViewModel _searchViewModel;
    protected override void Establish_context()
    {
        base.Establish_context();
        _searchViewModel = new SearchViewModel();
        _searchViewModel.Criteria = "foo";
    }
```

```
    protected override void Because_of()
    {
        _result = _searchViewModel.CanClear;
    }

    [Test]
    public void then_canclear_should_be_false()
    {
        _result.ShouldEqual(true);
    }
}
```

You've now written tests to make sure the user enters something to search for before he or she can actually search. You also wrote a test to make sure the user can always clear and start over. What happens if the user enters the search criteria and actually searches or clears? Start with the clear test. When the user clicks the Clear button, two things should occur. First, the criteria should be reset to blank. Second, if there are any results, they should be removed.

Because you're using the MVVM pattern, instead of writing code in the SearchButton_Click or ClearButton_Click events, you need to somehow write code that can be bound to the buttons. Using Caliburn.Micro, all you need to do is create methods in the ViewModel that have the same name as the control in the view. So, if you have a button with x:Name="Clear" in your view, all you need is a method in SearchViewModel also named "Clear". This is yet another reason to use frameworks such as Caliburn.Micro.

```
public class and_executing_clear : when_attempting_to_search
{
    private bool _canClear;
    private string _result;
    private ISearchViewModel _searchViewModel;
    protected override void Establish_context()
    {
        base.Establish_context();
        _searchViewModel = new SearchViewModel();
        _searchViewModel.Criteria = "foo";
    }

    protected override void Because_of()
    {
        _canClear = _searchViewModel.CanClear;
        _searchViewModel.Clear();
        _result = _searchViewModel.Criteria;
    }

    [Test]
    public void then_criteria_should_be_blank()
    {
        _result.ShouldEqual(string.Empty);
    }
}
```

Running this test results in a failure because the build failed due to the missing `Clear` method in `SearchViewModel`. After updating `ISearchViewModel`, you write just enough code to get the test to fail properly. Here's the updated `ISearchViewModel`:

```
public interface ISearchViewModel
{
    string Criteria { get; set; }
    bool CanSearch { get; }
    bool CanClear { get; }
    void Clear();
}
```

SearchViewModel.cs

Here's the simplest implementation of the `Clear` method in `SearchViewModel`:

```
public void Clear()
{
}
```

SearchViewModel.cs

The red bar appears with the following message:

```
Test 'OSIM.UnitTests.OSIM.WinClient.and_executing_clear
.then_criteria_should_be_blank' failed:
    Expected string length 0 but was 3. Strings differ at index 0.
    Expected: <string.Empty>
    But was:  "foo"
    -----------^
```

SearchViewModel.cs

To make this test pass, you need to modify the `Clear` method:

```
public void Clear()
{
    Criteria = string.Empty;
}
```

SearchViewModel.cs

You're back to seeing all green, but something is still missing. When the user clicks the Clear button, not only should the criteria be reset to blank, but any results that are present should be removed.

Now you simply add another test to the `and_executing_clear` class:

```
[Test]
public void then_results_should_be_cleared()
{
    _searchResults.ShouldBeNull();
}
```

SearchTests.cs

Because you can't build, you need to update `ISearchViewModel` and `SearchViewModel` to support search results. The results are `List<ItemType>`:

```
public interface ISearchViewModel
{
    // previous code not shown
    List<ItemType> Results { get; set; }
```

SearchViewModel.cs

Here's the simplest implementation:

```
Private List<ItemType> _results;
public List<ItemType> Results
{
    get { return _results; }
    set
    {
        _results = value;
        OnPropertyChanged(() => Results);
    }
}
```

SearchViewModel.cs

Instead of the red bar you might be expecting, the test passed! This is always a red flag to check on the code you just wrote, because it's never a good thing to expect a failure but then see the test pass.

If you look at the test, you can see what happened:

```
[Test]
public void then_results_should_be_cleared()
{
    _searchResults.ShouldBeNull();
}
```

SearchTests.cs

The simplest implementation of `Results` always returns `null` because you are not actually creating the results yet. You'll deal with that in the Search tests, but you can take a shortcut now and modify the `Establish_context()` method of the `and_executing_clear` test to set `Results` to new `List<ItemType>()`:

```
protected override void Establish_context()
{
    base.Establish_context();
    _searchViewModel = new SearchViewModel();
    _searchViewModel.Criteria = "foo";
    _searchViewModel.Results = new List<ItemType>();
}
```

SearchTests.cs

Running the test again gives you the familiar red bar and the failure you were expecting. To get the test to pass, you need to make sure that when `Clear` is executed, the `Results` are set to null. The `Clear` method should now look like this:

```
public void Clear()
{
    Criteria = string.Empty;
    Results = null;
}
```

SearchViewModel.cs

The green bar tells you that everything is working as expected, so it's time to move on to more tests to drive out the rest of the `SignInViewModel` class. The previous tests were all part of the `when_attempting_to_search` specification and were all related to the behavior that occurs before the user can even click the Search button. Now you're firmly in new territory: The user has entered the item to search for and clicked the Search button. Although you haven't created the view yet, much work still needs to be done in the ViewModel.

You start by creating another base class named `when_searching`:

```
Public class when_searching : Specification { }
```

SearchTests.cs

The first test to write checks for a user who is searching for an item that doesn't exist:

```
Public class and_searching_for_an_item_that_does_not_exist : when_searching
{
    Private List<ItemType> _results;
    Private bool _canSearch;
    Private ISearchViewModel _searchViewModel;
    Protected override void Establish_context()
    {
        base.Establish_context();
```

```
_searchViewModel = new SearchViewModel();
_searchViewModel.Criteria = "foo";
}
```

SearchTests.cs

Notice how the `Criteria` property of `_searchViewModel` is set to `"foo"`? That is a way of emulating a user's entering the name of an `ItemType` that doesn't exist. Remember, when you finally bind a text box in the `Criteria` property of `SearchViewModel`, anything typed into the text box is reflected in the ViewModel itself.

The `Because_of()` method exercises the `Search` method of `SearchViewModel`. When the search is complete, a value indicating whether results were returned is stored in the `_result` variable. Notice how you also store a copy of the `CanSearch` property:

```
Protected override void Because_of()
{
_canSearch = _searchViewModel.CanSearch;
_searchViewModel.Search();
_results = _searchViewModel. Results;
}
```

SearchTests.cs

The test `then_results_should_be_null` does a couple things. First, it ensures that the user can sign in. This helps catch silly errors such as not setting up the test correctly in `Establish_context`. Then the test checks to see if the `ErrorMessage` property was set correctly, because the password was incorrect when the `SignIn` method was called:

```
[Test]
Public void then_results_should_be_null()
{
    _canSearch.ShouldBeTrue();
    _results.ShouldBeNull();
}
}
```

SearchTests.cs

Again, the build fails because `SearchViewModel` doesn't contain the `Search` method. After you add the following to the `ISearchViewModel` interface, you can write just enough real code in `SearchViewModel` to get the test to fail:

```
Void Search();
```

SearchViewModel.cs

The most basic code you can write to implement the `Search` method in `SearchViewModel` to get a build running looks like this:

```
Public void Search()
{
    Results = new List<ItemType>();
}
```

Running this test should result in a failure and the red bar. Now it's time to refactor the `SignInViewModel` to get this particular test to pass:

```
public void Search()
{
    if(Criteria == "foo")
        Results = null;
    else
        Results = new List<ItemType>();
}
```

Once this test is passing, it's time to write `and_searching_for_an_itemtype_that_does_exist`. The setup is the same, except for this code:

```
protected override void Establish_context()
{
    base.Establish_context();
    _searchViewModel = new SearchViewModel();
    _searchViewModel.Criteria = "USB";
}

[Test]
public void then_results_should_be_null()
{
    _canSearch.ShouldEqual(true);
    _results.ShouldNotBeEmpty();
}
```

The red bar appears, telling you the test failed. Recall the implementation of `Search`:

```
public void Search()
{
    if(Criteria == "foo")
        Results = null;
    else
        Results = new List<ItemType>();
}
```

The simplest way to get this particular test to pass is to modify Search to return some hard-coded values:

```csharp
public void Search()
{
    if (Criteria == "foo")
        Results = null;
    else
    {
        Results = new List<ItemType>();
        if (Criteria == "USB")
        {
            Results.Add(new ItemType { Id = 1, Name = "USB Key - 2GB" });
            Results.Add(new ItemType { Id = 2, Name = "USB Key - 4GB" });
            Results.Add(new ItemType { Id = 3, Name = "USB Key - 8GB" });
            Results.Add(new ItemType { Id = 4, Name = "USB Key - 16GB" });
        }
    }
}
```

SearchViewModel.cs

Running the test results in the familiar green bar. In the grand scheme of things, instead of hard-coding data, you'll call methods in a service or possibly a repository class, pass in the criteria, and set results to the output from those methods.

Bringing It All Together

Finally, it's time to implement `SearchView`! Thankfully this is a simple process. You'll notice there are absolutely no binding statements due to the naming conventions used and the great things Caliburn .Micro brings to us. Our `Criteria` textbox is named Criteria. Caliburn.Micro looks at the ViewModel to find a property with a matching name. Once it finds a match, it will create the actual binding:

```xml
<UserControl x:Class="OSIM.WinClient.SearchView"
        xmlns="http://schemas.microsoft.com/winfx/2006/xaml/presentation"
        xmlns:x="http://schemas.microsoft.com/winfx/2006/xaml"
        Background="LightGray"
Height="200" Width="325">
    <Grid>
        <DockPanel LastChildFill="True">
            <StackPanel
                Orientation="Horizontal"
                DockPanel.Dock="Top">

                <TextBlock Text="Criteria:" Margin="0,0,5,0"/>
                <TextBox x:Name="Criteria" Width="100" Margin="0,0,5,0" />
                <Button x:Name="Search" Content="Search" Margin="5,0,5,0"/>
                <Button x:Name="Clear" Content="Clear" Margin="5,0,5,0"/>
            </StackPanel>
            <ListBox x:Name="Results" DisplayMemberPath="Name"/>
        </DockPanel>
    </Grid>
</UserControl>
```

SearchView.xaml

The project now looks like Figure 11-3.

To take advantage of Caliburn.Micro, you need to do a little setup work in the WPF project. The first step is to modify `App.xaml` to remove the `StartupUri` tag. `App.xaml.cs` should be trimmed so that it's not much more than this:

```
public partial class App : Application
{
    public App()
    {
    }
}
```

```
┌─────────────────────────────────┐
│ ▲ ▣▦ OSIM.WinClient               │
│   ▷ ▣▦ Properties                 │
│   ▷ ▣  References                 │
│   ▲ 📁 ViewModels                 │
│       ▣▤ SearchViewModel.cs       │
│   ▲ 📁 Views                      │
│     ▲ ▣▦ SearchView.xaml          │
│         ▣▤ SearchView.xaml.cs     │
│       ▣▥ app.config               │
│   ▲ ▣▦ App.xaml                   │
│       ▣▤ App.xaml.cs              │
└─────────────────────────────────┘
```

FIGURE 11-3

App.xaml.cs

The next step is to add a "bootstrapper" to the project that configures the framework. In the root of the WinClient project, you create a class named `WinClientBootstrapper` that looks like this:

```
public class WinClientBootstrapper : Bootstrapper<SearchViewModel> { }
```

App.xaml.cs

That's all you need. Remember that you write the simplest bootstrapper possible to get your project working. The Caliburn.Micro website (`http://caliburnmicro.codeplex.com/`) contains a lot of great content that describes all the things you can do with the bootstrapper, so be sure to check it out. Now you add a little XAML to `app.xaml`:

```xml
<Application x:Class="OSIM.WinClient.App"
             xmlns="http://schemas.microsoft.com/winfx/2006/xaml/presentation"
             xmlns:x="http://schemas.microsoft.com/winfx/2006/xaml"
             xmlns:local="clr-namespace:OSIM.WinClient"
             >
    <Application.Resources>
        <ResourceDictionary>
            <ResourceDictionary.MergedDictionaries>
                <ResourceDictionary>
                    <local:WinClientBootstrapper x:Key="bootstrapper"/>
                </ResourceDictionary>
            </ResourceDictionary.MergedDictionaries>
        </ResourceDictionary>
    </Application.Resources>
</Application>
```

App.xaml.cs

If you're writing a Silverlight application, `App.xaml` looks a little different:

```
<Application x:Class="OSIM.WinClient.App"
             xmlns="http://schemas.microsoft.com/winfx/2006/xaml/presentation"
             xmlns:x="http://schemas.microsoft.com/winfx/2006/xaml"
             xmlns:local="clr-namespace:OSIM.WinClient"
             >
    <Application.Resources>
        <local:WinClientBootstrapper x:Key="bootstrapper"/>
    </Application.Resources>
</Application>
```

App.xaml.cs

That's it. That's all you need to use Caliburn.Micro. Based on the conventions used, and with the modifications to `App.xaml` and the `WinClientBootstrapper` class, when you run the WinClient application, the basic search screen appears. Notice how the Search and Clear buttons are disabled until something is entered into the Criteria field. If something is in the Criteria text box and then you click the Clear button, the contents are cleared, and the Search and Clear buttons are disabled again. Entering some criteria and clicking the Search button displays a list of matching `ItemTypes`. Figure 11-4 shows the very basic search screen.

FIGURE 11-4

This project was approached from the standpoint of writing the ViewModel first and then writing tests to support the needed functionality. You could have just as easily started with the view, but either way, you have created an application that has been thoroughly unit-tested and that meets the requirements of the user story presented at the beginning of the chapter.

SUMMARY

WPF and Silverlight are powerful frameworks for creating rich applications using XAML. Writing unit-testing applications with these frameworks can be difficult, but it is not something you should avoid. As with WCF and ASP.NET, it is important to have a firm testing strategy for your varied clients.

Instead of working around the limitations of the code-behind paradigm and trying to instantiate the tightly coupled classes, the MVVM pattern facilitates a true separation of the user interface and the code that controls it.

Not only does using MVVM allow you to unit-test your applications, but it also makes your applications more maintainable. It also helps the developer/designer relationship by allowing designers to work only in the XAML without having to worry about the code. Several great MVVM frameworks remove the burden of implementing this pattern, letting you focus on the process of writing great software.

PART IV
Requirements and Tools

12

Dealing with Defects and New Requirements

WHAT'S IN THIS CHAPTER?

➤ Understanding why applications need to be flexible in a modern business computing environment

➤ Using TDD to deal with changes to your application

➤ Building more flexible applications through TDD

➤ Practicing TDD in a situation where a new feature has been introduced or a defect identified in an application

Application development efforts do not live in a vacuum. The increasing popularity of agile project methodologies is testament to that fact. Even in an agile environment, most development efforts span months — if not years — between the time the first requirement is documented and the day the application is deployed to production. That leaves a lot of time for requirements to change.

Change doesn't end after an application reaches production. No matter how good a job the development team and QA department do, most applications have some sort of defect that isn't discovered until the application reaches production. Even if an application makes it to production and no defects are found, actions and influences from a variety of external forces (customer, government, market forces) can demonstrate a need for changes in an application.

In TDD, defects and new requirements represent opportunities to create new tests. By approaching defects and new requirements with a test-first philosophy, you can more easily deliver a quality application without damaging existing functionality. Reading this book has helped you acquire the skills and knowledge you need to handle these situations. Now it's simply a matter of taking those skills and that knowledge and applying them in a slightly different manner.

HANDLING CHANGE

Change is inevitable. Historically, most business applications have not dealt with change well. This is because most applications, despite the best intentions of the developer and architects, become brittle and fragile. Without the security of a unit and integration test suite, most applications devolve into the code equivalent of a Jenga tower. Before long, the application is so unstable that most developers are afraid to touch it, lest the whole thing come tumbling down.

These applications lacked automated unit and integration tests. Without a method to automatically regression-test an application that had a change made to it, no one could guarantee that the application would function properly after the change. Developing an application while practicing TDD provides a suite of these tests to ensure that as changes are made, the application itself remains stable.

The practice of TDD has another side effect that makes applications more flexible in the face of change. Developers who practice TDD, whether by design or as a side effect of writing code for testability, seem to follow the SOLID principles more than developers who do not practice TDD. Adhering to the SOLID principles results in software that is easier to maintain and extend. This is clearly a benefit in an environment where change is inevitable.

Change Happens

An application might need to change after being deployed to production for a number of reasons. Perhaps the company has adopted a new business strategy or identified a new market to enter. Many business sectors such as finance and medicine are heavily regulated by state and federal government. New laws and regulations are being passed all the time. Customers who use an application might want new features to be added or changes to be made to existing functionality. And no application is immune to defects.

Whatever the source or reason for a change to your application, as a developer you must address new requirements and defects. In an application where TDD has been practiced from the start, the approach may be obvious. But even in cases where an application has not been developed using TDD, the practice can and should still be employed when developing new features and fixing defects. Tests ensure a degree of quality in your application, and this commitment to quality should be carried through post-deployment development work.

Adding New Features

New features can be introduced into an application at any time. New features introduced during the normal development cycle when an agile methodology is being used are nothing noteworthy. They are added to the project backlog and scheduled like any other feature. Features introduced after the application has been deployed to production, when the bulk of the development team has presumably moved on to another project, are a bit different.

It's important that features introduced after an application's primary development life cycle has ended are treated like features that are known and built during that application's primary development life cycle. Do not fall into the trap of thinking that corners can be cut and quality compromised in the name of speed because the application is "done." There will always be new features. There will always be defects. Allowing yourself as a developer to take a shortcut at the expense of quality sends you down a slippery slope that leads to a brittle, unmaintainable application with an incomplete test suite.

When a new feature for an application is added, it needs to go through the same process that other features of the application went through. The same discovery and design process that was used to build the other features of the application need to be employed again. This is true even if the new feature is small. There are no small features. A wise person once said, "Judge me by my size, do you?" An improperly designed and implemented "small feature" can wreak just as much havoc, cause as much damage, and anger a user base as quickly as a mishandled "large" feature.

As soon as the new feature has been properly designed, with input from the business and the technical side of the project, development can begin. Like the features developed during the primary application development life cycle, the development of the new feature begins with a test. Again, as with the previous development of the application, the test should fail. A failing test for a new feature signifies that your test is likely testing for the right (nonexistent) functionality and that the functionality in question is truly not implemented in the application. If your test passes without your having to write any additional code, you have some research to do. Is your test really testing for the new functionality? Is it testing in the correct place? Does the feature in question already exist in the application and is somehow being obscured by something else in the application? These questions must be answered before you proceed.

After the correct test is written, your goal is the same as during the application's primary development life cycle: You should strive to write just enough code to make the test pass. At the same time, you must make sure that no existing tests begin to fail. If they do, you should determine why and work to make those tests, in addition to the new tests, pass. After all the tests are passing, the new feature is complete and ready for deployment.

Addressing Defects

On my development teams, a defect is defined as functionality in code that does not reflect the documented specifications via the user stories and/or features. That means that a defect can exist only if the application functions differently than described by a specification the development team has in hand. When a business user tells a developer, "The application specifications say a tax rate of 7.5% should be applied in this situation, but the application is applying a tax rate of 6%," he is describing a defect. The specification states that the tax rate should be 7.5% for a given set of circumstances, but it is not. When a business user tells a developer, "I know the specification *says* that on Tuesdays customers who order more than five items get a 15% discount, but what I *meant* was that when a user orders $100 or more of merchandise on Friday, he gets free shipping," he is describing a new feature. Technically, the business user is describing two features if he really wants me to remove the functionality for the discount applied on Tuesdays.

The distinction can be important even if the approach is the same. When a new feature is requested, the work is scheduled for development based on the development team's bandwidth and the priority that the business has assigned to the new feature. If the business wants the feature implemented right away, another feature on the schedule must be postponed. When a defect is reported, depending on its severity, the development team reprioritizes their work to fix the defect as soon as possible. Defects always have a high priority because quality is important to the development team. The team is personally invested in the delivery of a quality application, and they will work to fix the defect and deliver the agreed-upon features by the end of the iteration.

When developing fixes for defects, the approach is the same as the development approach for features. The first step is to discuss the defect with the business to make sure the development team understands how the application should behave and how that behavior is different from how the application currently functions. After the business rules have been revalidated, you start by writing a test. As with new features, this test should fail. A nonfailing test may indicate that you are not testing the correct thing. The test should expose the defect. That way, you can be assured that not only is the defect fixed, but it won't reappear.

Starting with a Test

In Chapter 11, a potential defect was uncovered during the development of the `InventoryService` WCF service, as shown in Figure 12-1.

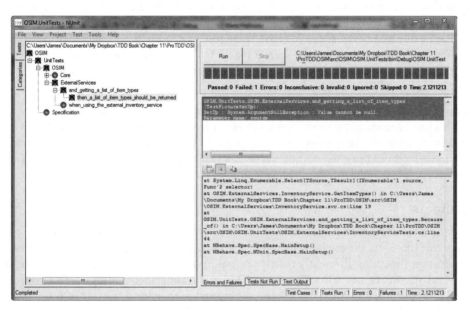

FIGURE 12-1

For review, here is the code that generated this error:

```csharp
public string[] GetItemTypes()
{
    var itemTypeList = _itemTypeService.GetItemTypes()
        .Select(x => x.Name)
        .ToArray();

    return itemTypeList;
}
```

InventoryService.svc.cs

The error occurs when the `GetItemTypes` method of `ItemTypeService` returns a null. This is an undesirable behavior for this method. Granted, the `GetItemTypes` method of `ItemTypeService` should never have cause to return a null. Even if no `ItemTypes` are in the data store, Fluent NHibernate still returns an empty instance of a list. The `GetItemTypes` method on `ItemTypeService` simply passes that empty list up the chain to the `GetItemTypes` method on `InventoryService`.

So why worry about it? On my team we have a requirement on all applications in production: The user should never see an unhandled exception. Aside from being a potential security leak, most users would not know how to recover from such a situation. Most users would also be upset that the application had died and must be restarted, causing them to potentially lose work. The user needs to be isolated and protected from the unhandled .NET exception.

I start working on this defect by creating a test. Specifically, I want to see a test where the stub on the `GetItemTypes` method of `ItemTypeService` returns a null:

```
public class and_getting_a_list_of_item_types_when_the_returned_list_is_null :
    when_using_the_external_inventory_service
{
    private IInventoryService _inventoryService;
    private string[] _result;
    private Mock<IItemTypeService> _itemTypeService;

    protected override void Establish_context()
    {
        base.Establish_context();

        _itemTypeService = new Mock<IItemTypeService>();
        _inventoryService = new InventoryService(_itemTypeService.Object);

        List<ItemType> itemTypeList = null;
        _itemTypeService.Setup(x => x.GetItemTypes())
            .Returns(itemTypeList);
    }

    protected override void Because_of()
    {
        _result = _inventoryService.GetItemTypes();
    }

    [Test]
    public void then_an_empty_list_of_item_types_should_be_returned()
    {
        _result.ShouldNotBeNull();
        _result.Count().ShouldEqual(0);
    }
}
```

InventoryServiceTests.cs

This test should look similar to the test written to verify the functionality of the `InventoryService` WCF service in Chapter 10. In fact, it's almost identical — with two exceptions. The first change to point out is that instead of returning a `List` of `ItemTypes`, the `GetItemTypes` stub on the `ItemTypeService` mock returns a null. This replicates a situation in which the `GetItemType` method on the `ItemTypeService` class returns a null. The other change is that the test method `then_a_list_of_item_types_should_be_returned` does not look for items in the `List`. It simply verifies that the `_result` member variable is not null and that it is empty.

After running this test, you can see in Figure 12-2 that it fails and thus represents the circumstances that cause the defect in `InventoryService` to appear.

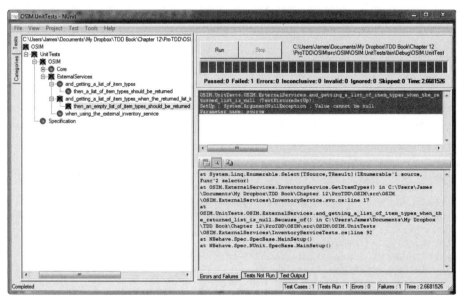

FIGURE 12-2

Changing the Code

You now have a test that exposes a defect in the `InventoryService` WCF service. Before you start writing code, you should run all the tests and verify that the test for the defect is in fact the only test that is currently failing. That test is shown in Figure 12-3.

The next step is to look at the code for the `GetItemTypes` method of `InventoryService` and find out where the defect is occurring. The entire `GetItemTypes` method is shown here:

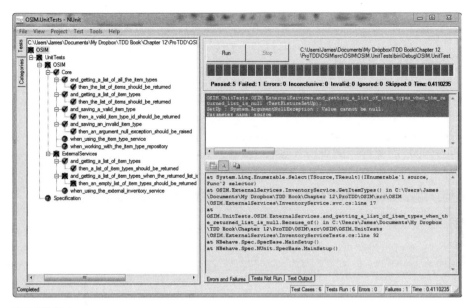

FIGURE 12-3

Available for
download on
Wrox.com

```
public string[] GetItemTypes()
{
    var itemTypeList = _itemTypeService.GetItemTypes()
        .Select(x => x.Name)
        .ToArray();

    return itemTypeList;
}
```

InventoryService.svc.cs

Line 17 of the `InventoryService.svc.cs` file is the line with the call to the `_itemTypeService`
`.GetItemTypes` method in the `GetItemTypes` method of `InventoryService`. The fix for this code
is simple. You need a way to capture the output of the `_itemTypeService.GetItemTypes` method
before the `Select` and `ToArray` extension methods are invoked and check the result for null. If the
result of the `_itemTypeService.GetItemTypes` method is null, you need to return an empty string
array:

Available for
download on
Wrox.com

```
public string[] GetItemTypes()
{
    var itemTypeList = _itemTypeService.GetItemTypes();
    if (itemTypeList == null)
    {
        return new string[0];
    }
```

```
      var itemTypeArray = itemTypeList.Select(x => x.Name)
         .ToArray();

      return itemTypeArray;
   }
```

InventoryService.svc.cs

Rerunning the test in `and_getting_a_list_of_item_types_when_the_returned_list_is_null` shows that the new code corrects this defect, as shown in Figure 12-4.

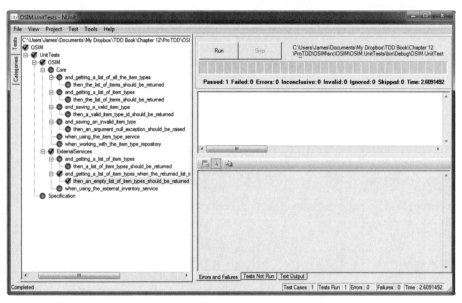

FIGURE 12-4

The new implementation of `GetItemTypes` in `InventoryService` works. But the code is starting to get a little complicated and long. It's also starting to flirt with no longer following the SOLID principles — specifically, the Single Responsibility Principle (SRP).

You should refactor this code a little to make it a bit cleaner. The main change to make to the `GetItemTypes` method is to extract the functionality that checks the result of the `_itemTypeService` `.GetItemTypes` method for null. If the returned `List` of `ItemTypes` is not null, it pulls the information out of the `List` and transforms it into a string array to be returned by `InventoryService`. You accomplish this by changing the code thusly:

```
public string[] GetItemTypes()
{
      var itemTypeList = _itemTypeService.GetItemTypes();
      var itemTypeArray = ReturnValidItemNameListArray(itemTypeList);

      return itemTypeArray;
```

```
    }

    private static string[] ReturnValidItemNameListArray(IEnumerable<ItemType>
    itemTypeList)
    {
        return itemTypeList == null ?
            new string[0] :
            itemTypeList.Select(x => x.Name).ToArray();
    }
```

InventoryService.svc.cs

This snippet adds a method called `ReturnValidItemNameListArray`, which takes as a parameter the returned `List` from the call to the `_itemTypeService.GetItemTypes` method. `ReturnValidItemNameListArray` checks the input parameter `itemTypeList` to determine if it is null. If it is, `ReturnValidItemNameListArray` returns an empty string array. If `itemTypeList` is not null, `ReturnValidItemNameListArray` selects the names from `ItemTypeList` and then transforms that list into an array that is returned from the `ReturnValidItemNameListArray` method. The `GetItemTypes` method simply needs to return the result of the `ReturnValidItemNameListArray` method.

The extraction of logic from the `GetItemTypes` method on `InventoryService` immediately makes that method more readable. Likewise, because `ReturnValidItemNameListArray` does only one thing, that algorithm is more readable as well. In the `GetItemTypes` method, you could have simply returned the result of the `ReturnValidItemNameListArray` method without storing it in `itemTypeArray`. In this case, however, storing the result of the `ReturnValidItemNameListArray` method in the `itemTypeArray` variable enhances readability, so I chose to keep the variable.

Running the test after performing this refactoring action shows that the refactoring didn't introduce any defects into the code, as shown in Figure 12-5.

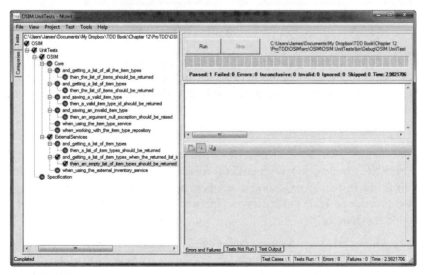

FIGURE 12-5

The test passes. By definition this refactoring is not all that is required to fix this defect. It's time to verify that the code changes have not introduced any more defects.

Keeping the Tests Passing

In addition to fixing a defect or adding a feature, it's important to make sure that you aren't breaking any preexisting functionality. I have a suite of unit tests that verify that all the other functionality in this application works. By running the whole suite of tests, you can verify that you have fixed this defect while not introducing any more defects into the application, as shown in Figure 12-6

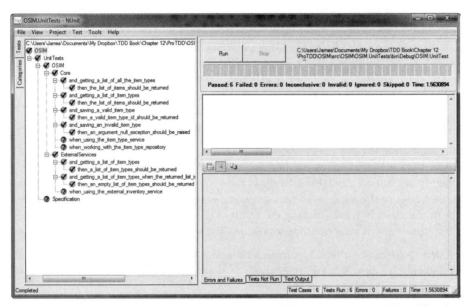

FIGURE 12-6

All the tests, including the new test created to address the defect in the `InventoryService` WCF service, are passing. This means that the defect has been fixed, and no other functionality in the application has been damaged. This application now can be sent to QA to be verified for production.

SUMMARY

Change in business is inevitable. Changes in laws, market forces, and business strategies are regular occurrences. Resistance is futile. Instead, application developers need to learn to embrace change. The correct and dedicated practice of TDD will give your application an advantage by making it more flexible and adaptable for change.

When you're working with a new feature, you must employ the same business analysis, design, and estimation protocols that were used to develop the application. This is true even for applications that have already shipped or been deployed to production. Do not fall into the trap of cutting corners under the claim, "Well, it's just a small change." Even small changes implemented poorly can severely damage an application and customer trust.

Whether you're working with a new feature or a defect, the first step in the development process is the same: writing a test. This test should initially fail. If this test passes, some investigation is required. Does your test test for the correct functionality or defect? Are you testing the right part of the application? Does the newly requested functionality already exist as a side effect of some other functionality? Remember that just because a test passes immediately doesn't mean that you have fixed the defect or that the new functionality exists in the application.

After your new test is written and you've seen it fail, the steps are the same as when you're doing primary development of the application. Write just enough code to make the new test or tests pass. When the new tests pass, you have either fixed the defect or implemented the new feature. Refactor where necessary, but do not add more code than is required. Use the entire test suite to verify that the other parts of the application have not been negatively impacted by your change. As soon as all the tests, old and new, are passing, your application is ready to be sent to QA for verification and deployment to production.

13

The Great Tool Debate

by Jeff McWherter

As with many other procedures in the software development industry, test-driven development and the tools used in this discipline can cause many debates among software developers. These debates are often religious wars over which tool is best. This chapter discusses the different types of tools that are useful with test-driven development processes and offers opinions about the tools. This chapter will help you decide which tools are best for you.

TEST RUNNERS

Having a test runner that you are comfortable with is crucial to following test-driven development practices. Many testing frameworks such as NUnit (used in the majority of examples in the previous chapters) ship with a GUI for running tests. You have learned that unit tests need to run fast, but having feedback about your tests and a way to run them that you are comfortable with ensures that you will run your tests. Often, alternatives to these GUIs that ship with unit-testing frameworks can make your life easier.

TestDriven.NET

TestDriven.Net is a popular test runner that supports running tests created in frameworks such as NUnit, MbUnit, and MSTest. TestDriven .Net personal edition is free to students and open source developers. Corporate developers must pay a modest fee, but it's worth not having to keep open the GUI interface to these testing frameworks.

TestDriven.Net integrates into Visual Studio. You can run a test by right-clicking it and selecting Run Test, as shown in Figure 13-1.

It's highly recommended that you create a keyboard shortcut so that you do not need to right-click each time you want to run your tests. To set up keyboard shortcuts in Visual Studio, select Options ⇨ Keyboard ⇨ Settings, as shown in Figure 13-2.

FIGURE 13-1

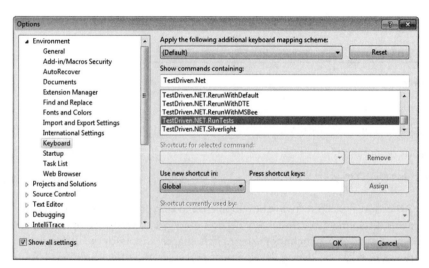

FIGURE 13-2

Many test runners such as TestDriven.Net also allow you to debug your tests. Stepping into a test is useful when you are trying to figure out exactly what is going on in a complex test. The commercial and personal versions of TestDriven.Net can be downloaded at `http://www.testdriven.net/ download.aspx`.

Developer Express Test Runner

Recent versions of Code Rush, the powerful coding assistance tool from Developer Express, include a well-written test runner. It is similar to other test runners but fits within Code Rush, providing users with a highly extensible tool. It also works great right out of the box. Code Rush has become known as the Visual Studio add-on that helps developers write code fast and provides suggestions in an aesthetically pleasing way. As with other test runners, you can perform testing by right-clicking the test/test fixture or by setting up a keyboard shortcut. Not only is the Developer Express test runner fast, but it also makes it easy to see which tests passed and failed, as with the test code shown in Figure 13-3.

```csharp
public class HTMLHelpersTests
{
    [Test]
    public void Should_Truncate_Text_Over_Five_Characters_Long()
    {
        string textToTruncate = "This is my text";
        string expected = "This ..";
        string actual = HTMLHelper.Truncate(textToTruncate, 5);
        Assert.AreEqual(expected, actual);
    }

    [Test]
    public void Should_Not_Truncate_Text_When_No_Length_Is_Passed_In()
    {
        string textToTruncate = "This is my text";
        string expected = "This is my text";
        string actual = HTMLHelper.Truncate(textToTruncate, 0);

        Assert.AreEqual(expected, actual);
    }

    [Test]
    public void Should_Not_Append_Ellipses_When_Truncating_Text_That_Is_Shorter_Than_Length()
    {
        string textToTruncate = "This is my text";
        string expected = "This is my text";
        string actual = HTMLHelper.Truncate(textToTruncate, 50);

        Assert.AreEqual(expected, actual);
    }
}
```

FIGURE 13-3

More information about Code Rush can be found at `http://www.devexpress.com/Products/ Visual_Studio_Add-in/index.xml`.

Gallio

Gallio is a highly extensible automation platform that provides a common object model for tools such as test runners and runtime services to interoperate. Simply put, Gallio is a GUI test runner that runs tests created using MbUnit, MbUnitCpp, MSTest, NBehave, NUnit, xUnit, csUnit, and RSPec. Gallio also provides various levels of support and integration with MSBuild, NAnt, Pex, CCNet, Powershell, Resharper, TestDriven.Net, dotCover, TypeMock, and Visual Studio. You can find out more about Gallio at `http://www.gallio.org`.

Figure 13-4 shows the Gallio Icarus GUI running tests created in MbUnit and NUnit in the same project. I once worked with a developer who had a bad habit of switching testing frameworks midway through a project. Gallio would have been beneficial on this project.

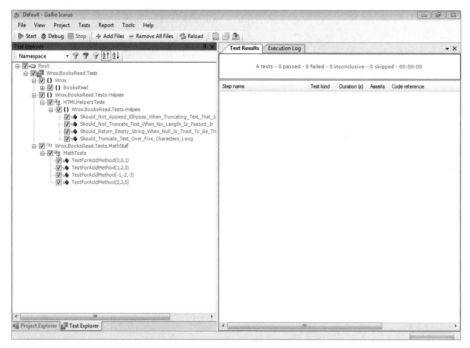

FIGURE 13-4

UNIT TESTING FRAMEWORKS

Unit-testing frameworks are like a good pair of work boots. You hate them at first because they are uncomfortable, but the more you wear them, the more you start to love them. By the time you have to get a new pair of boots, or a new testing framework in this case, you start to complain again because it's uncomfortable. Unit-testing frameworks tend to cause the most religious wars between the different testing tools.

MSTest

MSTest is the testing framework created by Microsoft that has been included in specific versions of Visual Studio since 2005. MSTest sparks many heated discussions among developers. When all is said and done, MSTest is similar to many of the other unit-testing frameworks, with a slightly different syntax. It has been my experience that the tests run slower, but you should make your own call.

The syntax for MSTest is much like that for NUnit, except that the Test Fixture has a `TestClass` attribute, and the actual tests have a `TestMethod` attribute:

```
[TestClass]
public class HTMLHelpersTests
{
    [TestMethod]
    public void Should_Truncate_Text_Over_Five_Characters_Long()
    {
```

```
            string textToTruncate = "This is my text";
            string expected = "This ..";
            string actual = HTMLHelper.Truncate(textToTruncate, 5);
            Assert.AreEqual(expected, actual);
    }

        [TestMethod]
        public void Should_Not_Truncate_Text_When_No_Length_Is_Passed_In()
        {
            string textToTruncate = "This is my text";
            string expected = "This is my text";
            string actual = HTMLHelper.Truncate(textToTruncate, 0);

            Assert.AreEqual(expected, actual);
        }
    }
```

MSTest.cs

As shown in Figure 13-5, MSTests are run in a similar fashion as using a test runner that is included with Visual Studio.

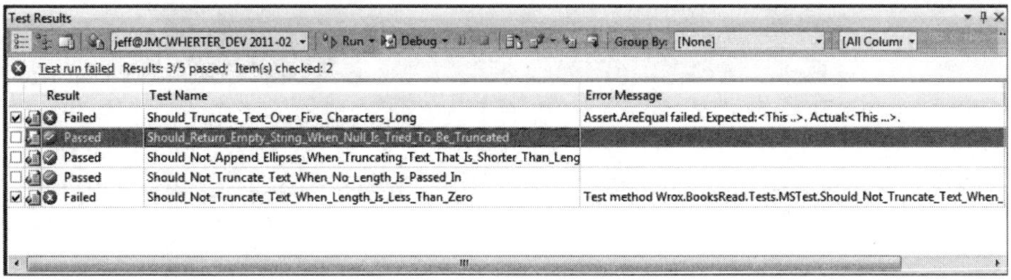

FIGURE 13-5

As a unit-testing framework, MSTest is ranked low on our recommended list because of its speed issues. But this is no reason to dismiss the other wonderful testing tools included, such as database-driven tests, performance testing tools, and ordered tests.

MbUnit

In 2004 Jonathan "Peli" de Halleux created MbUnit (called gUnit at the time) based on a series of articles by Marc Clifton. Out of the box, MbUnit supports a concept called row tests. You can create a single test and have multiple sets of data to execute the test against defined as method attributes. Each set of data is executed separately and treated as a unique test within the runner.

The following code is a test for a static method called Add that simply adds together two integers. The following test has three inputs: value a, value b, and the expected result. Using the Row attribute, you can create the input for the test.

```
[TestFixture]
public class MathStuffTests
{
    [RowTest]
    [Row(5, 3, 8)]
    [Row(0, 0, 0)]
    [Row(-1, -2, -3)]
    public void AddTests(int a, int b, int expected)
    {
        int test = MathStuff.Add(a, b);
        Assert.AreEqual(test, expected);
    }
}
```

MbUnit.cs

As shown in Figure 13-6, the MbUnit test runner treats this as three separate tests when reporting the test results.

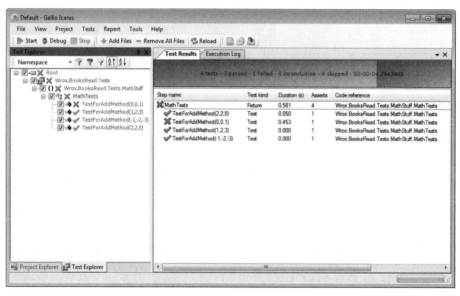

FIGURE 13-6

MbUnit can be downloaded at http://www.mbunit.com/.

xUnit

xUnit is an open source testing framework developed by Brad Wilson of Microsoft with cooperation from Jim Newkirk, one of the original authors of NUnit. xUnit takes a minimalist approach that provides framework features through method attributes. This minimalist approach helps keep tests simple and clean. One of the major differences between xUnit and the other testing frameworks discussed so far is the lack of `Setup` and `Teardown` method attributes. Keeping with the simplistic theme of xUnit, you use the constructor and a `dispose` method of your test class when you need to implement setup or teardown functionality.

Based on the knowledge of NUnit you have gained in previous chapters, the following code example should look very similar. xUnit tests have an attribute of `Fact`. The `[Fact(Timeout = 20)]` attribute is useful when you need to ensure that a method returns within a specified time.

Available for
download on
Wrox.com

```
[Fact]
public void AddTest()
{
    int expected = 10;
    int actual = MathStuff.Add(5, 5);
    Assert.Equal(expected,actual);
}

[Fact(Timeout = 20)]
public void TimeOutTest()
{
    System.Threading.Thread.Sleep(40);
    Assert.Equal(1, 1);
}
```

For more information about the minimalist syntax of xUnit, see the syntax comparison chart of NUnit, MbUnit, MSTest, and xUnit found on the xUnit project page on Code Plex at `http://xunit .codeplex.com/wikipage?title=Comparisons&ProjectName=xunit`.

MOCKING FRAMEWORKS

Chapter 2 discussed the basics of mocking objects, and throughout this book we have been using the Moq framework because of its simple syntax. Moq is becoming a popular mocking framework, but it is not the only framework available. Other frameworks have features that allow you to mock objects differently.

Moq uses a declarative syntax for mocking objects, which is different from the record/playback method of mocking that many mocking frameworks support. Many of these frameworks are moving away from the record/playback method in favor of an arrange, act, and assert (AAA) method because of its ease of use.

Rhino Mocks

Rhino Mocks is a free mocking framework created by Orin Eini, who is also known for his work on the nHibernate and Castle projects. Rhino Mocks is popular because of its ease of use and list of power features. Although the syntax is not as clean as Moq's, it is a worthwhile tool to check out. Rhino Mocks supports two different styles of mocking objects: the record/playback method and the arrange, act, and assert syntax. Record/playback is now considered to be the older way of mocking objects, but it makes sense to consider the differences.

The following example uses the AAA style of mocking objects, which is similar to mocking with Moq, as you learned in Chapter 2. The basic Rhino Mocks syntax looks like this:

```
MockRepository mocks = new MockRepository();
IDependency dependency = mocks.CreateMock<IDependency>();

// create our expectations
Expect.Call(dependency.GetSomething("parameter")).Return("result");
dependency.DoSomething();
mocks.ReplayAll();

// test the middle layer
Thing thing = new Thing(dependency);
thing.DoWork();

// verify the expectations
mocks.VerifyAll();
```

RhinoMocks.cs

This example sets up a mock object for the IDependency interface that will eventually get passed into the Thing class. Two expectations are set for the mock: The GetSomething method is called, with a string parameter and a return value, and the DoSomething method is called off the dependency. Expectations are verified with the VerifyAll method on the mock object.

You can take Rhino Mocks a bit further and create a test that is actually useful to a project:

```
[Test]
public void Mocking_With_Rhino_Mocks()
{
    MockRepository mocks = new Rhino.Mocks.MockRepository();

    // create the repository object; the real object would make calls to the DB
    IItemTypeRepository repository = mocks.CreateMock<IItemTypeRepository>();

    // mock the call to get an item with the ID of 2 and return null,
    // to mock not finding an item
    Rhino.Mocks.Expect.Call(repository.GetById(2)).Return(null);

    // get the mocking ready
    mocks.ReplayAll();

    // inject our mock into our service layer
    ItemPresenter presenter = new ItemPresenter(repository);

    // service.GetItem will call the mocked repository, which will call
    // repository.GetByID, which will return null
    ItemType item = presenter.GetItem(2);

    // should be null
    Assert.IsNull(item);
}
```

RhinoMocks.cs

In some cases you may want to throw an exception in your mock object instead of returning a value. It's a good idea to create tests that simulate faults. The following example simulates a `DivideByZeroException` error within the `MethodThatThrowsError` method:

```
itemRepository.Expect(m => m.MethodThatThrowsError("")).Throw(new
    DivideByZeroException("Error"));
```

RhinoMocks.cs

Working with events in Rhino Mocks is just as simple. First you need to gain access to the Event Raiser, and then you simulate an event being raised, as shown in the following example. The `MyEvent` event is simulated, and it returns a string value for `"result"`:

```
itemRepository.GetEventRaiser(v => v.MyEvent += null).Raise("result");
```

RhinoMocks.cs

You can also use the record/playback syntax to mock objects using Rhino Mocks. Record/playback is a two-stage process. In the record stage, you define how you want the mock to be interacted with. In the second stage of playback, you enter your test code and interact with the `Mock` object:

```
MockRepository mocks = new MockRepository();
IItemTypeRepository mock = mocks.CreateMock<IItemTypeRepository>();

using (mocks.Record())
{
    Expect.Call(mock.GetById(3)).Return(null);
}

using (mocks.Playback())
{
    Assert.AreEqual(null, mock.GetById(3));
}
```

RhinoMocks.cs

Rhino Mocks has a strong following and is a good mocking tool to consider. To start working with Rhino Mocks, visit `http://www.ayende.com/projects/rhino-mocks.aspx`.

Type Mock

Type Mock is different from Rhino Mocks and Moq in that it uses intermediate language (IL) to replace real implementations with the mock implementation at runtime. Type Mock can mock any object in your system at any time, so there is no need to worry about how to inject your model into the system. It's also important to note that Type Mock is a commercial product and therefore is not free.

The other major advantage of Type Mock is that the mock object does not need to inherit from an interface. Type Mock can mock concrete implementations of objects. With Type Mock, you can mock objects that are not in your control, such as third-party libraries or even parts of the .NET framework.

The following code is very similar to the Rhino Mocks syntax:

```
// Arrange
IItemTypeRepository repository = Isolate.Fake.Instance<IItemTypeRepository>();
Isolate.WhenCalled(() => repository.GetById(2)).WillReturn(null);

// Act
ItemPresenter presenter = new ItemPresenter(repository);
ItemType item = presenter.GetItem(2);

// Assert
Assert.IsNull(item);
```

TypeMock.cs

The true power of TypeMock comes into play when you don't have an interface and you need to mock something like `DateTime.Now`. Consider the following code. It has a method called `IsExpired` that looks at a constant value of `11/21/1981` and compares it to `DateTime.Now` to see if the item is expired:

```
public class Item
{
    private DateTime EXPIRATION_DATE = new DateTime(1981, 11, 21);

    public bool IsExpired()
    {
        bool tmpRtn = false;

        if (DateTime.Now > EXPIRATION_DATE)
            tmpRtn = true;

        return tmpRtn;
    }
}
```

TypeMock.cs

You could write logic to abstract your call to `DateTime.Now` out of this method and pass a date into the `IsExpired` method. But using TypeMock you can mock `DateTime.Now` and test to ensure that your `IsExpired` method is checking for expired dates.

In the following `Isolated` test, when `DateTime.Now` is called, a new date is returned. In the first test it is an expired date, and the second test returns a nonexpired date:

```
[Test, Isolated]
public void Item_Should_Be_Expired()
{
    Isolate.WhenCalled(() => DateTime.Now).WillReturn(new DateTime(1981, 11, 22));
```

```
        Item item = new Item();
        Assert.True(item.IsExpired());
    }

    [Test, Isolated]
    public void Item_Should_Not_Be_Expired()
    {
        Isolate.WhenCalled(() => DateTime.Now).WillReturn(new DateTime(1981, 11, 21));

        Item item = new Item();
        Assert.IsFalse(item.IsExpired());
    }
```

TypeMock.cs

With features such as the ability to mock any object, Type Mock is great for legacy applications, where testing was an afterthought. Information about the Type Mock isolation framework can be found at `http://www.typemock.com/`.

DEPENDENCY INJECTION FRAMEWORKS

If you think of your application as a puzzle, dependency injection (DI) frameworks are the tools that put these puzzle pieces together. Some might even say that dependency injection frameworks are just an implementation of a super factory design pattern. Chapter 5 discussed the basics of dependency injection. The examples used Ninject, but Ninject is not the only dependency injection framework on the market.

In the past, most dependency injection frameworks were configured by using XML files that soon became difficult to maintain. Most modern dependency injection frameworks still support this method of configuration, but this method is generally frowned on and has been traded in for cleaner approaches. This section explores a few alternative dependency injection frameworks using the example from Chapter 5 to inject dependencies into a business application.

When choosing a dependency injection framework, you should follow two rules:

➤ Keep the framework at a distance.

➤ Focus on the Inversion of Control pattern.

Structure Map

Structure Map is an open source container framework that has a fluent API that makes the code easy to read and maintain. One of the more powerful features of Structure Map is the automocking container.

The Structure Map automocking feature allows you to create stubs automatically when requested by the test. Even though you still need to set your expectations on the mocks, this saves time when you create mocks in your tests.

The following example re-creates the example from Chapter 5 that used Ninject to inject dependencies into a business application class. First you need to map interfaces to their respective concrete implementations. In Structure Map, as well as most DI frameworks, this step is performed only once, when the application starts. Depending on the number of objects you are mapping, this could be an expensive process. In web applications this is usually done in the Global.asax file, but for these short examples we will create a bootstrap class that is called to set up the mappings:

```
public static class StructureMap_IoCBootStrapper
{
    public static void SetupForIoC()
    {
        // the setup. If we were working with ASP.net this would occur in
        // Global.asax
        ObjectFactory.Initialize(x =>
        {
            x.ForRequestedType<ILoggingDataSink>()
                .TheDefaultIsConcreteType<LoggingDataSink>();

            x.ForRequestedType<ILoggingComponent>()
                .TheDefaultIsConcreteType<LoggingComponent>()

            x.ForRequestedType<IDataAccessComponent>()
                .TheDefaultIsConcreteType<DataAccessComponent>();

            x.ForRequestedType<IWebServiceProxy>()
                .TheDefaultIsConcreteType<WebServiceProxyComponentProvider>();

            x.ForRequestedType<IPersonRepository>()
                .TheDefaultIsConcreteType<PersonRepository>();

            x.ForRequestedType<IPersonService>()
                .TheDefaultIsConcreteType<PersonService>();
        });
    }
}
```

StructureMap.cs

The first thing you do in this example is create an instance of the object factory and call initialize. The initialize method takes an expression that allows you to configure Structure Map. With this logic added, you can inject dependencies into the business application.

```
public class StructureMap_ThingThatImplementsABusinessService
{
    public StructureMap_ThingThatImplementsABusinessService()
    {
        StructureMap_IoCBootStraper.SetupForIoC();

        // getting our objects to work with. This usually occurs in the
        // constructor of the class you need the objects for
        var logger = ObjectFactory.GetInstance<ILoggingComponent>();
        var personRepository = ObjectFactory.GetInstance<IPersonRepository>();
```

```
            // start working with our objects that have been loaded
            var person = personRepository.GetPerson(3);
        }


    }
```

StructureMap.cs

The last example here re-creates the example found in Chapter 5 that used Ninject. It does not map all the dependencies, as was done in Chapter 5 for simplicity. Mapping every dependency could get cumbersome on large projects. Another great feature of Structure Map is the autoregistration or autoscan feature. Structure Map looks at your interfaces and tries to match them to concrete implementations based on default conventions. For instance, if you have an interface of Ifoobar, it's more than likely that it matches the Foobar class. If the default mapping is incorrect, you can create profiles to set the correct mapping.

```
public static void SetupForIoC_Scan()
{
    // the setup. If we were working with ASP.net this would occur in
    // Global.asax
    ObjectFactory.Initialize(x =>
    {
        x.Scan(s =>
        {
            s.TheCallingAssembly();
            s.WithDefaultConventions();
        });
    });
}
```

StructureMap.cs

The Open Source Structure Map project can be found at http://structuremap.net/structuremap/.

Unity

From the Patterns and Practices group at Microsoft, Unity is the youngest of the DI frameworks discussed in this chapter. Unity does not support many of the advanced features that these other DI frameworks do, but it supports enough to get the job done.

To implement the example that you should be very familiar with by now, you need to add project references to the Microsoft.Practices.Unity assembly as well as the Microsoft.Practices .ObjectBuilder2 assembly. After that, in the bootstrap class, you create a UnityContainer object and then start the mappings, as shown in the following code:

```
public static class Unity_IoCBootStraper
{
    public static UnityContainer BaseContainer = new UnityContainer();

    public static void SetupForIoC()
```

```
    {
        // the setup. If we were working with ASP.net this would occur in
        // Global.asax
        BaseContainer.RegisterType<ILoggingDataSink, LoggingDataSink>();
        BaseContainer.RegisterType<ILoggingComponent, LoggingComponent>();
        BaseContainer.RegisterType<IDataAccessComponent, DataAccessComponent>();
        BaseContainer.RegisterType<IWebServiceProxy,
        WebServiceProxyComponentProvider>();
        BaseContainer.RegisterType<IPersonRepository, PersonRepository>();
        BaseContainer.RegisterType<IPersonService, PersonService>();
    }
}
```

Unity.cs

To get your dependencies in your business object, you can simply call the `resolve` method from the `UnityContainer` object:

Available for
download on
Wrox.com

```
public class Unity_BusinessApplication
{

    public Unity_BusinessApplication()
    {
        Unity_IoCBootStraper.SetupForIoC();

        // getting our objects to work with. This usually occurs in the
        // constructor of the class you need the objects for
        var logger = Unity_IoCBootStraper.BaseContainer
            .Resolve<ILoggingComponent>();

        var personRepository = Unity_IoCBootStraper.BaseContainer
            .Resolve<IPersonRepository>();

        // start working with our objects that have been loaded
        var person = personRepository.GetPerson(3);
    }
}
```

Unity.cs

By default, when you resolve an object in the `UnityContainer` object, you get a new instance of that object based on the default mappings. One of the nice features of Unity is that you can change this functionality and return a singleton of that object if needed. The `RegisterType` function has an overload that takes a `LifeTimeManager` object. Unity comes with a Container Controlled Lifetime Manager that is, in fact, a singleton:

```
BaseContainer.RegisterType<ILoggingComponent, LoggingComponent>(new
    ContainerControlledLifetimeManager());
```

Unity is open source and can be found on CodePlex at http://unity.codeplex.com/. The large amount of documentation and webcasts make Unity a good place to start for people new to the Inversion of Control pattern.

Windsor

Maintained within the Castle project, Windsor was one of the first open source dependency injection frameworks to appear for .NET. Out of all the dependency injection frameworks discussed here, Windsor has the largest following and provides the most mature and powerful implementation of dependency injection. Because this project has so many features, there may be a relatively high learning curve for using some of the more advanced features. The following code implements an example. As you can see, it's very similar to the other dependency injection frameworks:

```
public static class Windsor_IoCBootStraper
{
    public static WindsorContainer BaseContainer = new WindsorContainer();

    public static void SetupForIoC()
    {
        // the setup. If we were working with ASP.net this would occur in
        // Global.asax.
        BaseContainer.AddComponent<ILoggingDataSink, LoggingDataSink>();
        BaseContainer.AddComponent<ILoggingComponent, LoggingComponent>();
        BaseContainer.AddComponent<IDataAccessComponent, DataAccessComponent>();
        BaseContainer.AddComponent<IWebServiceProxy,
            WebServiceProxyComponentProvider>();
        BaseContainer.AddComponent<IPersonRepository, PersonRepository>();
        BaseContainer.AddComponent<IPersonService, PersonService>();
    }
}

public class Windsor_BusinessApplication
{

    public Windsor_BusinessApplication()
    {
        Windsor_IoCBootStraper.SetupForIoC();

        // getting our objects to work with. This usually occurs in the
        // constructor of the class you need the objects for
        var logger = Unity_IoCBootStraper.BaseContainer
            .Resolve<ILoggingComponent>();

        var personRepository = Unity_IoCBootStraper.BaseContainer
            .Resolve<IPersonRepository>();

        // start working with our objects that have been loaded
        var person = personRepository.GetPerson(3);
    }
}
```

Windsor.cs

Castle Windsor can be downloaded from http://stw.castleproject.org/Windsor.MainPage .ashx.

Autofac

Autofac was one of the first dependency injection frameworks to include an interface that allows configuration without XML files. Because of this, many developers started to work with this dependency injection framework. With Autofac, your components can be created using reflection, lambda expressions, or a ready-made instance. The `ContainerBuilder` object provides the `Register` functionality and all the methods needed to support the registration of objects, as demonstrated here:

Available for download on Wrox.com

```
public static class AutoF ac_IoCBootStraper
{
    public static IContainer BaseContainer { get; private set; }

    public static void SetupForIoC()
    {
        var builder = new ContainerBuilder();
        builder.RegisterType<IPersonRepository>().As<PersonRepository>();

        BaseContainer = builder.Build();
    }

    public static TService Resolve<TService>()
    {
        return BaseContainer.Resolve<TService>();
    }
}
```

AutoFac.cs

To inject dependencies into a business application, you simply need to call the `Resolve` method found within the bootstrap class:

Available for download on Wrox.com

```
public class AutoFac_BusinessApplication
{

    public AutoFac_BusinessApplication()
    {
        AutoFac_IoCBootStraper.SetupForIoC();

        // getting our objects to work with. This usually occurs in the
        // constructor of the class you need the objects for
        var logger = AutoFac_IoCBootStraper.Resolve<ILoggingComponent>();
        var personRepository = AutoFac_IoCBootStraper
            .Resolve<IPersonRepository>();

        // start working with our objects that have been loaded
        var person = personRepository.GetPerson(3);
    }
}
```

In most situations, the difference in performance between the dependency injection frameworks won't impact your decision about which one to use, but note that AutoFac is the fastest of the frameworks listed here. The Autofac framework can be found on Google code at `http://code` `.google.com/p/autofac/`.

MISCELLANEOUS USEFUL TOOLS

Some tools fall under the miscellaneous category. They are not required to perform TDD but are useful when it comes to testing your application.

nCover

nCover is a code coverage testing tool. It analyzes your tests and code and reports the percentage of code covered by the tests. There are two versions of nCover. One is open source, and the other is a commercial product that contains more features.

Figure 13-7 shows the test coverage for the `Wrox.BooksRead.Web` project. You can see that the `HTMLHelper` class has 100% test coverage, whereas the other projects have 0% test coverage. In this example, the only tests created are for `HTMLHelper`, so this makes sense.

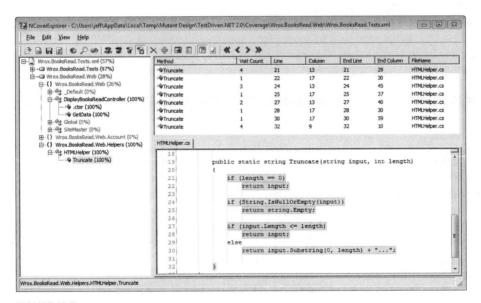

FIGURE 13-7

nCover can be downloaded at `http://www.ncover.com/`.

PEX

PEX, short for Program Exploration, is a project from Microsoft Research that generates unit tests from existing code. PEX is a Visual Studio add-in that with a small amount of configuration generates a suite of parameterized unit tests that give your code a large amount of code coverage.

Not only does PEX generate the tests, but it also provides suggestions on how to resolve tests that fail. PEX is great for running on legacy code or finding edge or corner cases that have been handled incorrectly. PEX is not a silver bullet and should be used with caution. Not only is TDD about testing; it's also about design. On the other hand, PEX is solely about finding bugs. Figure 13-8 shows that PEX created five unit tests for the `Truncate HTML` function, with one of them failing.

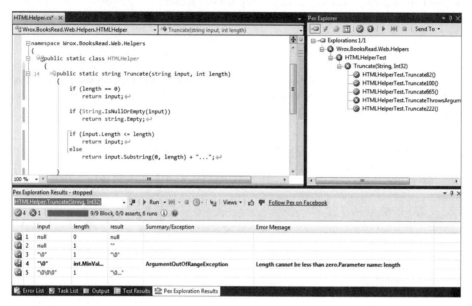

FIGURE 13-8

Test 4 failed because it passed in a negative number. This is the benefit of PEX: It caught an edge case that the original unit tests missed. You should go back and add a test within the `HTMLHelpersTests` class and add the following test to test for this edge case:

```
[Test]
public void Should_Not_Truncate_Text_When_Length_Is_Less_Than_Zero()
{
    string textToTruncate = "This is my text";
    string expected = "This is my text";
    string actual = HTMLHelper.Truncate(textToTruncate, int.MinValue);
    Assert.AreEqual(expected, actual);
}
```

You can learn more about PEX at `http://research.microsoft.com/en-us/projects/pex/`.

HOW TO INTRODUCE TDD TO YOUR TEAM

You might be wondering how a section on introducing TDD to your team is related to tools, but being able to change someone's core thinking is a valuable tool. We are asked this question so often and have debated it so many times that it simply boils down to this: Either you're working with people who want to better themselves by learning new processes, or you're not. If your workplace values quality and people over process, introducing TDD is easy.

Working in Environments That Are Resistant to Change

When you leave at the end of the day, the code you checked into version control is your mark on the project. If it does not work, you are responsible for it. TDD has an initial learning curve, but once you get past that, you will create code as quickly as ever. Even if a team is unwilling to change to follow TDD practices, *you* can change. Get past this learning curve on your own time by pairing with someone who practices TDD. When you are comfortable, slowly start implementing what you have learned about TDD into your projects. I suggest that you do not go back and refactor everything in your existing codebase; just start slowly and track metrics. Managers like charts, and when you can show them that the last release had 20% fewer defects than the previous one, you can tell them you implemented TDD on your portion of the project.

At that point, the manager will either be mad that you did this or happy that the system has 20% fewer defects. If the manager is upset, it's probably time to move on to a different position where your ideas are valued. This method of introducing a new concept to a team is told best in Chapter 1 of *The Pragmatic Programmer* by Andrew Hunt and David Thomas (Addison-Wesley, 1999, ISBN: 9780201616224). It relates two stories about stone soup and boiled frogs. In the latter example, if you drop a frog into a pot of boiling water, it jumps right out. However, if you drop the frog into cold water and then slowly heat the water until it boils, the frog keeps adjusting to the increasing temperature and stays in the water until it dies.

Working in Environments That Are Accepting of Change

Some companies allow employees to grow and learn new things. If you are working at a place like this, the best way to teach your team about TDD is to bring in a mentor. A pair programming strategy is the best way to get developers up to speed. The authors of this book learned TDD from pairing with other people. This is the best way to learn this process. Having a mentor who knows TDD well can help get the slower members on the team up to speed faster than having them read about TDD in a book.

If your company is unwilling to have someone come in for the day, events such as code retreats are a great place to pair with up someone for the day and write code. For more information about code retreats, go to `http://coderetreat.ning.com/`.

SUMMARY

This chapter has examined many tools that help with the TDD process. When you explore new tools, we suggest that you come up with a simple example, replicate it using the various tools, and then come to your own conclusion.

NUnit has been around for years and has a large following, but this does not necessarily make it the best tool for the job. xUnit is the new testing framework on the scene and is radically different from NUnit in many ways. Tools that are radically different are the tools you should be trying, because they are the ones that may make your life easier. Thinking outside the box and trying new things will help in many ways.

You will evolve as a software developer throughout your career. You should be able to look back at code you wrote in the past and wonder, "What was I thinking?" This is how you get better at doing your job. Exploring new tools is just one way to improve yourself.

When it comes to choosing which tools to work with, select the ones you are most comfortable with. In some business situations open-source tools are not allowed. Many times these tools are not allowed out of a fear of open source for various reasons. Excuses such as licensing issues or "I can't call someone on the phone and get support" are common. Learn how to make a case for how these tools make you more productive. When it boils down to selecting a tool, no one has ever been fired for using Microsoft.

14

Conclusions

WHAT'S IN THIS CHAPTER?

- ➤ Reviewing the concepts and techniques covered in this book
- ➤ Understanding best practices for working with TDD
- ➤ Reviewing benefits of developing with TDD
- ➤ How to introduce TDD to your development team

This book has given you much information to give you a good foundation for becoming a TDD developer. You have learned the principles and techniques to practice TDD. You can apply many of these techniques to your everyday development tasks to help ensure that you are delivering well-written, quality software.

In addition to the principles and techniques of TDD, you have learned many of the techniques, ideas, and principles that support the test-driven development of applications. You've learned that the SOLID Principles provide a set of guidelines for developing well-written and maintainable applications. You've seen how agile-based development methodologies give the development team the necessary time, space, and information to successfully develop applications using a TDD approach.

This book contains a lot of information. But even if you read this book 100 times, the only way these principles and techniques become real is through daily adoption in the real world. TDD is like learning a language: If you don't practice and use it every day, your skills will never reach their full potential. As you prepare to go forth in your practice of TDD, keep in mind the parting advice from this chapter.

WHAT YOU HAVE LEARNED

In addition to some pointers about incidental frameworks and patterns such as Fluent NHibernate and the repository, this book has given you a solid foundation in TDD principles.

You've learned some core patterns and techniques needed for the successful practice of TDD, such as dependency injection. You've also seen how adhering to the SOLID Principles and development using an agile methodology can support TDD developers in their work. This chapter offers a few last pointers to help you in the practice of TDD.

You Are the Client of Your Code

As a developer, you consume services and components when constructing your software. These pieces come together to form a whole greater than the sum of their parts. Usually, these services and components are things that you or a member of your development team has written. This means that the primary consumers of these services and components you develop are you and your development team. These services and components should be simple to understand and easy to use. A new member of your development team should quickly and easily be able to determine the function and usage of these services and components by their names and method signatures.

In TDD you are the first client of any service or component you create. By writing a test for the service or component you are creating, you are the first one to consume that service or component. Is the service or component easy to use? Do the naming and method signatures give you a clear picture of how the service should work? Is the interface clean and free of confusing names or duplicated functionality? By using TDD to develop these services and components, you make yourself the first consumer. Are you creating a service or component that you would find easy to use? By deriving your service and component interfaces from the practice of TDD, you will create interfaces and classes that are elegant, intuitive, and simple to use.

Find the Solutions Step by Step

Developing a software application is a big job. Approaching the development of any application as a single large step is a futile approach that sets up you and your team for failure. A well-known saying in software development is "Don't try to boil the ocean." It means that a large task may seem complex and impossible, but if you break it into several smaller tasks, suddenly the job doesn't seem so difficult. Software can be complicated. Instead of trying to address all the problems encompassed by a software application development effort at once, deal with it as several smaller problems. Tackle these smaller problems one at a time in a manageable way. Instead of thinking of a feature or user story as a 40-hour task, it might be easier to think of it as 10 four-hours tasks. Even better, you could break it into 20 two-hour tasks.

Dealing with smaller tasks offers many advantages. Smaller tasks are easier to understand. Instead of working with a macro problem that encompasses so many moving parts, deal only with a focused section of scope at a time. Smaller tasks are easier to implement. Instead of waiting a week to know if you have successfully addressed the problem at hand, you can know in a matter of hours. This enables a developer to build momentum and a sense of accomplishment.

Use the Debugger as a Surgical Instrument

Developers who do not use TDD tend to lean on the debugger as a primary development tool. For most developers who do not employ TDD, the first step in verifying code is often to watch that code execute in the debugger and see what it does. For these developers the debugger is a blunt instrument: a club they must use repeatedly to beat their code into shape. This approach is wasteful.

The process of verifying code in the debugger is slow. Developers usually have to set the break point several lines or even methods before the code they want to watch and step to the code in question. Because a developer is required to step through the code and manually view and evaluate the data, this process is slow. In the same amount of time it takes a developer to step through a unit of functionality with the debugger and verify that the functionality is correct, you could run the tests for all your features and know right away if they are working. Using a debugger also produces inconsistent results. In most cases, the application requires some form of user interaction to get to the functionality you need to verify, so there is room for error. You can easily input the wrong value or press the wrong button.

Developers who do use TDD tend to make conservative use of the debugger. The tests verify that the code works; there is no need to watch it execute line by line in the debugger. If your tests are well written and your code is simple, the debugger is simply not needed as often.

When you use TDD, your use of the debugger is much more focused and narrow. Because the tests isolate each unit of functionality, you know exactly where to look in your code for the defect. You can set a break point in the immediate vicinity of the defect and go directly to the trouble spot in the code. When you get there you know what you are looking for, because you have a failing test that describes the error you are getting. After you locate the cause of the problem, you can write a test that can be used to ensure that the problem does not occur again. The test is repeatable and fast, which means that you can continue to verify that the code is working correctly repeatedly without having to run the code in the debugger again.

TDD BEST PRACTICES

Ultimately, your practice of TDD should reflect your needs and those of your development team and application. There is a lot of room to customize your team's approach and methodology when practicing TDD. Most successful development teams follow similar strategies. In your continued practice of TDD, you should remember these guidelines.

Use Significant Names

Names are important. Good names make it easy to identify the purpose and function of a class, method, or variable. Conversely, bad names make it almost impossible to identify the intent of these objects. When naming your tests, be sure to be specific about what you are naming your classes and test methods. Class and method names should clearly spell out the preconditions or assumptions for your tests, the action or functionality you are testing, and what result you are looking for to constitute a successful test. Keeping names descriptive is a key component of keeping your code readable and maintainable.

Write at Least One Test for One Unit of Functionality

The first D in TDD stands for driven. This means that before writing code to add functionality to an application, you should write a test. By necessity this means that each unit of functionality has at least one test. For many types of functionality, one test is not enough. Tests that test only the "happy path" of your code are easy to write. Unfortunately, these tests often do not tell the whole story.

It's important to test your code not only for the acceptable range of input parameters, but also for cases in which the inputs fall outside the acceptable regions. The first step is to find out from the business what the acceptable range of input is for the method in question. Obviously, you should test for values that fall squarely in this range. But you should also test the boundaries of that range. Does the method work the same if you pass in the absolute minimum or maximum value for an input parameter as it does when the value for this parameter is squarely between the minimum and maximum? You should have a test to verify that. What about values that fall outside the defined boundaries? Remember, all input is evil. You should test for values that fall outside the acceptable range to ensure that your code can handle such occurrences gracefully.

Keep Your Mocks Simple

A strict mock has a set of rules or expectations as to in what order its methods are called, and how many times (and with what arguments) its methods are called. I haven't spent much time discussing them in this book. That's because in general I don't like using strict mocks. The need for a strict mock in a unit test indicates that the service or component being mocked may have a needlessly complicated interface. The knowledge necessary to consume and mock this service or component starts to blur the lines where a service or component's internal functionality is encapsulated from other classes. The functionality in question is abstracted for a reason: to make consumption easier. A litany of rules that must be obeyed and therefore mocked for a service or component to be used makes mocking that service or component difficult. It also results in brittle tests, because those rules may change and would require a corresponding change in the test.

In some situations, strict mocking is necessary. Certain services and components in the .NET framework or other toolkits may have a more complex interface than you would like. In these cases the framework or toolkit API is unlikely to change drastically (especially if you never upgrade it), so the tests are not as brittle as if you were strictly mocking your own components or services. In the end, a strict mock is better than no mock at all.

In general, mocks should be kept simple. Do not mock more than you need to. An interface may have a dozen methods, but you care about only one of them. Mock only the one you care about, and leave the 11 other methods unmocked. This makes your tests easier to understand and ensures that you are not writing more code than is necessary to make your test pass.

THE BENEFITS OF TDD

The primary benefit of TDD is having a suite of tests that you can call on at any time to verify the correct functionality of your application. This in itself is a tremendous benefit. It ensures that the application always works as described. A suite of passing tests ensures that as development continues, existing functionality is not damaged. Other indirect benefits of TDD are worth noting:

➤ **Better design** — To really take advantage of TDD, your application should make liberal use of the DI pattern. The use of DI promotes loose coupling in your application. No service or component is statically bound to another. This introduces a great deal of flexibility in your application, leaving it open to change and extension.

Most practitioners of TDD employ the SOLID Principles. Whether this is by design or is a side effect of writing testable code, the result is the same. The code that is written is easier to understand, more maintainable, and extremely flexible. This translates into code that delivers a high degree of quality to the client.

➤ **Fewer defects** — By practicing TDD, you are writing working business code, not defects. Because you have a suite of tests that accurately reflect the business needs and requirements, and because those tests pass, you can feel confident that your code contains few, if any, defects resulting from the business requirements being incorrectly implemented. Defects may still arise from defective or incomplete requirements. You handle these defects by first writing a test to identify them and then fixing them. The existence of this test verifies that the defect will not return.

The quality of your code is contingent on your tests. If they do not accurately reflect your application's business requirements, they cannot demonstrate that your code has a high degree of quality. It's important to make sure that the same eye for quality that you apply to your code is also applied to your tests.

➤ **A relaxed team** — Most developers do not like working with a codebase that is unstable or difficult to understand. When an application is developed using TDD, you can use a suite of tests to verify the correct functioning of the codebase at every step. Applications that are built through TDD tend to be better designed, making it easier for developers to quickly get up to speed and effect positive change in a codebase. This includes the tendency for applications built with TDD to employ smaller, more focused classes that are easier to work with. All this leads to fewer defects, which developers also like. In turn, this creates a happy, more relaxed team that can be more productive.

HOW TO INTRODUCE TDD IN YOUR TEAM

TDD can be intimidating to some developers. This is especially true for developers who do not spend the requisite amount of time away from work learning new technologies and techniques. The TDD approach is quite a departure from the traditional way of developing software. This drastic change can be difficult for some developers to understand and deal with. Some strategies can help members of your development team understand and adopt TDD. Telling them about this book is a good start. In addition, you can use some strategies to get your teammates interested in TDD.

TDD is easiest to introduce in greenfield or new projects. When a project is being planned, or development has just started, it's easy to design the application around dependency injection (DI). If you are just starting to develop a new project, start by introducing the team to DI. Adopting DI is a big step, and for a team unfamiliar with TDD, DI is a good introduction to the principles they will learn in their continued practice of TDD. As soon as the team understands and feels comfortable using DI, begin introducing them to the idea of writing automated unit tests. After the team has developed the needed skills to write unit tests, introduce the concept of test first. Take small steps; don't overwhelm your team. Wait between each step until the team is comfortable with the new practice, pattern, or technology. There is no set timetable for this; you know your team, and you'll know when they are ready for the next step.

Most developers work on brownfield projects — those that have been under development for some time or are in maintenance mode. These projects are the most difficult to introduce TDD to. Most of these applications do not employ DI, which makes true unit testing difficult. I do not advocate stopping all feature development or maintenance on a system for a long period of time to introduce DI. This is simply not cost-effective. A better approach is to start introducing the concepts of TDD as you continue writing or maintaining the application. Add DI where you can and where it will not damage or destabilize the application. As new features are written or defects fixed, write tests around this new work. Initially it will be easier to write integration tests instead of unit tests. That is fine; integration tests are better than no tests at all. The book *Working Effectively with Legacy Code* by Michael C. Feathers (Prentice Hall, 2004, ISBN: 9780131177055) provides many strategies and techniques for testing in applications that were not built with testability in mind.

Getting management buy-in for TDD can be a difficult task. TDD, especially for a developer or development team who is learning it, represents a significant learning curve that can make initial development much slower. Managers are tasked with getting software delivered on time, at or below budget. You must learn to speak to them about TDD in their language. A good tactic is to demonstrate that although the upfront development takes longer, the dramatically lower defect count after the application reaches QA and the higher customer satisfaction after the application is deployed more than make up for the perceived slower start-up. Managers like charts and figures. Quantify this information, and demonstrate real savings. Many studies on the Internet can support your point. Take advantage of these. Show that TDD provides more value than development without TDD, and your manager will have to pay attention.

SUMMARY

This book has taught you the principles and techniques of TDD. However, there is more to TDD than what can be contained in any book. TDD is a journey, not a destination. This book can prepare you to start the journey to becoming a TDD developer, but it is up to you to make it happen.

You are the primary client of your code. The TDD approach can help you create and define interfaces to services and components that make development easy. As you write your tests, think about how you are using the method or class under test. Does it make sense? Is it intuitive? Does it require a lot of training or explanation to use properly? If you don't like the answers to these questions, consider redesigning the interface to make it better.

Do not try to boil the ocean. Large tasks with lots of moving parts can be difficult to complete. Break these larger tasks into smaller, simpler ones. Completing these smaller tasks makes the work easier. Being able to complete several small tasks quickly will help you build momentum and feel a sense of accomplishment.

Through your practice of TDD, you'll reap many benefits. Your application will have fewer defects, because your code will reflect your business requirements. As a side effect of the principles you'll employ to keep your code testable, you'll enjoy a system of better-defined classes, interfaces, and methods. Your code will represent the business's needs and requirements, creating a happy user base. Finally, your development team will enjoy the satisfaction of delivering a well-designed application with a high-quality codebase.

When introducing TDD to your team, start slowly. TDD is a dramatic change from what they are used to. Start with DI, a bedrock principle of TDD. Once your team understands and feels comfortable with DI, introduce the idea of writing tests. As your team becomes comfortable and proficient with each principle, practice, or technology, you can introduce the next one. Do not introduce change too quickly. Keep your finger on the pulse of your team. When they are ready for the next step, you'll know.

APPENDIX

TDD Katas

Kata is the Japanese word for practice. I first heard the term when I was 8 and started taking tae kwon do classes. A kata is a series of choreographed moves designed to help students sharpen their technique and commit to memory specific patterns of attacks and blocks. If you've ever seen two highly skilled and trained martial artists fight, you've no doubt noticed the incredible speed with which they move and string together attacks and blocks. That is the result of hours upon hours of kata.

Practice makes perfect. Talent helps. But most athletes, musicians, and anybody else who has achieved great success in their field will tell you that practice is what turns the potential of talent into the reality of success. In his book *Outliers* (Little, Brown and Company, 2008, ISBN: 9780316017923), Malcolm Gladwell defines the "10,000-Hour Rule." In short, the rule states that the key to success is mostly a matter of practicing a specific task for approximately 10,000 hours. He makes a compelling argument, citing the success of the Beatles, Bill Gates, and Tiger Woods.

WORKING WITH TDD KATAS

Practice is important for building the skills required to be a productive TDD developer. You must master new technical skills such as dependency injection, MVC/MVVM, unit-testing frameworks, and supporting frameworks such as NBehave. You also must make many mental adjustments when approaching TDD, such as adopting the SOLID Principles and becoming comfortable with the idea of test-first development.

For the purposes of creating a TDD kata, this appendix provides a series of user stories for the OSIM application. This application is sparse and incomplete by design. My hope is that you will take these user stories and complete the OSIM as a form of kata. Do it once. Then do it again. Then do it again. Keep doing it until you are comfortable with your TDD skills. This is especially necessary if you are not currently working in an environment that supports TDD. Your skill is like a saw. It could be made by the best craftsman using the finest materials, but if you do not maintain it, it will not stay sharp for long.

SHARE YOUR WORK

Several years ago I started playing ice hockey. A big part of hockey (I would say 90%) is the ability to skate. I already knew how to skate a bit, but I hadn't really reached a level where I could be competitive. I started practicing in earnest; I grabbed every bit of available ice time and spent hours practicing. I was getting pretty good, but one thing still bothered me: my turns. A professional hockey player can make tight, fast turns without losing any speed. I wanted to be able to do that, so I spent countless hours practicing. The problem is I never got any better at it. I didn't understand. I thought I was doing exactly what I saw everybody else doing, so why wasn't I improving? It became frustrating.

One day I was at an open practice, and I spoke to a friend who does some coaching. I explained my problem and asked if he could help. He had me skate out and make a few turns. He knew right away what my problem was: My feet were too far apart. I made the prescribed change to my technique, and before long I could make turns the way I wanted. I would never have known that if someone hadn't looked at what I was doing and given me another perspective.

It's the same with software development — specifically, learning a new technique such as TDD. It's important to share your code with others. Other people will see problems that you are blind to. Other people will have a viewpoint you have not considered. Other people will see sloppy technique creeping in where you think you are being honest. Other people will be able to see where you might be going wrong in work that you are emotionally attached to. Do not underestimate the power of sharing your work and getting feedback from others. I spent many hours practicing the wrong way to turn. That was a huge waste of time and effort. Do not make the same mistake I did; start showing your code to others as soon as possible.

OSIM USER STORIES

The following is a list of user stories for the OSIM application. Notice that they describe only the system's desired functionality, not how it should be implemented. It's up to you to make that decision. Make a copy of the OSIM application, and start implementing these user stories. Add some user stories of your own if you feel you need to practice a specific area. When you are done and have shown the code to someone else, throw it out and start over.

➤ The user must be able to log into the application and be authenticated.

➤ The user must be able to log out of the application.

➤ The user must be able to view a list of available item types.

➤ The user must be able to add item types to the system.

➤ The user must be able to delete item types from the system.

➤ The user must be able to log in new inventory and record the quantity received.

➤ The user must be able to log out inventory as being distributed.

➤ The system must keep track of what supplies (type and quantity) are distributed to which department.

➤ The system must keep track of a per-item internal price for each item type (the price the supply department charges other departments for supplies).

➤ The system must keep a running total of current inventory.

➤ The system must keep a running total of each department's monthly supply bill.

➤ The system must allow users to specify a reorder level for each item type.

➤ The system must alert the users when the current stock of an item type has fallen below the reorder level.

➤ The system must prepare a bill for each department on a monthly basis.

➤ The system must keep track of the per-item vendor price for each item type (the price the external vendor charges for each item).

➤ The system must produce a monthly usage report (how many of each item were distributed).

➤ The system must produce a monthly cost report (how much was paid to external vendors, and for what).

➤ The system must produce a monthly internal revenue report (how much was paid by internal departments, and for what).

INDEX

INDEX

XAML (Extensible Application Markup
    Language), 245
XML files, dependency injection and, 289
XP (Extreme Programming)
    history of agile methodologies, 6–7
    test-first programming in, 8

xUnit
    Gallio supported for, 281
    unit-testing with, 284–285

YAGNI (You Aren't Going to Need It), 42